SQL Server
Source Control
Basics

Robert Sheldon, Rob Richardson & Tony Davis

First published by Simple Talk Publishing, 2014

Technical Review: Rob Richardson
Editor: Tony Davis
Cover Image: Andy Martin
Typeset: Peter Woodhouse and Gower Associates

Table of Contents

Chapter 8: Automating Database Versioning and Deployment from Source Control

Foreword: A Brief History of Source Control

By Phil Factor

The fledgling computer industry did not invent source control. It merely adopted practices that were already well established in the industrial manufacturing and design industries. The design and manufacture of large, complex machines such as aircraft, tanks or motor cars required a great deal of discipline, particularly in the technical drawing of components. The engineering process involved identifying the assemblies and components in a design, and representing them in a hierarchical map. Each component was defined by its technical drawing, and the "spec" which specified the materials and manufacturing techniques.

Having defined the context of a component within the overall design, for example the dimensions within which the component had to fit, and the tolerances within which it had to work, a team of engineers could work on each one relatively independently. Over the course of the engineering process, they would construct and test the various assemblies, and change the drawings and specifications as required. Each version of every component had a version number. At this stage, or perhaps retrospectively, variants would be designed. For an estate version of an automobile, for example, a stronger back axle and suspension might be required. However, any drastic changes to the design, such as a change in width, which affected all variants, would require a new version of all the affected components. At the stage of testing the prototypes, some changes would have a knock-on effect, requiring changes to other components.

The drawing office and project office evolved a robust system for dealing with all these processes; thus were born the fledgling change control and releasing systems, and much of the software engineering process and terminology still shows signs of these roots.

Source control for software mimicked the established techniques of the drawing office, but only the parts that were possible within the crude technology of the time. Back in the days of punch cards, once the programmers had finished with their routine, they would take the punched cards, change cards, or coding forms to the source-control or config-uration-management team who would duly update the library, and build the customer-ready product from the official source. At the same time, there was an office process that recorded the work and managed the "versioning" task. The work was treated as if it were a technical drawing. To alter source, you checked the code in and out as though it were a technical drawing that had to be altered.

Evolution and refinement of the process proved to be slow.

As soon as programs became text files, there was an automation of the manual process, using programs such as Source Code Control System (SCCS). At this stage, there wasn't the concept of storing just the difference between file versions. The technology was there but we weren't culturally ready. This practice of delta-storage became mainstream in the 1980s with Revision Control System (RCS), but the whole process still used the analogy of the file being the unit of work, as if it were a technical drawing. The idea of being able to deal with a whole lot of files at once took a long time to catch on. Also absent for a long time was the idea of having more than one person working on a file at the same time. Although Concurrent Versions Systems (CVS) was the first to break free from the idea of locking out the file to work on it, it was unreliable until the introduction of Subversion. Even now, it is only too easy for the source control system to fail to sort out the merging of two simultaneous alterations of a source file, and "merge failure" is still a phrase to be dreaded by most developers.

The original source control software was mainframe-based, and individual programmers accessed the system via a terminal. UNIX systems were the first to introduce server-based, or "centralized" source control systems that relied on a single, shared repository, and these eventually became available on MSDOS and Windows. Whilst these worked well when a team was co-located on the same file-sharing server, they were useless where some of the team were outside the domain. In the mid-nineties, source control became network-based, but still ultimately hosted on a server. From this point, the idea of a hosted service on the Internet was just a short step.

More fundamental was the change to a distributed model for source control, in which no single computer held the master copy. The distributed model became mainstream with BitKeeper, followed by Git and Mercurial, and it made the process of forking, branching and merging far easier and more reliable.

Source control has always been an intrinsic part of software development. The recent advances in source control have led to a fundamental change to the way we develop software. It has made possible the current surge of collaborative open-source software and made the rapid delivery of software achievable. It has revolutionized team-working in the past decade.

If we've seen rapid improvements in source control over the past decade, I suspect we'll see even more, since the recent advances have been fuelled by frustration with the existing system and that frustration still remains, in large part manifest in the pain inherent in many merge operations.

The problem with merging boils down to the fact that source control systems still stick to the idea of the text file as the unit of work, just as if it were the generic technical drawing or engineering specification. Comparing the textual differences between source files isn't always a good way of merging, or of detecting the repercussions of a change. Without the ability to perform any a semantic analysis of the source file, it cannot, for example, judge whether a change is a code logic change, or merely the addition of comment blocks. I long for the day of a generic version-control system that understands any language once I've added the appropriate parser as a plug-in. In the meantime, in order to achieve rapid delivery of software, some teams avoid the pain of the merge by avoiding branches altogether, and keeping all the development work in the trunk, using software "flags" to disable the functionality of the components that are not ready for release.

However complex a software system may be, there is no "opt-out" alternative to source control. A database, for example, can be of startling complexity but everything can be scripted, even if built step-wise, using a GUI. Whatever the system, the ultimate source of that system, and the script to build it, is what lies in the script repository. Despite the occasional frustrations, the benefits far outweigh the effort. Any team development, even a one-person team, needs source control.

About the Authors and Technical Reviewers

Robert Sheldon

After being dropped 35 feet from a helicopter and spending the next year recovering, Robert Sheldon left the Colorado Rockies and emergency rescue work to pursue safer and less painful interests – thus his entry into the world of technology. He has worked as a technical consultant and written numerous books, articles, and training material related to Microsoft Windows, various relational database management systems, and business intelligence design and implementation.

He has also written news stories, feature articles, restaurant reviews, the novel, *Dancing the River Lightly*, the publishing guide *Ebook Now*, and six books in the 5-Spot ebook travel series. You can find more information at HTTP://RHSHELDON.COM.

Bob contributed Chapters 1–7 to this book.

Rob Richardson

Rob Richardson is a software craftsman from Phoenix, Arizona building web properties in ASP.NET and Node. Rob specializes in translating business requirements into technical solutions for small- to medium-sized businesses. He has created software applications ranging from enterprise-scale applications to PDA-based systems, web applications to embedded database synchronization and postscript processing systems.

He's a frequent speaker at conferences, user groups, and community events, and a diligent teacher and student of high quality software development. You can find recent talks on his blog at HTTP://ROBRICH.ORG/ and follow him on Twitter at @ROB_RICH.

Rob contributed Chapter 8 to this book, plus additional material elsewhere, and was the technical reviewer for Chapters 1–7.

Tony Davis

Tony is an editor with Red Gate Software, based in Cambridge (UK), specializing in databases, and especially SQL Server. He edits articles and writes editorials for both the Simple-talk.com and SQLServerCentral.com websites and newsletters, with a combined audience of over 1.5 million subscribers. You can sample his short-form writing at either his Simple-Talk.com blog at HTTP://TINYURL.COM/NT2WNAB his author pages at HTTP://TINYURL.COM/OTQ9RWF, or at his SQLServerCentral.com author page at HTTP://TINYURL.COM/MS3D6DD.

As the editor behind most of the SQL Server books published by Red Gate, he spends much of his time helping others express what they know about SQL Server. He is also the lead author of the book, *SQL Server Transaction Log Management* for which, see HTTP://TINYURL.COM/O89OCXL.

In his spare time, he enjoys running, football, contemporary fiction and real ale.

Tony contributed additional material throughout the book, and was the technical reviewer for Chapter 8.

Introduction

For efficient team-based database development, and reliable and repeatable database deployments, source control is not optional. The job of a source control system is to maintain a change history of all the files in a project. As soon as we enter a new file into source control, the system assigns it a version. Each time we commit a change to that file, the version increments, and we have access to the current version and all previous versions of the file. For good reason, we often refer to a source control system as a **version control system**, or VCS.

Few software developers would consider building an application without the benefits that a VCS offers, but its adoption for databases has been slower, partly because of the added complication of the need to preserve data during database upgrades. However, unless we have in the VCS the correct versions of all the scripts necessary to create our database objects, load lookup data, add security accounts, and take any other necessary actions, we have no hope of a reliable and repeatable database deployment process, let alone of coordinating database upgrades with changes to the associated application. We also run a very real risk that our "ad hoc" database patching will cause inconsistencies and data loss.

Version control can and should play a key role in the database development and deployment process, and this book will show you exactly how to get started. It provides "just enough" detail about the core components of a source control system, and the operations that allow us to commit our database changes and retrieve others' changes. It then focuses on getting a database into source control and working with it, covering:

- **Database source control architecture** – what needs to be in there, how to structure it all.

- **Collaborative editing** – working as a team on a database project, while minimizing the potential for conflicting changes and data loss.

- **Change auditing** – what changed between one version and another, and who changed it?

- **Branching** – allows teams to work independently on separate features, and control what they deploy and when.

- **Merging** – what happens if one user changes the name of a column while another updates its data type? A merge operation lets the team decide the correct outcome.

- **Building and deploying databases** – building new databases and upgrading existing databases from source control, both manually and using automation tools.

Every chapter follows the same "half theory, half practice" template, so you learn the concepts and then immediately see how they work in a particular source control system, in this case, Subversion (SVN).

It's important to state up front that this is not a book *about* Subversion. It will explain conceptually the purpose and function of some of the primary source control operations, and familiarize you with their implementation in SVN, but it is not a reference for SVN commands. We focus on the advantages and challenges of working with databases in source control, and on what's required for efficient, repeatable database deployments, from source control.

Intended Audience

The primary audience for the book is the database developer, though it is relevant to any developer, data architect, DBA, or anyone else who needs to work with or deploy databases from a version control system.

This is an entry-level book, suitable for anyone not currently using a version control system (VCS), or using it for the application only, and not the database. It does not assume any prior knowledge of source control operations, although some familiarity would be an asset. It assumes basic technical competency with SQL Server.

Required Tools

For the majority of this book (Chapters 1–7), you will need only access to:

- **A SQL Server installation** – even if it is the evaluation edition available free from Microsoft. We tested the code examples on SQL Server 2008 and SQL Server 2012, though most should work on later editions, as well as on SQL Server 2005.

- **A source control management system** – we used VisualSVN Server standard edition, which is free (see Chapter 2 for details).

- **A native source control client** – we used TortoiseSVN, again freely available (see Chapter 2 for details).

If you wish to work through Chapter 8, you will also need access to three Red Gate Software tools (or suitable alternatives): SQL Source Control, SQL Compare and SQL Data Compare. You can download free trial versions of each of these tools (see Chapter 8 for details).

The Hands-on Examples

The practical sections of each chapter work progressively through an example of getting a database for a fictional Bookstore application into source control and working with it.

The book provides various scripts, shown as listings, to create the `Bookstore` database, and various database objects, and then progressively modify them while tracking changes through the VCS.

You can download all of these scripts from: HTTP://TINYURL.COM/LUM8RYL.

The example builds sequentially through each chapter, but to make it easier to jump in at any point, we also provide a **SVNBackups** folder, containing a backup repository as it existed at the end of a given chapter, which you can restore to recreate the repository. To do this:

1. In VisualSVN Server Manager, create a new *empty* repository (not with the trunk/ branch/tag structure) e.g. called **MyBookstoreProject**.

2. At the SVN Server level, select **Action | All Tasks | Start Command Prompt**.

3. Restore the appropriate repository backup. E.g. to restore the repository as it existed at the end of Chapter 2:
   ```
   svnadmin load D:\Repositories\MyBookstoreProject < D:\SVNBackups\
   BookstoreProject_Ch02.bak.
   ```

4. Check out the **BookstoreProject** to a new working folder, using the **SVN Checkout** command (described in detail in Chapter 2).

Chapter 1: Core Source Control Concepts

This opening chapter takes a conceptual, "big picture" approach to explaining core source control concepts, using diagrams and anecdotes as necessary to describe how all the pieces fit together.

- **Why source control** – the basic purpose of source control and the benefits it offers, including:
  - maintaining an "**audit trail**" of what changed, who made the change, and when.
  - allowing **team collaboration** during development projects.
- **Basic source control components and concepts**, including:
  - the **repository**, which stores the files and maintains their histories.
  - the **working folder**, which provides an isolated environment (sandbox) for creating, editing, and deleting files without affecting those in the repository.
  - workflow concepts, such as **versioning**, **branching** and **merging** files.

Why Source Control?

A source control solution provides users with the tools they need to manage, share, and preserve their electronic files. It does so in a manner that helps minimize the potential for conflicting changes and data loss, in other words one user inadvertently overwriting another user's changes when multiple users work on the same files. If one user changes the name of a column while another one updates its data type, the source control system will alert us to the conflict and allow the team to decide the correct outcome, via a **merge** operation.

Critically, a source control solution maintains a version history of the changes made to every file, over time, and provides a means for users to explore those changes and compare different file versions. This is why we often refer to a source control system as a **version control system**, or **VCS** for short.

These days, few software developers would consider building an application without the benefits that a VCS offers, but its adoption for databases has been slower. This is mainly because of the nature of a database, which must preserve its "state" (i.e. business data) between database versions. It means that having, in source control, the files that define the schema objects and other code is not the whole story. When upgrading a "live" database to a newer version, as it exists in the VCS, we can't just tear down objects that store data and re-create them each time.

Nevertheless, despite this added complication, there is no reason why we should exclude databases from our source control practices. In fact, a VCS can be one of a database developer's most valuable tools and the foundation stone for an effective and comprehensive change management strategy.

A Brief History of Source Control

If you skipped straight to Chapter 1, you missed Phil Factor's trawl through the recent history of source control, and its roots in the mechanisms used to control the process of designing and manufacturing large, complex machines such as aircraft and tanks. I recommend you go back and read his Foreword at some point. From here in, we focus on the use of source control to store and manage electronic files, and database files in particular.

At its heart, the purpose of a VCS is to maintain a change history of our files. As soon as we enter a new file into source control, the system assigns it a version. Each time we commit a change to that file, the version increments, and we have access to the current version and all previous versions of the file.

This versioning mechanism, which we discuss in more detail in Chapter 3, serves two core purposes:

- **Change auditing**
  - Compare versions, find out exactly what changed between one version and another.
  - Find out who made the change, and when; for example, find out when someone introduced a bug, and fix it quickly.

- **Team collaboration**
  - Inspect the source control repository to find out what other team members have recently changed.
  - Share recent changes.
  - Coordinate work to minimize the potential for conflicting changes being made to the same file.
  - Resolve such conflicts when they occur (a process called **merging**).

By maintaining every version of a file, we can access the file as it existed at any revision in the repository, or we can roll back to a previous version. Source control systems also allow us to copy a particular file version (or set of files) and use and amend them for a different purpose, without affecting the original files. This is referred to as creating a **branch**, or fork.

I hope this gives you a sense of the benefits a source control system offers. We'll look at more as we progress. The following sections paint an initial picture of the source control components and workflow that enable this functionality. We review the most important concepts in terms of the content creation, the storage, and the tracking strategies they enable, but we won't go into detail, because we'll cover these topics in depth from Chapter 2 onwards.

The Source Control Repository

At the heart of a VCS is the **repository**, which stores and manages the files, and preserves file change histories.

Centralized source control systems support a single, central repository that sits on a server, and all approved users access it over a network. In **distributed** source control systems, each user has a private, local repository, as well as (optionally) a "master" repository, accessed by all users. We'll discuss both centralized and distributed repositories in more detail in Chapter 2, but assume a centralized model for the conceptual examples in this chapter.

Regardless of the model used, when we add files to the repository, those files become part of a system that tracks who has worked on the file, what changes they made, and any other **metadata** necessary to identify and manage the file.

Repository storage mechanisms

The exact storage mechanism varies by source control system. Some products store both the repository's content and its metadata in a database; some store all content and metadata in files (with the metadata often stored in hidden files); other products take a hybrid approach and store the metadata in a database, and the content within files.

The repository organizes files and the metadata associated with each file, in a way that mirrors the operating system's folder hierarchies. In essence, the structure of files and folders in a source control system is the same as in a typical file management system such as Windows Explorer or Mac OS Finder. In fact, some source control systems leverage the local file management system in order to present the data in the repository. Figure 1-1 shows the server repository structure for a **BookstoreProject** repository, typical of the one we'll see throughout this book, with the **Databases** folder expanded to reveal a **Bookstore** database. Don't worry about the details of this structure yet, as we'll get to them later.

Figure 1-1:   Typical hierarchical folder structure in the repository.

What sets a source control repository apart from other file storage systems is its ability to maintain **file histories**. Everything we save to a repository is there for ever, at least in theory. From the point that we first add files to the repository, the system maintains every version of every file, recording every change to those files, as well as to the folders that form the repository structure.

Source control of non-text files

Ideally, a VCS manages and tracks the changes made by all contributors to every type of file in the system, whether that file is a Word document, Excel spreadsheet, C# source code, or database script file. In reality, however, traditional source control solutions usually track changes only on text files, such as those used in application and database development, and tend to treat binary files, such as Word or Photoshop files, as second-class citizens. Even so, most solutions maintain the integrity of all files and help manage processes such as access control and file backup.

The Working Folder

Most users care less about how their source control system stores the file content and metadata, and more about being able to access and work on those files. Each repository includes a mechanism for maintaining the integrity of the files within their assigned folder structure and for making those files accessible to authorized users.

However, to be able to edit those files, each user needs a "private workspace," a place on his or her local system, separate from the repository, to add, modify, or delete files, without affecting the integrity of the files preserved in the repository.

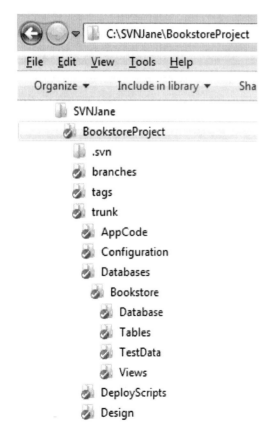

Figure 1-2:   Typical working folder structure.

Most VCSs implement this private workspace through the **working folder.** The working folder is simply a folder, and set of subfolders, on the client computer's file system, registered to the source control repository and structured identically to the folders in the repository. Figure 1-2 shows the working folder structure for a user of the **BookstoreProject** repository. This user has copied the entire repository to a working folder called **BookstoreProject.**

Each user stores in their working folder copies of some or all of the files in the repository, along with the metadata necessary for the files to participate in the source control system. As noted above, that metadata is often stored in hidden files.

We can update our working folder with the latest version of the files stored in the repository, as illustrated in Figure 1-3.

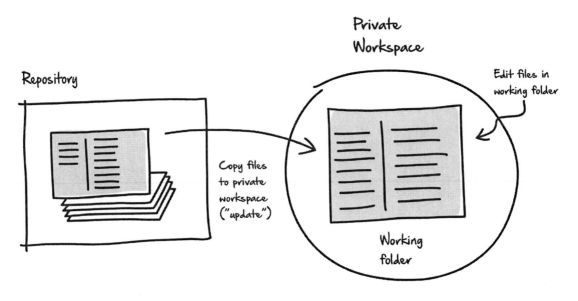

Figure 1-3:   Copying files from the repository to the working folder.

We can edit the files in the working folder as necessary and then, eventually, commit the edited versions back to the repository. This process of "synchronizing" the working folder with the repository, i.e. updating the local working folder with any changes in the repository and committing any local changes to the repository, works differently from product to product and depends on whether the repository is centralized or distributed.

Regardless of repository type or product, the source control system always keeps the files in the repository separate from changes made to files in the working folder, until the user chooses to **commit** those changes to the repository.

Versioning and Collaborative Editing

The exact architecture and mechanisms that underpin versioning and collaborative editing vary by VCS, but the basic principles are constant. A user can obtain a local "working copy" of any file in the repository, make additions and amendments to that file, and then commit those changes back to the main repository. At that point, other users can request from the repository the amended version of the file or any of the previous versions. The VCS maintains a full change history for each file, so we can work out exactly what changed from one version to another.

In this section we'll discuss, at a high level, how the repository maintains these file versions, as users make progressive changes to those files. Chapter 4 will discuss versioning in much more detail, along with the specifics of how it works in various source control systems.

Notionally, this versioning process is easy in a single-user system. A user updates his or her working folder with the latest versions of a set of files, and then edits those files as appropriate in a suitable client, such as Notepad for a plain text file, Visual Studio for an application file, or SQL Server Management Studio for a database file. The user then commits the changes to the repository, creating new versions of the files.

However, another key function of source control is to enable a group of people to work *collaboratively* on the set of files that comprise a development project. In other words, the VCS must allow multiple users to modify a file concurrently, while minimizing the potential for conflicts and data loss. Here, we'll take a first look at how source control systems allow for and manage these concurrent changes, but we'll discuss this topic in more depth, and with worked examples, from Chapter 3 onwards.

How versioning works

Let's assume we've created a project directory in source control for an **Animal-Vegetable-Mineral** (AVM) application and that we've established a working folder for this project.

Figure 1-4 depicts the progressive changes to the application over three revisions. Notice that the repository preserves all the changes to the files, with each version assigned a **revision number**. Note that Figure 1-4 is not in any way a depiction of how a VCS maintains different file versions internally. It is merely to help visualize the process of how it can allow us to access different file versions, and provide a history of changes to our files over time.

In Revision 1, we committed to the repository (from our working folder) two new files, Animals.txt and Vegetables.txt. Revision 1 represents the first and latest file versions in the AVM repository.

We edited Animals.txt to replace *skunk* with *elk*, and created a third file called Minerals.txt, and committed the changes to the repository. Collectively, these changes form Revision 2. Vegetables.txt remains unchanged from Revision 1.

Next, we edited Vegetables.txt, changing *sprouts* to *carrots*, and edited Minerals.txt, changing *potash* to *pyrite* and adding *silica*. These changes form Revision 3, with Animals.txt unaltered from Revision 2.

Mostly, users are interested in working with the latest folder and file versions in the repository, but we can also request to see the repository as it existed at any earlier revision, with each file exactly as it existed at that point in time. For example, if we were to pull Revision 2, we would get the Revision 2 copies of the `Animals.txt` and `Minerals.txt` files, as well as the Revision 1 version of the `Vegetables.txt` file. In this way, we can build and deploy a specific "version" of the application or database.

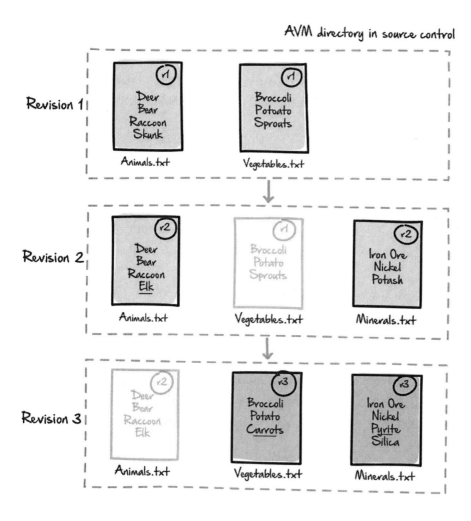

Figure 1-4:   Working with files from the AVM project in source control.

Conceptual versus actual source control implementation

*At this stage in the book, the descriptions of the versioning process are conceptual in nature. An actual source control implementation will vary according to product. It might not store this many different file versions, or it might build a given version by storing a record of the differences (the **delta**) between a current version and the previous version. We'll discuss this fully in Chapter 4.*

Since developers usually want to ensure they are working with all the most recent versions of their project files, they update their working folders regularly to get the latest versions. When they view their working folders, they are viewing the latest version of the repository and all its folders and files, at the point in time they did their last update.

However, we can also request to view the revision history for the repository (for example, by accessing the repository's log – more on this in Chapter 3). Exactly what we see when viewing the revision history depends on the VCS, but it's likely to include information such as the revision number, the action, who made the changes, and when, and the author's comment, i.e. a description of the change. Figure 1-5 on the next page shows what the log might look like for the AVM project folder, after the sequence of changes (and assuming two users, Fred and Barb).

A VCS, as noted earlier, often stores the differences between each file version, rather than the full file for every version. We refer to each set of differences as the **delta**. If we request to view a file as it existed at a particular revision, the VCS might, for example, retrieve the last stored complete file and then apply the deltas in the correct order going forward.

Likewise, a VCS will usually provide an easy visual way for users to see a list of what changed between any two revisions in the repository. We call this performing a **diff**, short for "difference between revisions." We'll cover deltas and diffs in more detail in Chapter 4.

Revision	Action	User	Date/Time	Description
3	Update Minerals.txt	Fred	March 22, 2014 10:18:39 AM	Delete "Potash" Add "Pyrite" and "Silica"
3	Update Vegetables.txt	Fred	March 22, 2014 10:18:39 AM	Delete "Sprouts" Add "Carrots"
2	Add Minerals.txt	Barb	March 21, 2014 12:40:22 PM	Add the Minerals.txt file
2	Update Animals.txt	Barb	March 21, 2014 12:40:22 PM	Delete "Skunk" Add "Elk"
1	Add Vegetables.txt	Fred	March 20, 2014 6:20:40 PM	Add the Vegetables.txt file
1	Add Animals.txt	Fred	March 20, 2014 6:20:40 PM	Add the Animals.txt file

Figure 1-5: Storing files in the repository of a source control system.

Collaborative editing

Any source control solution must provide the structure necessary to permit collaboration on different file versions in the repository, while preserving every version of each file.

The potential difficulty arises when more than one user works on the same version of a file at the same time. Let's say both Fred and Barb have in their respective working folders Revision 2 of our AVM app. Fred edits **Vegetables.txt**, changing *sprouts* to *carrots* and commits the change. At roughly the same time, Barb edits the same file, changing *sprouts* to *peas*, and commits the change. What should be the result in the source control repository? If the "last commit wins," we'd simply lose Fred's changes from the current version of the file.

Older source control systems (often referred to as "first generation") get around such difficulties by imposing an **isolated editing** (or locking) model, whereby only one user at a time can work on a particular version of a file.

Most modern source control systems enable a group of users to work collaboratively on the same version of a file. Referred to as a **concurrent editing** model, this process allows them to reconcile, or **merge**, the changes made by more than one user to the same file and, in the process, resolve any conflicting changes.

Isolated editing

A traditional "first-generation" source control solution, such as Source Code Control System (SCCS), developed at Bell Labs in 1972, uses a central repository and a locking model that permits only one person at a time to work on a file.

To use a database metaphor, we can liken the isolated editing model to SQL Server's pessimistic concurrency model. It assumes, pessimistically, that a conflict is likely if multiple users are "competing" to modify the same file, so it takes locks to prevent it happening.

A typical workflow in source control might looks as follows:

1. Fred performs a **check-out** of the latest version of the `Animals.txt` file, in this case, Revision 1.

    a. If the file does not exist in Fred's working folder, the source control system will copy it over.

    b. The source control system "**locks**" the file in the repository. (The exact "locking" mechanism varies by system.)

2. Fred edits the file in his editor of choice. He deletes *skunk* and adds *elk*.

3. Fred saves the changes to his local working folder.

4. Barb attempts to check out `Animals.txt`, but cannot because Fred has it locked. Although Fred saved his changes locally, he has yet to perform a check-in to the repository and so the file remains locked and no one else can check it out.

5. However, Barb can download `Animals.txt` to her working folder as a read-only copy, so she can at least see the latest version as it exists in the repository.

Figure 1-6 provides a pictorial overview of this process, to this point.

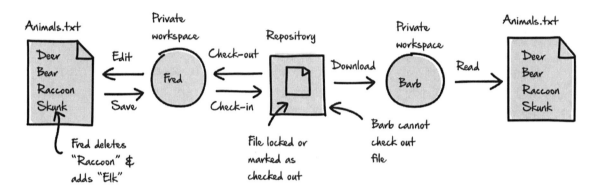

Figure 1-6: Allowing only one user at a time to modify a file.

From this point, the workflow might proceed as follows:

6. Fred performs a **check-in**, which copies the updated file from his working folder into the repository.

   a. The repository stores Revision 2 of `Animals.txt`, while retaining Revision 1.

   b. The source control system releases any locks, so both versions of the file are available for check-out.

7. Barb can now work freely on `Animals.txt`. She can:

   a. View Revision 2, with an elk instead of a raccoon, by re-syncing her working folder.

b. Compare the two versions to determine what changed.

c. Check out the file for editing. The source control system will automatically copy the latest version, Revision 2, to her working folder and lock the file in the repository.

Remember that source control terminology can vary a lot depending on the system. For example, some systems refer to the check-out operation as a "get," and the check-in operation as an "add," a "delta," or a "commit."

An important point in all this is that the repository only increments the revision number in response to the check-in operation. A user can check out a file, edit it and save it to his working folder but then decide to "revert" to the original version of the file. The source control system will release the file, and the revision number will remain unchanged. The user's local changes are lost, unless he or she saved them elsewhere.

Concurrent editing

If working on the files in isolation is the safest route to controlling changes and avoiding conflicts, it's also the slowest. For a more efficient workflow, modern source control systems allow for the possibility that two or more users will edit the same file at the same time. The notion of a check-out operation, with its attendant locking, disappears and instead each user performs an "update" to refresh his or her working folder with the most recent copies of the repository files. Users can then work on these files concurrently, then commit their changes to the repository.

If isolated editing is akin to SQL Server's pessimistic concurrency model, then the concurrent editing model is more like SQL Server's optimistic concurrency model. It hopes, optimistically, that no other user will "interfere" with a file on which another user is working, but it has to deal with the consequences if it happens.

Let's see how this might alter our typical workflow. Our description of the various processes uses the most common terms associated with centralized version control systems, with the usual proviso that you will see differences even among centralized systems, and certainly for distributed systems where these processes work slightly differently.

1. Fred performs an update to retrieve the latest files. In this case, he now has in his working folder Revision 2 of `Animals.txt`.

2. Barb does likewise.

3. Fred edits his working copy of the file by adding *wolf*.

4. Barb edits her working copy of the file by adding *fox*.

5. Fred saves the changed file to his working folder.

6. Fred commits the changed file to the repository. The updated file becomes Revision 3 in the repository.

7. Barb saves her edited copy to her working folder.

8. Barb tries to commit to the repository, but the repository detects that the version of the file has changed since Barb's last update. The commit fails.

9. Barb performs an update, retrieving Revision 3 into her working folder, and must now "merge" the changes in her working copy of the file with those in the Revision 3 copy of the file. This merge process might be automated, manual, or a combination of both.

10. Barb commits the merged file to the repository. The updated file is designated as Revision 4.

Figure 1-7 provides an overview of this process.

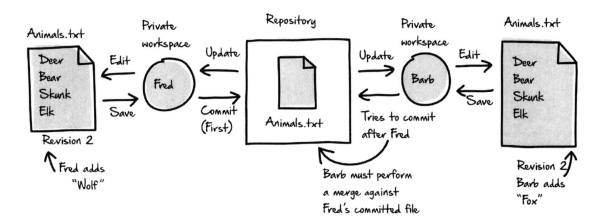

Figure 1-7: Concurrent editing of the `Animals.txt` file.

In this simple example, Fred and Barb each make changes that do not really conflict; the wolf and the fox can easily co-exist, at least within the confines of a text file. In such cases, the source control system will probably perform this sort of merge automatically, but in this case even merging the documents manually is a relatively painless process whereby Revision 4 simply contains both the users' changes, as shown in Figure 1-8 overleaf.

Again, this may not be exactly how a VCS implements a merge, but it gives a good idea of how it works conceptually. Some users don't even consider this a merge operation, since it can occur automatically as part of the update operation. Some merges, however, are not quite so straightforward.

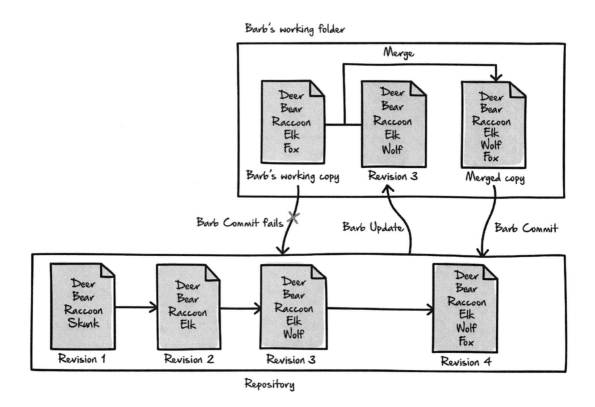

Figure 1-8: Merging two versions of a file to create a third version.

Dealing with conflicts during concurrent edits

A VCS can sometimes auto-merge changes made by different users to the same file. Sometimes, however, concurrent changes to the same version of a file will cause a real conflict, and to resolve it one of the users will need to perform a manual merge operation, within his or her working folder.

Let's rewind to the stage of our `Animals.txt` example, where each user was working with Revision 2. Suppose that, in addition to adding *wolf* to his file, Fred changed *bear* to *black bear*, and committed the changes (creating Revision 3). At the same time, in addition to adding *fox* to her file, let's assume Barb changed *bear* to *brown bear*. Now when Barb tries to commit her file, an actual conflict emerges, one that Barb must resolve, as shown in Figure 1-9.

The source control system can't merge the two file versions until Barb resolves the conflict between *black bear* and *brown bear* (the additions of *wolf* and *fox* still cause no problem).

When conflicts of this nature arise, someone must examine the comparison and determine which version of *bear* should win out. In this case, Barb decides to go with *black bear*.

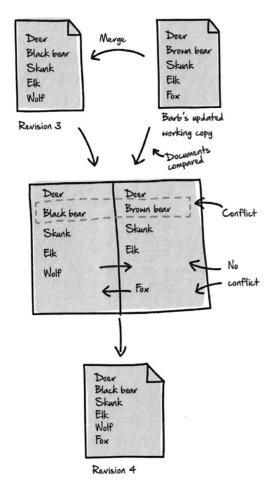

Figure 1-9: Addressing conflicts when trying to merge files.

We're going to discuss the practicalities of merging in much more detail later in the book, but it's worth considering the risk associated with this merge process. Barb's commit fails, so she can't save her changes to the repository until she can successfully perform a merge. If something goes wrong with the merge operation, she risks losing her changes entirely. This might be a minor problem for small textual changes like these, but a big problem if she's trying to merge in substantial and complex changes to application logic. This is why the source control mantra is: *commit small changes often.*

Merging in distributed source control systems

In distributed source control systems, each user's client hosts a local repository as well as a working folder. In the distributed model, Barb commits to her local repository, saving her changes, and then pushes the updated file to the central repository, which would fail because Fred got there first. We won't go into detail on what comes next, but it means we'd see different file versions and version numbers in the central repository from what we saw in our "centralized" example. The main point at this stage is simply that merging is "safer" on distributed source control systems because users can always commit their local changes to their local repository.

Another wise practice is: *update often.* The earlier and more often we update our working folders and commit our changes, the better the processes work for everyone and the easier it is to merge files and resolve conflicts.

Branching

The way in which we organize files within a repository depends on the team's preferences, the project, and the source control system itself. One common approach is to organize files by project, with each set of project files, whether related to database development, application development or something else, stored within the main project folder.

We organize the project folder itself according to the standards set for the organization. In many cases, we will store the files related to the main development effort in a common root subfolder, often named **trunk**, but sometimes referred to by other names, such as **master**. We then create subfolders in the trunk folder as required; for example, as we saw earlier in Figure 1-1, a subfolder for database development and another for application development, and so on.

However, relying exclusively on the trunk folder assumes that everyone on the team is working simultaneously on the project files associated with the main development effort. In reality, it is common that certain team members will wish to "spin off" from the main effort to work on separate, but related projects, often referred to as **branches**. For this reason, you'll find that the main project folder will also contain a branches folder (or a folder with a comparable name), in addition to trunk.

Let's assume that we've created a project folder in our repository for our AVM project, added the trunk and branches folders, and built our data-driven application. At this point, all our files are stored in the trunk folder.

At Revision 100, the team releases the latest version of the application to customers as v1.0. They're now ready to begin developing v2.0. At the same time, customers are submitting feedback and bug reports for v1.0. This is a classic example in software development of where it will be useful to create a branch (we'll discuss various other branching strategies in Chapter 5). We create a branch at a particular revision in the repository. When we do this, the repository creates a new path location, identified by whatever we call the branch.

In this case, we'll create a branch at Revision 100 and call it **1.0_bug fixes**. From the user's perspective, this process creates a separate **1.0_bug fixes** subfolder in the branches folder, at Revision 101, and populates it with project files that point back to the Revision 100 files in the trunk folder. Developers can work on the branch files as they would in the trunk, but their efforts remain independent of the trunk development efforts, while preserving the fact that each set of files shares the same roots.

Tags and build numbers

Closely related to the concept of a branch is a tag. In fact, a tag is virtually identical to a branch in that it is a named location for a set of files in the repository, created at a particular revision. We can think of creating a tag as a way to name a set or subset of files associated with a particular revision. The big difference is that we don't ever modify tags. They represent a stable release of a product, with the tag usually representing some meaningful build number. In our example, we might create a tag at Revision 100, called "v1.0." We won't discuss tags again until Chapter 5.

While part of the team works on the 1.0 bug fixes in the branch, the rest of the team continues the 2.0 development in the trunk. Those assigned to the bug fixes can work with the trunk folders and files as they would in the trunk. They can edit the files in their working folders and commit changes to the repository, which will maintain revision histories for the life of each branch file, starting from the point of branch creation.

For example, let's say Barb creates a branch of the AVM project, containing all the project files, called **1.0_bug fixes**, in preparation for the first maintenance release (v1.1). This means that the branch folder is at Revision 101, and contains, among other files, the latest revision (let's say Revision 100) of `Animals.txt`, as it existed in the trunk at the time she created the branch. Meanwhile, Fred is working in the trunk in preparation for the release of v2.0.

Fred updates his working folder with the latest file versions in the trunk. He retrieves Revision 100 of the `Animals.txt` file, adds *chipmunk* and *walrus* and deletes *fox*. He saves the file and commits his changes to the repository. This creates Revision 102 in the repository.

Barb updates her working folder with the latest file versions in the branch. She retrieves the latest version of the `Animals.txt` file in the branch, which is still Revision 100; Fred's commit has no effect on the file versions in the branch. Barb changes *black bear* to *bear* and commits the change, creating Revision 103 in the repository, as shown in Figure 1-10.

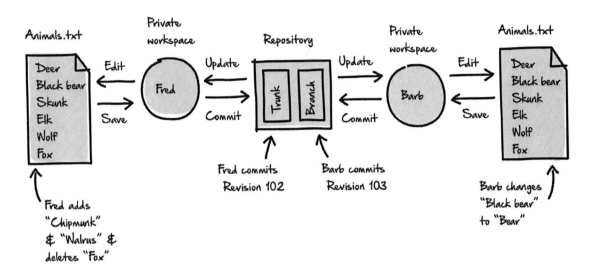

Figure 1-10:   Creating a branch for the Animals.txt file.

As you can see, at this point, we have two simultaneous but separate development efforts. Of course, at some point the team may want to merge changes made in the **1.0_bug fixes** branch back into the trunk so the next full product release can benefit from the maintenance fixes.

Merging

Previously, we discussed the need to perform a **merge** operation to resolve conflicting changes to the same version of a file in the repository. Similarly, when we create a branch, we'll at some point want to merge the changes made to the branch into the trunk. Conversely, we will also need to merge changes from the trunk into a branch. For example, this might be necessary so that a long-running "feature branch" can catch up with the changes in the trunk. As you can imagine, a merge in either direction could be a complex process, especially if conflicts arise across many project files.

The type of comparison made when merging between branches is similar to merging files during normal concurrent editing. In fact, within a particular source control system, the two processes might seem nearly identical. Conceptually, however, they are somewhat different in intent. When merging during concurrent editing of the same file, we're trying to resolve all conflicts to produce a copy of the file that represents a single source of truth. When merging a branch to the trunk, or vice versa, we're retaining two sources of the truth and we're interested only in incorporating the changes from one into the other.

For example, suppose Barb wishes to merge into the trunk the changes she made in the branch. Barb's latest commit to the repository was Revision 103 (*+bear, −black bear*), affecting the `Animals.txt` file in the branch. Meanwhile, Fred's latest commit to the repository was Revision 102 (*+chipmunk, +walrus, −fox*), affecting the **Animals.txt** file in trunk. The resulting merge operation will produce a new version of the `Animals.txt` file in the trunk (Revision 104), while the branch version will remain untouched at Revision 103.

Let's consider each of these changes in turn, in the context of the merge operation.

Fred's additions of *chipmunk* and *walrus* present no problem because they affect only the file slated for v2.0 (the trunk) and have nothing to do with version v1.1 (the branch). In other words, Revision 104 will still contain the *chipmunk* and *walrus* entries.

The next potential conflict is with the *fox* listing. Fred removed *fox* from the file in trunk, but Barb did not remove it from the version in her branch. You might think that in merging from branch to trunk, we'd add *fox* back in to the trunk version. However, in effect, this would simply overwrite Fred's change and any effective source control solution will recognize the potential for this sort of problem and avoid it. It may help to think of the merge in terms of the branch change set, in this case all the changes in the current branch revision compared to the revision on creating the branch. Barb wishes to apply this change set (*−black bear, +bear*) to the trunk file. This means, in SVN at least, that it will retain all other entries as they currently exist in trunk, and so *fox* will still *not* exist in the merged version in the trunk. Another VCS might mark this as a possible conflict, and the fact that the branch version assumes that the fox entry exists, but it doesn't exist in the trunk, is a potential problem. Ideally, before performing the merge, Barb would have updated her working copy of trunk and merged from trunk to branch, or at least inspected the differences and raised any possible issues with the team before performing her merge in the opposite direction.

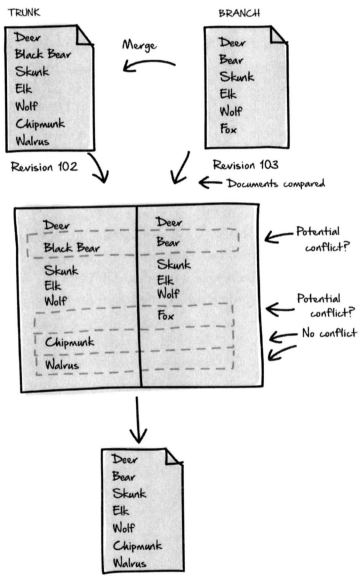

Figure 1-11: Resolving conflicts in the `Animals.txt` file.

Merging works differently in different source control systems

The methods used to perform the branch comparisons and merges vary from product to product, as does the amount of manual input involved to ensure that the merge does not do more damage than good. Each product is different and each configuration within a product can vary.

Finally, we have the potential conflict between *bear* and *black bear*. Just because Barb changed it in the trunk does not automatically mean it should be changed in the new release. Even so, SVN does not treat this as a conflict, though another VCS might. Only if Fred had also changed the *black bear* listing would SVN treat it as a conflict. The result is that the merged file in the trunk will contain the entry *bear*. Again, the onus is on Barb to ensure that this change to the maintenance release will cause no problems when applied to v2.0.

Branching usually comes off without a hitch; we point to the files and folders in the trunk that we want to branch and within seconds, off we go, with a new branch. Merging is the tricky part. The risks and overhead associated with merging can sometimes keep organizations from taking advantage of these capabilities. They might branch, but they don't merge, often resulting in duplicated development efforts and manual copy-and-paste operations.

On top of this, it's arguable that some source control systems are better at merging than others. Git, for example, was designed to merge, whereas SVN has a reputation for inflicting its fair share of agony on those trying to merge files.

Ultimately, though, the ability to branch and merge is crucial to any organization that needs to expedite their projects and work on those projects in parallel. The mantra is to merge early and often. If you do so, then it's not usually too painful.

Summary

In this chapter, we've discussed many of the primary benefits of a source control system, and taken an initial, largely conceptual, look at the components (repository and working folder) and processes (branching and merging) of such a system, which help us realize these benefits.

Application developers have been reaping these benefits for many years, but database developers are only just starting to catch up. It's true that database development is different from application development and we'll discuss these differences, and the extra challenges they pose for version control, in Chapter 3. Often database developers have to remind the rest of the development team of those differences, but that does not mean they cannot benefit from a proven system to store and manage files, track changes, work with different versions, and maintain a historical record of the file's evolution.

In the next chapter, we're going to take a deeper look at the role of the repository, for both centralized and distributed source control systems. We'll discuss briefly the factors to consider when choosing a source control system for database development work, and then install our chosen system and prepare it so we're ready, in Chapter 3, to start source controlling our databases.

Chapter 2: The Source Control Repository

All source control systems have a **repository**, a mechanism for storing and managing the files and preserving their histories. The repository organizes into a hierarchical tree structure every version of every file that comprises each branch of work. It also maintains comprehensive metadata that describes details about each file and folder, including who made the changes, when those changes occurred, comments submitted with those changes, and any other information the system needs in order to track each file and folder and maintain its version history.

All source control systems also provide a means to coordinate the efforts of a group of users working with those files. Via a **working folder**, users can add, modify, or delete files, without affecting the integrity of the files preserved in the repository. When changes are then committed back to the repository, the new versions are available to other users, and the repository retains the file version history. Together the repository and private workspace provide the structure necessary to support all other source control components and actions.

In this chapter, we examine the two primary types of repositories, **centralized** and **distributed**, looking specifically at how the two compare and how they differ. We also consider briefly the many factors that can influence the choice of a source control system for database development work.

In order to offer practical examples of the concepts, we had to pick a VCS for use in this book, and opted for **Subversion (SVN)**, a centralized repository. It is just one of a number of systems we could have chosen as a vehicle to demonstrate universal source control concepts; this is not a book *about* the SVN product, but SVN is free, easy to set up, and implemented widely, which made it a good candidate. The concluding sections of this chapter describe how to install Subversion and configure the repository and working folder, in preparation for putting a database under source control.

Centralized Versus Distributed Repositories

Source Control systems with a centralized repository are client-server applications that use a central server to host the repository, which stores the files and their version histories, along with any metadata necessary to manage those files and versions. All client computers communicate with the repository over a network, updating their working folders with the latest files in the repository, and committing changes in the opposite direction. All user interaction is between a local working folder and the remote repository, on the central server, which in turn oversees all operations related to the repository. These centralized solutions emerged into the market in the 1990s and dominate it still.

In the last decade, a new generation of source control tools has emerged that use a **distributed** model (also referred to as **decentralized**). In a distributed version control system (a **DVCS**), each client has a local repository, which is a clone and a peer of the repository on every other client. Most user interaction is between a local working folder and the local repository. Distributed systems are still as common as centralized ones, but they're quickly gaining popularity among the development community.

Many of the concepts fundamental to source control, such as updating working folders, committing changes to a repository, and so on, remain more or less the same regardless of the repository type, although individual features are implemented in different ways and the presence of local repositories in the distributed model alters the workflow. More notable differences come to the fore mainly when performing more complex operations such as merging, which we won't cover in detail until Chapter 6.

Centralized repositories

A VCS with a centralized repository, often referred to as "second generation," remains at the heart of the industry. When most people think of a VCS, they're usually thinking in terms of a centralized repository. Major document management systems, such as SharePoint Server, clearly rely on a central management server.

Figure 2-1 illustrates how a centralized system works. At the heart of the system is a central server that manages the repository, controls versioning, and orchestrates the update and commit processes. It maintains all the files, and tracks who made what changes, and when, via a series of **deltas**, which describe the modifications to the files over time, from one version to the next. In such a system, only the central repository stores the metadata necessary to describe these changes and maintain version history. Since there is a single central repository, it is an easy task to back up all the files stored in the repository.

Deltas and diffs

Sometimes the term delta is used interchangeably with **diff***, a dynamically generated comparison between two versions of a file. However, the two are not the same. Chapter 4 covers deltas and diffs in detail.*

In short, the central repository serves as the *single source of truth*. The users are, for all practical purposes, isolated from each other and all interactions are with this one repository, via a working folder on the client machine. Each user can update the files in the working folder, edit those files, and then commit the changes to the central server.

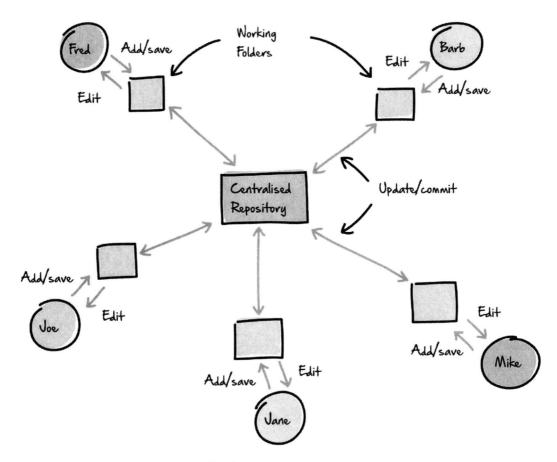

Figure 2-1:   Working with a centralized repository.

Following is a summary of a few of the core source control operations depicted in Figure 2-1. Of course, there are many more, some of which we'll encounter as we progress through the book.

- **Add** – Register a new file or folder in the working folder. When a user creates a file or folder for the first time (a file or folder that is currently no part of the source control system) they save it to their working directory. However, the user must then perform an **Add** operation to "register" it as part of that structure. Thereafter, the user can simply open the file in his or her editor of choice to edit it and then save the changes.

50

- **Commit** – Save to the repository changes made to the files and folders in a working folder.

- **Update** – Retrieve files and folders from the repository into the working folder so it has the correct version.

As noted in Chapter 1, you will see and hear different terms used to refer to the same operation, or even the same term used to refer to different operations! For example, in many second- and third-generation source control systems, developers tend to use the term **update** interchangeably with **checkout**. You might also hear the term **get** used in the same sense as checkout or update. In SVN, however, checkout has a specific meaning and refers to the initial synchronization of the working folder to the repository; essentially it's the first-ever update of a working folder.

An obvious drawback of a centralized system is that the users need the central server to be accessible in order to commit changes or update their working folders, as well as to carry out administrative tasks such as performing a diff or viewing file histories in the log. Users can, and do, work offline when editing the files in their working folders, but there is no history saved for any of these changes and, of course, no other user can access those changes until the user commits them to the repository. In general, a down server, as well as slow network connections or unavailable networks, can wreak havoc on the workflow.

Distributed repositories

A VCS based on the distributed model, often referred to as "third generation," is becoming an increasingly popular choice, because these address some of the limitations of centralized systems. In a DVCS, users each have a local clone of the repository on their client computer. Each local instance of a distributed repository maintains the entire project history of all changes to the files, as well as other metadata. In a DVCS, users can work offline and independently of each other, while still having a fully functioning source control system available at all times, thanks to their local repository.

In a centralized system, we saw that most of a user's interactions were across a network, between a local working folder on a client and a remote repository. In a distributed system, most of the interactions are between a local working folder and a *local* repository. When users wish to update their local repositories with other users' changes, or make their changes available to other users, they **synchronize** their local repository with any other remote repository, by **pushing** their changes to a remote repository and **pulling** others' changes into their local repository. Each repository can push changes to, and pull changes from, any other repository. Figure 2-2 shows an example of a DVCS that includes four users (Fred, Barb, Jane and Joe), each running a client machine with a local working folder and repository.

Users of a DVCS are likely to adhere to the following workflow, or some variation of it.

1. **Pull** the latest files and folders from a remote repository into their local repositories.

2. **Update** their working folders with the latest versions in their local repository.

3. **Edit** those files.

4. **Commit** changes to their local repositories.

5. **Push** files and folders to a remote repository.

A peer-to-peer relationship exists between each of the repositories. No one repository has any special significance over any other; each is a clone of the others. Of course, if users do not regularly push and pull changes, the repositories will quickly get out of sync, but eventually all will be consistent. Users can choose to pull only the branches, folders, or files that are relevant to their current work. However, this is not the default behavior and, culturally, most teams frown on this way of working. Such a process can become unwieldy, particular for large projects with a large number of users, and it becomes much harder to obtain a "master" view of the project as a whole.

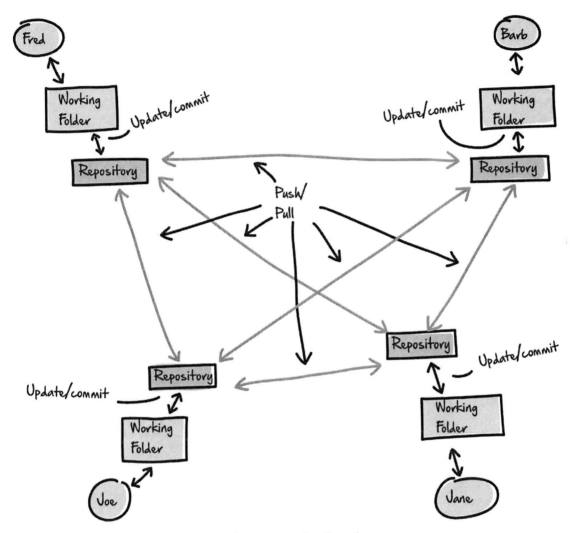

Figure 2-2:   Working without a central server in a distributed system.

In some DVCS architectures, a team often designates one of the peer repositories as a "central server" to which all users push their changes and from which they can pull recent file versions. In this sense, the central server is no different from any other peer, but it does represent the "one version of the truth" for the whole project, to which any local repository can refer.

Figure 2-3 shows an example of a distributed source control system in which we have designated one of the peers, Jane's computer, as the central server. Notice, however, that all peers can still push and pull from all other peers.

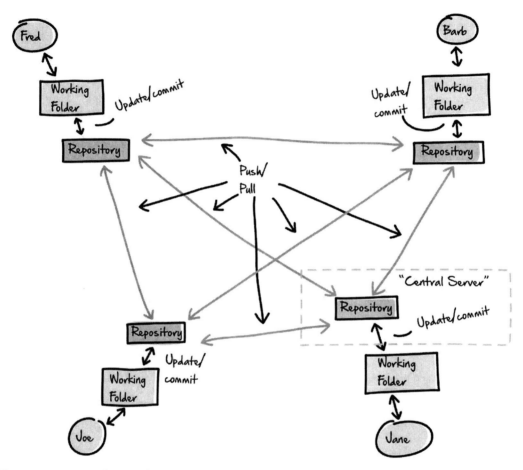

Figure 2-3: Working with a central server in a distributed system.

It is also possible to designate a separate computer to use specifically as a central server for the repository in order to support all users as well as provide a mechanism for backing up the repository at regular intervals. In this case, there would be no specific user associated with the machine in the sense of adding, editing and committing changes, although the server would still be considered a peer.

Comparing centralized and distributed repositories

Having seen the basic architecture for a centralized versus a distributed VCS, let's compare and contrast the two in terms of basic source control functionality, as well as administration.

Versioning

In the centralized model, users commit changes to, and update their local working folders from, a single central repository, which maintains the full version history for every file. The central server assigns a **global sequential revision number** to each commit. As a result, each file or set of files associated with a particular commit receives a revision number that represents a specific file version. The revision numbers increment sequentially making it easy to identify file versions at a specific point in time.

In a distributed model, users commit changes to their local repositories and then push and pull changes with any other remote repository. A distributed system will assign a commit hash to every change (for example, Git uses 40-character SHA1 hashes), but global sequential versioning is more difficult to achieve.

Chapter 4 provides a more detailed discussion of versioning.

Concurrent editing and merging

In the **centralized** model, all commits and updates require a connection to the central server, as does performing a diff or viewing revision history, and so on. Users can work on files offline, but what they do on their clients within their working folders is neither tracked nor versioned by the repository. A user can edit and save a file multiple times within a working folder, but it is only upon commit that those changes register in the repository as a new revision. At this point, other users can update their working folder to retrieve those changes into their working set.

If a conflict arises during a commit or an update, a user must perform a merge operation on their client and then commit the new, merged file. It's a potentially tricky operation and, in a centralized system, merges tend to be something to avoid, although modern centralized systems have become better at handling them. Although most centralized systems no longer exclusively lock a file upon checkout, it is possible to do so and, used sparingly, this is a possible solution in cases where you want to maintain absolute control over the versioning process and avoid issues of contention.

As discussed in Chapter 1, merging is much easier if the team adopt the "update often, commit often" philosophy. Counter to this, however, is the problem that with a single, central repository, every commit means inflicting the change on the rest of the team. It means users have a tendency to delay committing until they are sure the change won't cause disruption, which can sometimes result in a "big bang" merge operation.

In the **distributed** model, users commit changes locally and then push them to a remote repository as necessary, and pull the changes of others. A user can work offline, safe in the knowledge that their local repository maintains a full revision history. Users can also perform locally operations such as comparing versions (diffs) or viewing the log. In short, each user has a local, fully operational version control system.

Merge operations are safer, in that the user commits changes locally before performing a merge. After committing their changes locally, they can pull others' changes, update their working folder, perform a merge if necessary, commit again, and then push their changes. A user can make many small commits to their local repository, and then "publish" them all to a peer repository in one go, once debugging and testing is complete. This avoids potential disruption to the work of others while still offering each user the full benefit of a VCS.

A DVCS is designed from the ground up to support branching and merging, so it is optimized for that specific use case and encourages a culture of frequent merging. As a result, branches don't get stale enough to require a "big bang merge," as is often the case with second-generation systems.

Generally, third-generation systems have more sophisticated diffing algorithms, which often makes user intervention during merges less necessary. Centralized systems tend to track changes on a **file by file** basis. For example, let's say that during concurrent editing, one user renames a file, while another modifies the contents of the same file (with its original name). A system such as SVN will recognize this internally as a rename, rather than a "delete old file create new one" (as was the case for first-generation source control systems like CVS and SourceSafe). However, such situations will still raise a conflict and require a manual merge operation.

An important feature of distributed systems is that they **track changes across all files collectively**, rather than on a file-by-file basis. The text in a file has associated metadata that stores the filename. In our previous example, where one user renames a file, while another modifies its contents, a system such as Git records the former as a modification of the metadata attached to the text, and the latter as a modification of the text. Generally, it will be able to merge such changes without any manual user intervention.

Even so, if the possibility of conflict exists, the source control system will call for the user to step in to resolve those conflicts. The degree to which the user must get involved depends, in part, on the source control system itself as well as the files being compared.

If distributed systems offer much stronger support for merging (and therefore branching), the flipside is that you have much less control over what other users are doing. Although a distributed system can prevent changes from being lost or overwritten, it cannot prevent time being wasted on duplicate efforts.

Ease of backups

In a centralized system, the repository represents a single, consistent *source of truth* for all the files and folders, and all version histories. As such, it also provides the mechanism necessary for making reliable backups.

Even if a distributed system uses a central server, and we take backups off that repository, it can be difficult to guarantee that the backup represents a single, consistent view of the system. Of course, through repeated push/pull operations, each repository becomes a clone of any other repositories. In other words, we can achieve *eventual* consistency in a distributed system, as opposed to *immediate* consistency in a centralized system, and in that sense, each distributed peer could be considered a backup.

Repository size

Most modern source control systems are very efficient at storing file version histories while taking up minimal extra storage space. Using clever packing and compression techniques, a modern repository containing mainly text-based files can store decades of history with a total repository size of little more than that for a single working folder, and still maintain the current version of every file.

However, the *type* of file stored can and will affect the overall repository size. Binary files can take up lots of space. Each commit, after a change to one of these files, is likely to result in a whole new copy of the file. Under such conditions, the repository can rapidly grow in size.

The repository in a centralized system can, at least from a user's perspective, grow as large as it likes, as long as we can scale up the central server to accommodate the entire repository. Users can easily retrieve only a subset of files into their working folders in order to conserve space on their client machines.

However, size is more of an issue in a distributed system, with each user's client hosting a repository. Even if users quickly delete those large files, the repository maintains a permanent history of all changes, so the repository size is never reduced. This is true for first-, second-, and third-generation systems. For database developers, this might not be much of an issue, but it should be a consideration.

Security

A centralized system can restrict access to certain specific files and folders. In a distributed system, every peer gets all files and all history. This can become a concern, for example, if a contractor should have access to only a portion of the files. However, many teams get around this limitation by creating multiple smaller repositories, rather than maintaining one large one, as is more often the case in a centralized system.

Choosing a VCS for Database Development

There are many factors to consider when choosing both the repository type (centralized or distributed) and the specific source control product that is most appropriate for the needs of the organization, team, and project. It is necessary to consider the needs, not only of application developers, but also of the database developers, the administrators who will access the VCS to manage operations, the QA testers who must be able to test applications, the project managers who must be able track progress, and so on.

That said, perhaps the most important factor is continuity and consistency among teams. If the application development team uses a specific source control system then there will be a strong pull toward using the same one for the databases, and for good reason. Having the database content in the same repository as the application content provides a single, consistent versioning scheme across all project assets. Most source control solutions support different configurations within the same system, in order to maximize user flexibility.

The geographical distribution of your development team is also an important factor. A centralized source control solution can become a hindrance if your team is distributed to the extent that network bandwidth and connectivity become an issue. Under such circumstances, a distributed system might offer the necessary flexibility that a centralized one cannot.

Many application developers now work in Agile team environments, where code changes are rapid and frequent. They appreciate the flexibility of a distributed source control system, the strong support for concurrent editing of files via branching and merging, and the freedom to work locally as much as possible. When we want to replace the existing version of a client application with the version in source control, it doesn't really matter *how* we apply the changes as long as the modified version still builds and runs correctly.

For database developers, accustomed to a more sedate rate of change, this can seem an alien environment. In contrast to upgrading a live application, when we want to upgrade an existing database, for instance to add or remove a column, change a data type, split a table, and so on, we must be certain that what we have stored in the VCS describes, not only the required changes, but the exact order and manner in which to perform these changes in order to preserve data integrity.

Historically, most teams haven't had in place the processes, tools, checks, and controls that allowed frequent modification of live databases without significant risk of data loss, database downtime and subsequent disruption to users and to the business. Therefore, historically, database development work, in contrast to application development, has tended to be more conservatively paced, with longer upfront design and less frequent subsequent changes. In this sense, database development seems to be a better fit with the higher degree of control afforded by a single, centralized "master" repository, rather than the speed and high flexibility of a multi-repository distributed system.

However, with better tools, processes, and automated testing procedures in place, most teams now embrace a unified approach to the development and deployment of both application and database, and therefore a unified strategy for versioning a project, with all project resources organized side by side in the same repository. When all these are versioned together, everything can, in theory at least, change as often as necessary. Ultimately, in such teams, it's highly likely that the database will be absorbed into the existing VCS strategy for the application.

Versioning a Project in the Repository

As noted in the previous section, the secret of successful source control is to have all project assets versioned together, in the same repository. This will, of course, include the database, which is our primary interest in this book, but also the application code, QA resources including automated and functional tests, certain configuration details for each environment, scripts and tools for accomplishing various tasks, deployment scripts, and so on.

In many development projects the **trunk**, often referred to as **master**, is where the mainstream development effort takes place, and so this is where all the project folders live. The team create branches off of trunk as it becomes necessary to separate out certain strands of the development effort. However, different teams take different approaches, and we'll discuss this topic in more detail in Chapters 3 and 5.

The important point is that, with all the assets together, it's possible to use a single version number to represent a point in time for the entire application. This is immensely useful for fulfilling one of the main purposes of source control, namely being able to reproduce the entire project as it existed at a particular revision. For example, let's say a customer reports a bug with a release version of our software. We can re-create the project, from the revision in the repository that corresponds to this release, reproduce the reported defect, debug it, create a fix, and redeploy the new version to customers.

Each user checks out to their working folder at different levels of the repository structure, according to their role. In Figure 2-4, Jane, a data architect, checks out the entire repository. She creates a **BookstoreProject** folder on her client, linked to the root of the **BookstoreProject** repository on the server. Fred, a database developer, only needs the database assets so he creates a subfolder of **BookstoreProject** on his client, called **BookstoreDatabases**, and during checkout links it to the **Databases** sub-directory of the **BookstoreProject** repository.

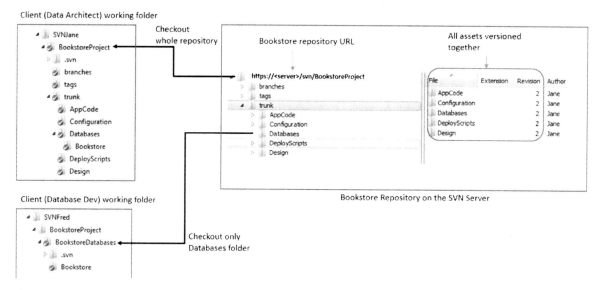

Figure 2-4:   Project versioning.

Getting Started with Source Control

In order to turn concepts into practical examples, we needed to choose a source control system for this book. We decided to use a centralized system over a distributed one, and out of all the available centralized solutions, we chose Subversion (SVN), a system created by Collabnet and provided as an open source Apache project.

In addition to the above considerations, with regard the specific nature of database development work, we also took into account the following factors:

- SVN is an open source solution, so it's free.

- It is relatively easy to set up and runs on multiple platforms.

- It is one of the most widely implemented source control solutions, so you can find plenty of information about how it works, and people who are currently using it.

Ultimately, though, it is just one of any number of systems we could have chosen, and our choice of SVN in no way implies that we endorse this product above all others. For demonstrating the concepts in this book, SVN is a good fit, but you must decide what will work best for you.

Setting up Subversion

The best way to get started with source control is to jump right in; fortunately, SVN makes that very easy. All we need to do is create the repository and configure the working folder and we're good to go. To help us do this, we use the tools below.

- **VisualSVN Server standard edition** – A free SVN management program that lets us create and manage an SVN repository on a Windows computer.
  For information about downloading, installing, and running VisualSVN Server, see HTTP://WWW.VISUALSVN.COM/SERVER/.

- **TortoiseSVN** – A free, user-friendly interface that integrates with the Windows Shell, making most SVN-related commands available through Windows Explorer. We'll use this tool for all interactions between a user's working folder and the repository.
  For information about downloading, installing, and running TortoiseSVN, see HTTP://TORTOISESVN.NET.

In any real development environment, we'd have a separate server for the central SVN repository, and each user would work on their own machine, interacting with the central server through their working folder. If a proper client-server architecture is available to you, perhaps via virtual machines, then that's the setup to use. However, for convenience, we create both the SVN repository and the working folders for all users on a single machine, specifically a Windows 7 virtual machine running an instance of SQL Server 2012.

Avoid using TortoiseSVN for both working folder and local repository

Built into TortoiseSVN is a feature that lets us create a local repository. This configuration permits one user to connect to the repository on the same machine as the working folder. If you plan to try out the examples in this book, this approach works fine except when we need two users to demonstrate such concepts as branching and merging. However, if you plan to use the same computer to participate in a server-based SVN system, you're better off not using this feature because it can complicate any subsequent participation in the server-based implementation.

For the VisualSVN Server installation, we used the following default settings:

- **Location** – Default location (**C:\Program Files\VisualSVN Server**).

- **Repositories** – Default folder (**C:\Repositories**), where VisualSVN Server stores the repository data and metadata.

- **Server Port** – Default port (443) – if another service, such as Internet Information Services (IIS), uses port 443, you will need to select a different port, such as 8443.

- **Use secure connection** – Option selected.

- **Authentication** – Subversion authentication (we cannot use Integration Windows Authentication with the VisualSVN Server Standard edition, but it is available in the Enterprise Edition).

You can change the default settings in the server properties. To access the properties, open VisualSVN Server Manager, right-click the **VisualSVN Server** node and then click **Properties**. In the **VisualSVN Server Properties** dialog box, select the appropriate tab and configure the settings as necessary. For example, to change the authentication mode, go to the **Authentication** tab.

For the TortoiseSVN installation, simply follow the onscreen prompts and accept all the default settings.

With both tools installed, we're ready to go. The rest of this chapter is devoted to setting up a repository and working folder.

Setting up the repository

Not surprisingly, to set up a source control environment, one of the first tasks is to create the repository. Our repository will host a fictitious development project called **BookstoreProject**. As its name implies, it relates to a bookstore and its inventory.

Before we actually create the repository, we will add a few users to VisualSVN Server so we can control access to the repository and its files. We open up VisualSVN Server Manager.

Create repository users

We want to create three authorized repository users: **Jane**, the data architect, and two database developers, **Fred** and **Barb**. We'll make sure that no other user accounts can access our repositories.

1. In the left window, right-click the **Users** node, and then click **Create User**.

2. In the **Create New User** dialog box, create the first user, **Jane**, assign a password, and then click **OK**.

3. Repeat Steps 1 and 2 to create the users, **Fred** and **Barb**. The **Users** node should now look similar to Figure 2-5.

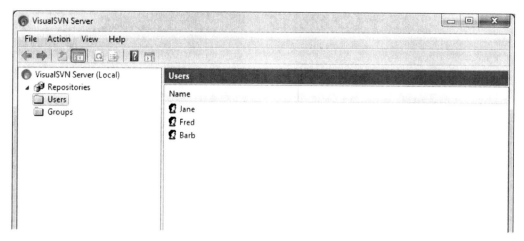

Figure 2-5:   Viewing users in VisualSVN Server Manager.

Create the repository

Our next task is to create the actual repository, which we'll name **BookstoreProject**.

1. Right-click the **Repositories** node, and then click **Create New Repository** to launch the wizard.

2. Enter **BookstoreProject** in the **Repository Name** text box, and then click **Next**.

3. On the **Repository Structure** screen, select the option **Single-project repository** (more on this below) and click **Next**.

4. In some cases, we would select the default option, **Empty repository**, but for now we want to use the predefined **trunk**, **branches**, and **tags** folders, a structure common to many development projects.

5. On the **Repository Access Permissions** screen, select the **Customize Permissions** option and then click the **Custom** button.

6. In the **Customize Permissions** dialog box, click the **Add** button.

7. In the **Choose User or Group** dialog box, select the users **Barb**, **Fred**, and **Jane**, and then click **OK**.

8. The three users should now appear in the **Customize Permissions** dialog box. Ensure that they all have **Read/Write** permission, and then click **OK** to close the dialog box.

9. On the **Repository Access Permissions** screen, click **Create**.

10. The R**epository Created Successfully** screen should appear and provide details about the **main** repository. Click **Finish** to complete the wizard.

Beneath the **Repositories** node in VisualSVN Server Manager, you should now see the **BookstoreProject** repository, with three folders: **branches**, **tags**, and **trunk**, as shown in Figure 2-6.

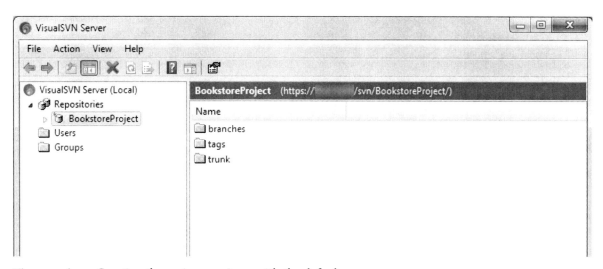

Figure 2-6:   Creating the main repository with the default structure.

11. Notice that the URL for the **BookstoreProject** repository appears above the right window. We will need it later, so right-click the **BookstoreProject** node and click **Copy URL to Clipboard** to get the URL.

As we progress, we can create the subfolders needed to store our project files, but we'll do that through the users' working folders. Interaction with the repository and its structure via Visual SVN Manager should be kept to a minimum, and should be the preserve of the project administrator only.

That's all there is to setting up the repository. If you want to test access to the repository, you can use your browser by going to HTTPS://LOCALHOST:443/SVN/ (or whichever port you selected). If prompted, enter one of the usernames and passwords. You should then be able to see the repository content. Note, however, that the URL and port number may vary depending how you initially configured the repository.

Setting up the working folders

Now that we've set up the repository on the server, it's time to set up a working folder on each client so that our users can access the repository and interact with it.

In this chapter, we'll define the high-level structure for the project as a whole. The focus of the book is purely on the database development but, as discussed, it's important to have all project assets stored side by side in a single repository. Subsequently, the database developers can update their respective working folders with this structure or, more specifically, the parts of it that are relevant to them, and start development work.

Each user's client, in this example, is TortoiseSVN, which integrates into Windows Explorer. As discussed earlier, you will ideally set up each user on a separate client. If you're working on a single machine, you'll need to remember to clear TortoiseSVN's authentication data each time you want to switch between users.

Multiple users on the same client: clearing authentication data

To clear out the previous authentication details, and connect as a different user, right-click the working folder, or one of its subfolders, navigate **TortoiseSVN | Settings**. *Go to the* **Saved Data** *node, and click* **Clear All** *for the* **Authentication data** *listing.*

Create a working folder: checkout

In order to set up a working folder for each of our three users (Jane, Fred, Barb), we simply need to create a regular folder in Windows Explorer (or use an existing *empty* folder), and then perform what SVN calls a **checkout**. As we discussed earlier, a checkout has a very specific meaning in SVN and what it does is register the working folder with the repository and perform the initial synchronization necessary to copy over the repository folder structure (trunk, branches and tags) and files.

To start, we'll create a working folder in the VCS for **Jane**, the data architect, who is responsible for defining how to structure the whole project. Jane will connect to the repository to register her working folder and perform an initial **checkout** of the whole **BookstoreProject** repository.

To create Jane's working folder:

1. In the root of the **C:** drive on your client machine (or use whatever drive and name you wish), create a folder called **SVNJane**. This allows us to distinguish each user when working on the same client. If you have each user on a separate client this folder is unnecessary.

2. Within the **SVNJane** folder, create a subfolder named **BookstoreProject**. This directory will form the root of Jane's working folder and will correspond to the root folder of the **BookstoreProject** repository (see Figure 2-4).

3. Right-click the **BookstoreProject** directory, and then click **SVN Checkout**.

4. In the **Checkout** dialog box, you should find a URL that points to the repository and the path to your working folder, similar to what is shown in Figure 2-7.

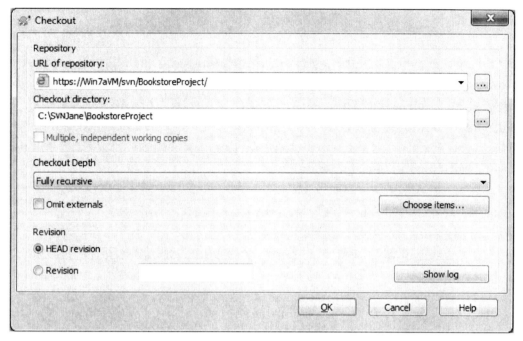

Figure 2-7:   The repository URL and working folder.

5. If you've already connected to a different SVN repository from your computer, another URL might be listed in the **URL of repository** text box. In such cases, you can retrieve the correct URL from within VisualSVN Server Manager by right-clicking the **main** repository and then clicking **Copy URL to Clipboard**.

6. Having verified that the information in the **Checkout** dialog box is correct, click **OK**.

7. When the **Authentication** dialog box appears, enter Jane's credentials, select the **Save authentication** check box and click **OK**.

8. When the **Checkout Finished** dialog box appears, it should confirm the update of Jane's working folder to reflect the initial trunk/branches/tags structure that we established when we created the repository. Creation of this initial repository structure formed Revision 1 in the repository, so Jane's folder is now "synchronized" with Revision 1 in the repository.

That's all we need to do to create a working folder! Jane's folder, as it appears in Windows Explorer, should now look similar to the one shown in Figure 2-8.

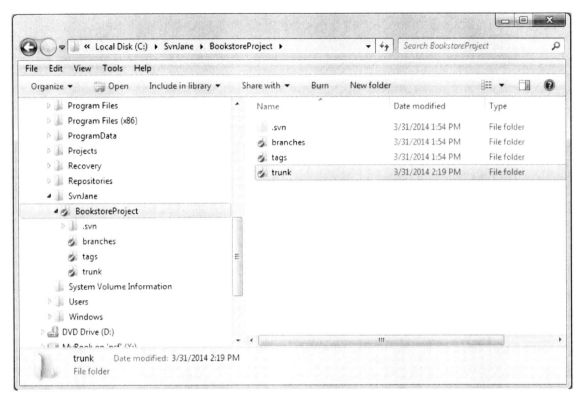

Figure 2-8: Jane's working folder in Windows Explorer.

The white-on-green checkmark on each folder except the **.svn** folder indicates that those folders are in sync with the latest revision in the repository. The **.svn** folder contains the metadata necessary to manage the files and folders in the working folder and to keep them in sync with the repository.

When viewing the working folder, be aware that TortoiseSVN can sometimes be slow in applying the appropriate icons to the various folders and files, especially with old hardware, very large repositories, or when the system is under load. Sometimes, refreshing Windows Explorer can help hurry things along.

Create the project structure in the repository: Add and Commit

Jane can now add the subfolders to her working directory that will establish the high-level project structure within the VCS. For this project, the major development effort will take place in trunk, so this is where we need to locate all the project assets. To establish the basic project structure in the repository we'll use two very common source control operations:

1. **Add** the file or folder to the working folder – **Add** is a formal source control process that "registers" the file or folder within the working folder.

2. **Commit** the file or folder (or both) to the repository – **Commit** is a formal source control process to move data from the working folder to the repository.

Remember, that these terms might have subtly or even very different meanings in a different VCS. In Git, for example, **Add** means to add to the staging area. However, for our purposes here, we referring specifically to the registering of the file or folder with the source control process.

We can commit empty folders to source control, we can commit individual files to source control, or we can commit a folder and all its subfolders and files in one go. In each case, we follow essentially the same process. We create the folder in the working folder, or save the file to it, and then perform an **Add** followed by a **Commit**.

Updating the working folder

*When we commit the changes in the working folder to the repository, we only move data from the working folder to the repository, not in the other direction. Any changes committed to the repository by other users in the meantime are not copied to our working folder until we explicitly do an **Update**. The working folder is only as current as the initial checkout or the last update. Chapter 3 covers the **Update** operation in more detail.*

Add the folders

In Windows Explorer, navigate to Jane's working folder (**SVNJane**), and then to the **trunk** folder, and create several new subfolders for **AppCode**, **Configuration**, **Databases**, **DeployScripts**, and **Design**. Since we are interested primarily in the database, let's also create a folder for our **Bookstore** database, as a subfolder of **Databases**. All of the other asset folders are empty, and are included simply to emphasize the importance of versioning all project assets together. We won't discuss them further.

Figure 2-9:   Creating new folders in the working folder.

The "?" icon overlay for each folder indicates that it is currently "untracked" by the repository.

At this stage we've created the folders but not registered them as part of the working folder structure. In order to do this, we need to **Add** them. Right-click the **Bookstore-Project** folder, point to **TortoiseSVN**, and then click **Add**. The **Add** dialog box lists the new folders, all selected by default, as shown in Figure 2-10.

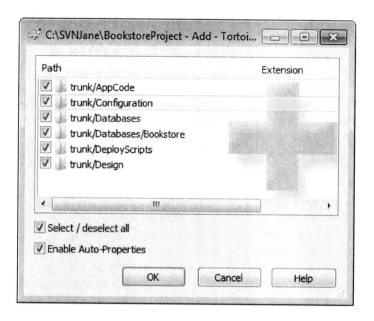

Figure 2-10:   Adding new folders to the working folder.

Jane can deselect any folders she doesn't want to add to her working folder at this time, but in this case she wants to add all of them, so click **OK**. We'll see confirmation of the folders that TortoiseSVN added to the working folder. With the **Add** complete, Jane's working folder should look as shown in Figure 2-11.

We see a blue plus sign next to each of our new folders, indicating that they have been newly added to the working folder, and white-on-red exclamation points on all the **trunk** and **BookstoreProject** folders, higher in the hierarchy, indicating one or more changes or additions to these folders that we are yet to commit to the repository.

Figure 2-11:   Folders added, but not committed.

We can verify the current mismatch between the working folder and the repository using the Repository Browser, a built-in tool for TortoiseSVN. Right-click the **BookstoreProject** folder, point to **TortoiseSVN**, and then click **Repo-Browser**. There you'll see that the **trunk** folder in the repository contains none of the new subfolders. For the subfolders to appear, we must commit our changes to the repository.

Commit the folders

During general development, we'd probably add files to a new folder and commit them together, but here we're only interested in establishing our initial project structure. Back in the working folder in Windows Explorer, right-click the **BookstoreProject** folder and then click **SVN Commit**. In the **Commit to** dialog box (shown in Figure 2-12) we can and should add a comment to the **Message** text box to describe what we're committing to the repository. Some organizations have specific guidelines for commit messages but even if

75

not, it's a very good practice to provide a description, as it can make auditing tasks much easier down the road.

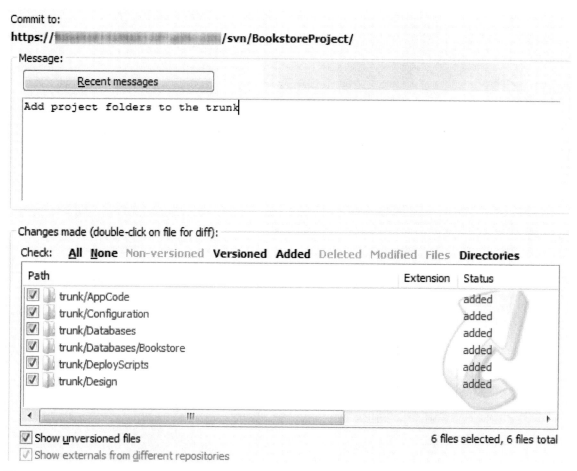

Figure 2-12: Committing new folders.

Click **OK** to close the **Commit to** dialog box. The subsequent **Commit Finished** dialog box reports which folders we committed and a revision number, in this case Revision 2. We'll discuss revision numbers in much more detail in Chapter 3, but for now simply note how our source control system increments the revision numbers with each commit operation.

Action	Path	Mime type
Command	Commit	
Adding	C:\SVNJane\BookstoreProject\trunk\AppCode	
Adding	C:\SVNJane\BookstoreProject\trunk\Configuration	
Adding	C:\SVNJane\BookstoreProject\trunk\Databases	
Adding	C:\SVNJane\BookstoreProject\trunk\Databases\Bookstore	
Adding	C:\SVNJane\BookstoreProject\trunk\DeployScripts	
Adding	C:\SVNJane\BookstoreProject\trunk\Design	
Completed	**At revision: 2**	

Figure 2-13: A successful commit creates a new revision in the repository.

Click **OK** to close the **Commit Finished** dialog box. White-on-green checkmarks should now overlay each of the folders we added to the working folder and then committed to the repository. In fact, this icon now precedes all folders (except **.svn**), indicating that the working folder contains no additions or changes that need to be committed to the repository, as shown in Figure 2-14.

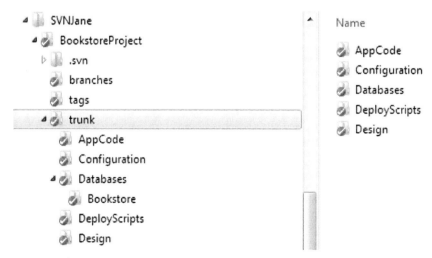

Figure 2-14: Jane's working folder with no changes to commit.

If desired, we can reopen the repo-browser to confirm that the subfolders now also exist in the repository.

Setting up working folders for the database developers

It's now time to set up the working folders for our developers, Barb and Fred. Barb is the lead developer and will need to check out the entire project. Fred is a database specialist and will be working only with the files in the **Databases** folder.

For Barb, we perform a checkout to a **BookstoreProject** folder, exactly as we did for Jane (except within a parent folder called **SVNBarb**). If you are working from a single client, remember to right-click **BookstoreProject**, choose **Settings**, and under **Saved Data** clear the authentication data, as described previously, before right-clicking again and performing the checkout. This will update Barb's working folder with the project structure Jane created.

Fred, instead of checking out the entire repository structure, will check out only the **Databases** folder, as follows:

1. In **Windows Explorer**, create a working folder named **C:\SVNFred** and then a subfolder called **BookstoreProject**.

2. Create a subfolder in **BookstoreProject** called **BookstoreDatabases**. This is the folder to which we will check out the **Databases** folder in the repository.

3. Right-click the **BookstoreDatabases** folder.

    a. If you are working from a single client, reset the authentication data. If not, go straight to b.

    b. Select **SVN Checkout**.

4. Provide a URL to the repository's **Databases** folder. Simply append the repository's root URL with **/trunk/Databases**, or click the ellipsis button and navigate to the folder in repository browser.

Figure 2-15: Mapping server to client URLs during checkout.

5. Click **OK** to close the **Checkout** dialog box.

6. If you receive a message that your certification failed, click **Accept the certificate permanently**.

7. When the **Authentication** text box appears, enter Fred's credentials and then click **OK**.

The **Checkout Finished** dialog box will appear and provide an overview of the folder you checked out. Fred's working folder is now at Revision 2 and he has in his working folder only the contents of the **Databases** folder.

Figure 2-16: Fred's working folder.

Remember that Fred checked out the **trunk/Databases** folder, so he doesn't actually have the **trunk** folder in his working directory, but implicitly all the work he does in his working folder will be committed to trunk.

We've Only Just Begun

At the end of this chapter, you should understand the fundamental differences between centralized and distributed repositories and have a better appreciation of the factors that will affect your choice.

Given the number of source control solutions now available to database developers, there's no reason that anyone who creates, modifies, or manages database components should not be taking advantage of source control both personally and across their organization.

Of course, this is just the start of our journey. We've set up a source control repository and a working folder with which to interact with it, and now it's time to put a database under source control!

Chapter 3: Getting Started with Source Control for Databases

Over the course of the previous chapters, we've discussed many of the primary benefits of source control systems in coordinating the efforts of the development team, ensuring a complete audit trail of all changes to the code files, and allowing the team to reproduce any specific revision or build. I hope by this stage you are convinced that a source control solution can and must play a key role in pulling together the database development process in a way that makes it more productive and efficient, while maintaining a history of database changes.

Database developers can and should benefit from source control's audit history and change-tracking capabilities, but there's more to it than simply placing a few database build scripts into a subfolder of the application development team's project folder in source control.

This chapter discusses many of the factors that will influence how a development team works with a database via the VCS, and how the team creates, organizes and updates the relevant database files in the VCS. Unlike application developers, database developers are not assembling files into a neat little application package, but are instead running scripts that feed off each other and off existing database objects, while negotiating the close interdependency between the code and the data.

However, with the appropriate planning, our VCS will not only protect our files and provide a single authoritative source for our schema, so we can incorporate changes into our database design in a controlled and consistent manner; it will also allow us to build any version of the database stored in the VCS and use it to upgrade any existing database, without fear of causing data loss or data integrity issues.

Planning for Database Source Control

The majority of this book concerns itself directly with the practicalities of using a version control system in a development environment to improve the efficiency of team-based database development. Regardless of the type of source control repository they choose, team members need to give thought up front to their **development model**, while coordinating their efforts through that VCS. They must also consider how they wish to **build and deploy** databases from source control. Both factors, and others, will affect how the team uses the VCS, how they organize the source files in the VCS, and how they handle modification of those files.

Integrated Development Environment (IDE) integration

Application developers work on files within their preferred IDE, usually Visual Studio for Windows platform developers. The IDE provides tools, either built in or via a plug-in, for syntax checking, debugging, compiling, and other development-related tasks. To give one obvious example, VisualSVN, a plug-in for the Visual Studio IDE, makes it very easy to work with a VCS, allowing developers to add and edit files directly from within the Visual Studio IDE. When developers modify an application, they retrieve the necessary code files from the VCS, build the application in their IDE, edit the underlying files directly, and commit the changed files back to the VCS. This is a natural fit for working with a VCS, and a very natural development model.

In recent years, good VCS plug-ins have also emerged for database development IDEs such as SQL Server Management Studio (SSMS) and SQL Server Data Tools (SSDT), offering some degree of source control for database development. The majority of this book does not rely on any particular plug-ins, but in Chapter 8 we demonstrate a database build and deployment scheme using the Red Gate SQL Source Control SSMS plug-in, which allows developers to work on a live database while ensuring every change gets checked into source control and becomes immediately available to other team members.

Disconnected versus online database development

The model whereby developers work in their preferred IDE, directly modifying the files stored in source control, is great for application development but a less natural fit for database development. It means that database developers need to work on a source-code "representation" or "model" of the database, in the form of the SQL scripts that create or alter the database objects, rather than working directly with a live database (the term "live" does not necessarily refer to a production database, but rather any running database, usually one used for development).

We call this a **disconnected** development model. For example, for each modification to a database object, a developer might generate a separate **change script** (we'll discuss other options shortly) and commit it to the VCS, and then run the script against the live database.

Some database developers, however, update the live database directly. In this **online** development model, we construct retrospectively the scripts necessary to describe the change (i.e. the source code), once the change is complete. Many teams use a schema comparison tool to generate the change scripts by comparing the updated live database with the latest revision in the source control repository.

Some teams favor the disconnected model because it is a highly controlled process, but the online model is equally viable, as long as the team has in place the tools, workflow, and business processes to ensure that all changes get from the live database into source control. These requirements are really no different from those used to control how application code gets from a developer's workstation to the repository. As the tools and processes to support the online database development model improve, it will likely become more common because it represents a much faster, more intuitive way to build databases.

You can work through the majority of this book using either development model, but Chapter 8 follows the online model.

Shared versus dedicated database development

It is a very common practice for every application developer to have their own "sandbox" environment, rather than have everyone work in a shared server environment. It means every developer can work in relative isolation, unaffected by the changes made by others. As soon as a change is completed and tested, the developer commits the change to the VCS, so that it is available to other developers the next time they update their working folders.

Most developers would prefer to use the same model for database development, working on their own dedicated sandbox databases, and committing changes to a shared database directory in source control, from where they are available to other team members.

However, for various reasons, many teams develop against a single shared database. It can mean lower licensing costs, the need to generate only one copy of test data, and the ability for the DBA to manage the environment much like a production instance, applying the correct security configuration, as well as instance and database properties.

The biggest impact on the development team, however, is the need to ensure non-interfering changes in the shared database environment. There are ways to achieve this. For example, if the database design makes intelligent use of schemas, such that each schema represents a logical area of the overall application then, notionally, we could assign each developer to a logical area, and there would be few overlapping changes.

However, most developers relying on a shared database have no doubt found that changes made by others can and do break things and affect their work, causing delays and frustration. Given a choice, most developers would likely choose the dedicated model.

Source control and Application Lifecycle Management

No VCS is an island, and in most development teams the VCS will be integrated into a larger suite of tools and policies that govern how the team design, build, test, and deploy applications and databases. The umbrella term for this suite of tools and policies is **Application Lifecycle Management** (ALM).

Not surprisingly, the ways in which these tools integrate varies from solution to solution, and tools can, and often do, cross multiple categories. For example, Microsoft offers the Visual Studio ALM solution, which includes Team Foundation Server for version control, bug tracking, build automation, reporting, and other functionality. The solution also includes the Visual Studio IDE for coding, debugging, and testing. SourceGear Fortress, on the other hand, is a cross-platform ALM solution that integrates version control, work item tracking, and other tasks into a single environment that can be integrated with IDEs such as Eclipse and Visual Studio.

The choice of ALM strategy will largely define the team's approach to source control issues such as support for concurrent editing, when and how to create branches and tags, how to name and comment on files, and how to organize the folder structure. We'll discuss good practices for each of these issues as we progress through the book, but it's essential to establish that there are many possible approaches, and that the one you choose will depend on many other factors, including the overall ALM strategy.

Database build and deploy considerations

Source control protects our files and provides a single authoritative source for our schema so that we can incorporate changes into our database design in a controlled and consistent manner during development. Of course, at some point the development effort will be complete, and the team will need to build and deploy the database to a target environment, such as **test**, **staging** or **production**, either to create a new database or to update an existing one in that environment.

At the deployment stage, our goal is to have in source control a single source of "truth" that defines precisely the database we wish to deploy. In other words, source control provides the foundation for reliable and repeatable database deployments to a range of environments.

Always deploy from source control

As tempting as it might be, never "sneak in" a direct modification to a test, staging, or production database, whether to add a feature or to quickly solve a customer concern. Always make the effort to make the change in the VCS, retest, and redeploy through the official deployment process. If someone modifies a target database directly, then it renders invalid the scripts we have in source control to roll that database from one state to another. This is a problem termed **version drift** *and it can and will cause failed deployments (see Chapter 7 for further details).*

We won't discuss the intricacies of database build and deploy until Chapters 7 and 8, but it's a potentially complex process with many moving parts, all of which rely on the fact that the correct versions of all the required files are in the VCS and accessible by the build engine. The developers must ensure, for example, that the VCS contains the correct versions of the scripts necessary to create objects, load reference (lookup) data, migrate data, add security accounts, set configuration settings, provide parameter values, or take any other necessary actions. If batch files, PowerShell files, or other types of script files are necessary, those too must be ready to go.

One of the major issues to address is how to apply those scripts and, particularly, in what order to apply them. The most basic solution is to document each step and ask the DBA to execute the scripts in the prescribed order. A slightly better option is to create a batch file that executes them in the preferred order. We can maintain (in source control, of course) a "change log" that supplies the batch file with an ordered list of scripts.

However, considering that building or upgrading a database might require hundreds of script files, this is clearly a task crying out for automation. Many organizations turn to tools that automate most or all of the steps necessary to build and deploy their applications and databases.

We have numerous options. For example:

- **Red Gate's Deployment Manager** is a package-based management tool for deploying databases.
- **Microsoft's Visual Studio Team Foundation Server** includes Team Foundation Build, which automatically compiles and tests applications.
- **BuildMaster** automates build management and supports workflow-driven approvals, database change scripts, and production deployments.
- **CruiseControl** provides a framework for a continuous build process that includes plug-ins for email notification, Ant build software, and various source control tools.

Each tool helps automate the process of getting from Point A (source control) to Point B (the deployed application or database) and has its own methods for getting there.

Chapter 7 will discuss build-and-deploy issues and others in a lot more detail, as well as demonstrating a very basic but reliable build scheme based solely on a build table and a PowerShell script. Chapter 8 will discuss and demonstrate a more automated, tool-based approach to building and upgrading databases.

Database versioning challenges

When developers modify an existing code object during application development, they simply change the code file as appropriate and save the modified file over the top of the old version. In other words, a developer saves an object's code file to source control and then, during the development cycle, continually modifies that same file, as required. This is a natural fit with the standard source control model; the repository stores one file per object, regardless of how often we change it, and it can reproduce the exact state of that file at any given revision number. Whenever developers update their working folder they get the latest version of each object.

Working with database objects is sometimes different. We can work with the code modules that form our database interface, such as stored procedures and views, in much the same way as any other code object. We simply write the script that creates the object if it doesn't exist, or alters it if it does, and then we continually refine that same script in source control. However, when working with tables, we need a different approach, one that accounts for the complex dependencies between these objects and, critically, the need to preserve the table's state, in the form of its business data, from one version to the next.

This need to preserve state when upgrading an existing database is the main factor that distinguishes working with databases in a VCS from working with standard application files. Let's say a developer adds a field to a C# class in source control, and then later someone else changes the type of that field. It doesn't usually matter exactly how we apply those changes to the application as long as it builds correctly in its final state. For the equivalent database changes (adding a column then changing the data type), the exact manner in which we apply each change matters a great deal, as each one has implications for the business data.

We have two basic approaches to versioning a database:

1. **Save the current state of the schema** – we store one `CREATE` script per object and edit each file over time, to reflect each schema modification.

2. **Save the migration scripts** – for each schema object, we store the string of migration scripts (`ALTER <ObjectName>...`), usually one change per script, required to advance the object from one defined state to the next.

Most teams would prefer to use Scheme #1 during development, since it's analogous to the way they work with all other application files. However, when it comes time to deploy an upgrade, Scheme #1 implies that we can simply tear down any database object that already exists in the target database and re-create it with the version from source control. As we've just discussed, this is not possible when that target database stores business data.

For this reason, many teams adopt Scheme #1 during development, and then switch to Scheme #2 after deployment of v1, stringing all of the migration scripts together in the right order, to arrive at a build script to go from v1 to v2.

Ideally, however, we'd have a unified process in place that could take us through initial development and subsequent upgrade, at least as far as possible. We can use Scheme #1 for most cases, as long as we have tools we trust to automate the synchronization of the latest schema as it exists in the VCS, with the database schema of the target database. This may include, for example, use of a schema comparison tool, such as Red Gate's SQL Compare, among others. However, sometimes modifying a **CREATE** script is not sufficiently descriptive to allow our automation tools to handle the data correctly during the state change, and we must create a migration script to nudge the tool in the right direction. In other words, the team optimizes its general VCS and deployment processes around Scheme #1, but incorporates migration scripts for the "hard" cases. We cover migration scripts in great depth in Chapter 8.

Chapter 4 will discuss each of these schemes in more detail. Throughout Chapters 3 to 6, we adopt Scheme #1 when working on a database in the development environment. Chapter 7 demonstrates a build-and-deploy scheme that assumes Scheme #1 during development, but switches to Scheme #2 after deployment. Chapter 8 demonstrates a build-and-deploy mechanism that follows Scheme #1, but incorporates migration scripts as necessary.

Database source control architecture

As we've discussed, our chosen source control architecture will reflect the needs of the organization, the needs of those who will use source control, and all of our ALM processes, including how we design and develop applications and databases, the manner in which we deploy them, how we assign version and build numbers, and the general strategies for working with source control on a day-to-day basis.

There are many possible architectures and it's impossible to be prescriptive, but it's worth discussing general considerations, in terms of what needs to be in the VCS and how we organize those folders and files. Our goal should be to define our source control structure and the policies that govern that structure, *before* we actually start the first project, rather than waiting till we're in the middle of it.

What needs to be in source control?

The first step to getting a database into source control is to create a script file for each database object and then add each one to the VCS, in the appropriate directory. As we'll demonstrate later in the chapter, we can simply write the script to create each database object and save it as a separate file, or we can generate script files from existing database objects or diagrams.

Primarily, the development team needs to ensure that the scripts in source control represent the correct and most recent versions of all database **schema objects**, including the base tables and indexes, as well as the code modules (views, stored procedures, triggers, and so on) that define the interface to the base tables and indexes. The developers must also ensure the VCS contains the latest versions of the scripts to load any necessary **static data**, including both reference data and data from other sources.

While, in this book, we'll focus only on database schema objects and reference data, a lot more goes into a database. To get a feel for what else is involved, it's instructive to view the permission hierarchy of SQL Server instance and database objects, as shown in Figure 3-1.

As you can see, building and deploying a database is about more than just implementing the schema. Separately from the schema objects, but still a part of the VCS, we'll need scripts to create all other necessary database objects, notably the users, roles, and permissions that govern who can access which objects. Again, these scripts will form a separate but integral part of the overall database build-and-deploy process.

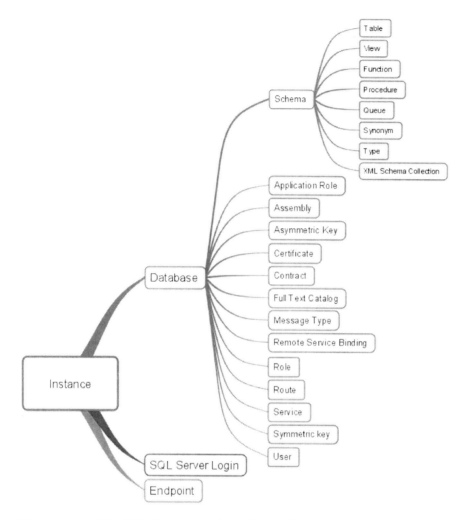

Figure 3-1:   The SQL Server permission hierarchy.

Other script files that go into a database build

Even Figure 3-1 doesn't tell the whole story. A database build might also include scripts to perform administrative tasks, such as define database configurations, schedule tasks, define file groups, perform Extract-Transform-Load (ETL) operations, or any number of interrelated and interdependent tasks. We don't cover this in the book, but HTTP://TINYURL.COM/KO99FNU provides a good overview of what's required.

On top of all this are the scripts necessary to define the deployment itself, such as batch files that list the order in which SQL scripts should be executed. The developer will have to work hand in hand with the DBA to provide all necessary scripts and to ensure that everyone is implementing the scripts through the change control processes that have been put into place.

Of course, in addition to the database, we have the applications that rely on it. As discussed in Chapter 2, right alongside the database in the VCS will be the files that comprise the relevant application, plus other related files, such as QA resources, test and design resources, and so on.

In short, only when the repository contains *everything* associated with the project, both database and application, are we truly gaining the benefits of the VCS audit trail.

Organizing the database source files

After *what*, the next question becomes *how* to store all of this in the VCS, i.e. how to determine the most appropriate folder and file structure for the database.

One simple but common organizational structure for database source control is to have a project folder (named after the database) and within it a series of subfolders for each relevant type of database schema object (a subfolder for tables, one for views, and so on). For simplicity, it's a model we use in this book, though some developers prefer an even simpler structure, with just a dedicated folder for tables (which need to maintain state) and a dedicated folder for all code modules that define the database interface.

Another approach to organizing files is to group schema-related objects together. For example, in a book-related application, we might subdivide the database objects and functionality into schemas such as **BookOrders, Accounts, Dispatch**, and so on. As a result, in our source control repository, we might create a subfolder named **SchemaObjects** under the database project folder. Within **SchemaObjects**, we would then create a subfolder for each schema (e.g. **BookOrders, Accounts, Dispatch**, etc.).

Finally, within each schema folder, we would create subfolders such as **Tables**, **Views**, **Types**, and so on. All files not related to schemas, such as database-level objects, batch files, or test data scripts, would be stored in folders outside of the schema hierarchy.

Simplifying the permission architecture

Although it's out of scope to go into detail here, such a schema-driven design also simplifies permissions, since we simply create a database login and role that has access only to the relevant schema and the objects therein.

For more information, see: HTTP://TECHNET.MICROSOFT.COM/EN-US/LIBRARY/MS191465.ASPX.

Again, for simplicity and because we need to focus on source control concepts, we don't make use of schemas in this book. We use only the default (dbo) schema in our Bookstore database. As a result, the way we organize the files in repository might be quite different from what you've seen elsewhere.

Getting the Bookstore Database into Source Control

Now that we've covered the basics, it's finally time to get our sample Bookstore database into source control and start developing it! In light of all the previous "planning" discussion, the following summarizes our basic approach to working with our example database and storing it in SVN:

- We'll develop our database in SSMS and from there we'll script it into the VCS.

- We assume online database development with a dedicated database for each developer (though the alternative model in each case will work equally well).

- We don't, at this stage, assume reliance on any particular ALM toolset.

- We'll subdivide our database project folder in source control according to database object type. As noted in Chapter 2, this folder forms just one part of a larger folder structure that accommodates all the project files.

- We'll version the database by saving the latest CREATE script for each object (i.e. saving the current state of the schema).

When we left off in Chapter 2, we'd used the VisualSVN Server Management tool to create a single-project **BookstoreProject** repository and three users (Jane, Fred, Barb) for our fictitious bookstore development project. As part of this process, VisualSVN Server automatically created our initial project folders (**branches**, **tags**, and **trunk**) at the root level. We could have just as easily taken a different approach, such as to create a single repository (often named after the organization, for example) to hold multiple projects, with each individual project containing its own branches/tags/trunk structure, or any number of other approaches.

Within the trunk folder, our data architect, Jane, via her working folder, created and committed all the required high-level project folders, such as **AppCode**, **Databases**, **DeployScripts**, and so on. If you followed along precisely, launching the Repository Browser (**TortoiseSVN | Repo-browser**) from the **BookstoreProject** folder, in one of the users working folders, should reveal a structure that looks as shown in Figure 3-2.

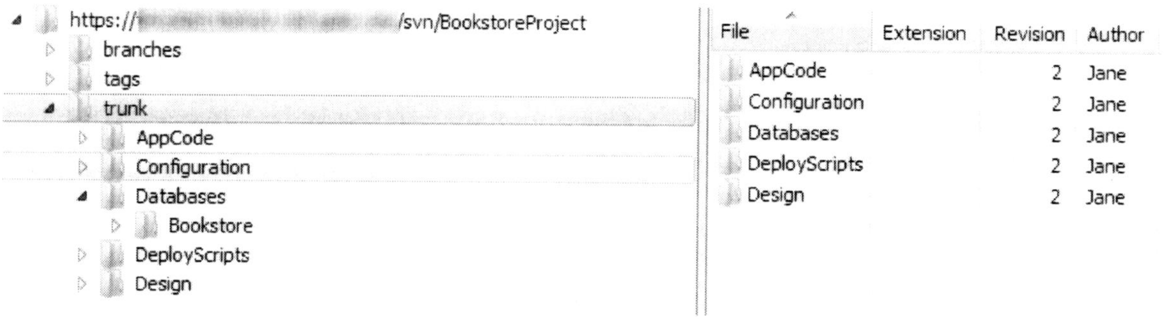

Figure 3-2:   The current structure of the BookstoreProject repository.

Don't worry if your revision numbers don't match exactly. Every **commit** creates a new revision in the repository. For example, if you committed the **Bookstore** folder as an additional commit, separate from the other folders, then the **Databases** folder would be at Revision 3.

For our lead developer, Barb, we created a **BookstoreProject** folder and checked out the entire project structure, as created by Jane. For our database specialist, Fred, we created a working folder called **BookstoreDatabases**, and linked it to the **Databases** folder in the repository (**https://<server>/svn/BookstoreProject/trunk/databases**).

Right now, though, all our developers have in their working folders is an empty subfolder called **Bookstore**, in which to house our `Bookstore` database and all its required objects and data. We're now ready to start creating all of the necessary database script files in our working folder, and committing them to the repository.

Script database objects for source control

When it comes to using source control for database development, one of the most important points that will emerge from our example is the need to create a script file for each database object and then add each one to source control. We can simply write the script to create each database object and save it as a separate file, or we can generate script files from existing database objects or diagrams.

For a large, existing database, scripting out every object can seem a daunting process. However, most tools, including SSMS, support methods for scripting out all database objects at one time, and putting each object in its own file. Simply right-click the database in **Object Explorer**, point to **Tasks**, and then click **Generate Scripts**. The interface walks through the process of scripting selected objects, each to a separate file in the chosen destination, in this case the working folder. Of course, as discussed earlier, when we need to build the schema from those files, we'll have to run them in the correct order, but we'll save the details on that for Chapter 7.

To get started with source controlling the `Bookstore` database, we'll create four T-SQL DDL scripts: a databases creation script and a script for each of the three tables. We'll add each file to our working folder, in the appropriate subfolder, and then commit these folders and files to our **BookstoreProject** repository. All interactions with the repository will be through the working folders of our developers, starting with Fred.

Create, Add and Commit database scripts

When working on database projects, we need to organize the necessary files into subfolders of our working directory, and then commit both to the repository, at which point they are available to the other source control users. As discussed earlier, we're going to subdivide our database directory according to database object type.

Each time we save a new file, folder, or both, to our working folder, we then add it to the working folder and then commit to the repository, as described in Chapter 2.

To get us started, within Fred's **Bookstore** folder, create two new subfolders, as follows:

- **Database**, which will hold script files related to the `Bookstore` database as a whole, including our database creation script.
- **Tables**, which will hold script files specific to tables.

Don't worry about whether to add or commit them yet, as we'll get to that shortly, after we've created our first database script.

The database creation script

Let's start with the script to create the `Bookstore` database. The database needs to be only a basic one that uses the default configuration settings. Therefore, in its very simplest form, we can open a SSMS query window, or even a text editor such as Notepad, and create a script such as that shown in Listing 3-1.

```
USE [master]
GO

CREATE DATABASE [Bookstore] ;
GO
```

Listing 3-1:   A basic script to create the `Bookstore` database.

Of course, we can customize the CREATE DATABASE statement as required, to specify values for configuration settings such as data and log file locations, file sizes, file growth increments and so on. We then simply save the file as `Bookstore.sql` to the appropriate location in our working folder, in this case to the **Database** directory in the working folder (i.e. **SVNFred\BookstoreProject\BookstoreDatabases\Bookstore\Database**).

Alternatively, we can create the database through SSMS (right-click the **Databases** node in Object Explorer, and select **New Database**), and then right-click the newly created `Bookstore` database and script it out (**Script Database As | CREATE TO | File**), choosing the same file name and path.

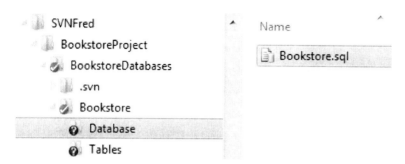

Figure 3-3:   Saving `Bookstore.sql` to the Database folder.

Having created our database creation script file, we need to add this file to the working folder and then commit it to the repository. In fact, we'll commit our two new folders, and the file, in one step. We'll keep this brief, as Chapter 2 already described the **Add** and **Commit** steps; refer back there if you need more detail.

Right-click on the **BookstoreDatabases** folder and perform the SVN **Add** operation (**TortoiseSVN | Add**), ensuring that it selects the two folders and the `Bookstore.sql` file. After the add, TortoiseSVN displays the blue "add" overlays for the folders and the script and the white-on-red exclamation points for the **Bookstore** folder and all folders higher in the hierarchy.

Next, right-click again on the **BookstoreDatabases** folder and perform the SVN commit (remember to clear the current authentication data first, if you have all three users on the same client, as mentioned in Chapter 2).

We've chosen to commit from our root folder, in order to include in the commit everything we've added to this folder and subfolders.

Committing from the root folder

*We could, instead, have committed from the **Database** folder, or just committed the* `Bookstore.sql`
*script, in which case we'd include that folder and its file in the commit, but not the **Tables** folder or*
any of its files. It's a good practice, as far as possible, to commit from the root folder to keep everything
in sync.

Enter a descriptive commit message along the way and, ultimately, we should see
the **Commit Finished** dialog box, informing us of what we committed and the new
revision number.

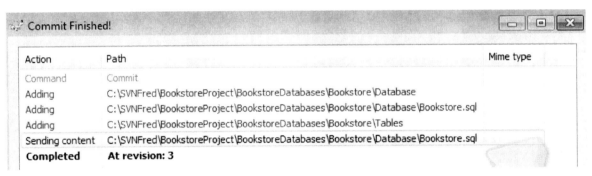

Figure 3-4:   Commit the **Database** and **Tables** folders and `Bookstore.sql`.

Having committed to the repository all additions to our working folder, we should see
plenty of those white-on-green checkmarks next to our folders. We can also open the
Repository Browser and confirm that this structure and the database creation script are
now versioned in the repository.

The table scripts

Our next step is to create three script files for three tables, Author, Book, and AuthorBook, in the Bookstore database, one file per table. The database diagram in Figure 3-5 shows the three tables and the one-to-many relationship that exists between the Author and AuthorBook tables and between the Book and AuthorBook tables.

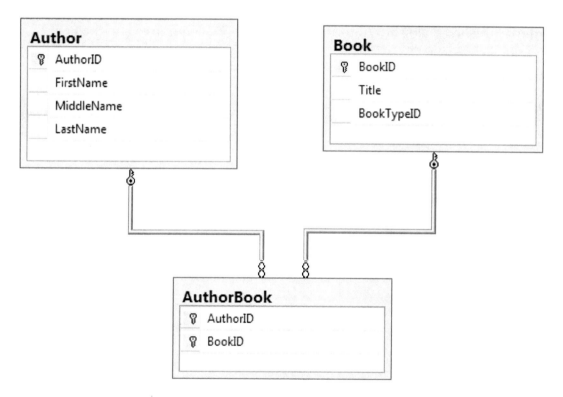

Figure 3-5:   The Author, Book, and AuthorBook tables in the Bookstore database.

Listing 3-2 provides a single T-SQL script to create all three tables. To implement the one-to-many relationships, we create two FOREIGN KEY relationships on the AuthorBook table, one to Book and one to Author.

```
/*Author.sql*/
USE Bookstore;
GO
CREATE TABLE dbo.Author
    (
        AuthorID INT IDENTITY
                    PRIMARY KEY ,
        FirstName NVARCHAR(30) NOT NULL ,
        MiddleName NVARCHAR(30) NOT NULL ,
        LastName NVARCHAR(30) NOT NULL
    );
GO

/*Book.sql*/
USE Bookstore;
GO
CREATE TABLE dbo.Book
    (
        BookID INT IDENTITY
                    PRIMARY KEY ,
        Title NVARCHAR(1000) NOT NULL
    );
GO

/*AuthorBook.sql*/
USE Bookstore;
GO
CREATE TABLE dbo.AuthorBook
    (
        AuthorID INT NOT NULL ,
        BookID INT NOT NULL ,
        CONSTRAINT pk_authorid_bookid PRIMARY KEY CLUSTERED
                                    ( AuthorID, BookID ) ,
        CONSTRAINT fk_authorid FOREIGN KEY ( AuthorID )
                                    REFERENCES Author ( AuthorID ) ,
        CONSTRAINT fk_bookid FOREIGN KEY ( BookID )
                                    REFERENCES Book ( BookID )
    );
GO
```

Listing 3-2:   Creating the tables.

To save these scripts to our working folder, we can place the code for each table in a separate query window in SSMS and save each as a separate script file (`Author.sql`, `Book.sql`, and `AuthorBook.sql`) to the **Bookstore\Tables** folder.

Alternatively, simply run Listing 3-2 to create all three tables, and then script out each table to an individual file, as described earlier (or we could even use **Tasks | Generate Scripts** for the database to generate them in one go).

Whichever way we choose to save the script files to the folder, we then need to add them to the working folder (right-click the **BookstoreDatabases** folder and select **TortoiseSVN | Add**) and then commit them to the repository (right-click **BookstoreDatabases**, select **SVN Commit**), exactly as described previously. The **Commit Finished** dialog box will verify the files committed and report the new revision number (in this case, Revision 4).

Windows Explorer should now show the reassuring green ticks next to the files we just added and committed to the repository.

On the server, we can confirm that everything has been properly synced with the repository by opening the Repository Browser and verifying the contents of our **BookstoreProject** folder, as shown in Figure 3-6.

Notice that we see the same revision number (in this case, 4) for each one of the files we committed. SVN assigns the same revision number to each object that is part of the same commit operation. It increments the revision numbers for each commit, across the entire repository, without regard to folder structures or file types or to how many different projects we might have within the repository, which is why the numbers are referred to as global sequential revision numbers.

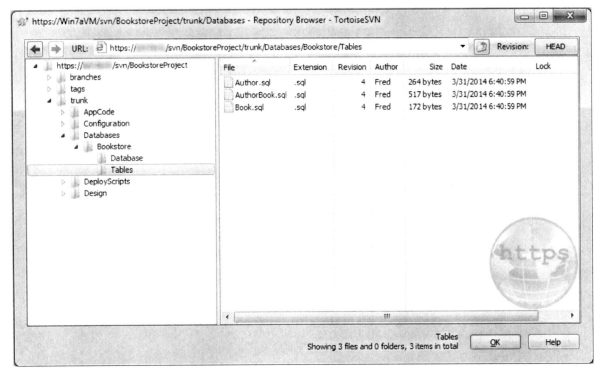

Figure 3-6: Viewing our files in the Repository Browser.

In other words, the **BookstoreProject** repository, as a whole, is at Revision 4. Within the root folder, each subfolder reflects the last revision to affect it or its contents. So, if you explore the repository, you'll see that the last revision to affect the Databases subfolder was Revision 4, whereas for the **Database** subfolder it is Revision 3, and for the other project folders that we created in Chapter 2, it is Revision 2.

We can review in more detail what SVN committed at each revision by using the SVN log. We're not going to discuss the log in detail until the next chapter, but to take a sneak preview, right-click on the **BookstoreDatabases** folder, point to **TortoiseSVN**, and then click **Show Log**.

Revision	Actions	Author	Date	Message
4		**Fred**	**02 April 2014 15:11:52**	**Initial commit of Author, AuthorBook and Book tables**
3		Fred	02 April 2014 14:47:20	Database and Tables folder and the Bookstore.sql database creation script.
2		Jane	02 April 2014 11:31:21	Add project folders to the trunk
				For complete history deselect 'Stop on copy/rename'

Initial commit of Author, AuthorBook and Book tables

Path	Action	Copy from path	Revision
/trunk/Databases/Bookstore/Tables/Author.sql	Added		
/trunk/Databases/Bookstore/Tables/AuthorBook.sql	Added		
/trunk/Databases/Bookstore/Tables/Book.sql	Added		

Figure 3-7: Viewing the log.

When we first set up the repository, VisualSVN Server added the **branches**, **tags**, and **trunk** folder, to which it assigned 1 as the revision number. However, that's not shown here because Fred did not sync to the entire repository, only to the **Databases** folder and its subfolders, so he sees only those revisions.

When Jane added and committed the project folders to the trunk, those were all grouped together as Revision 2. Fred then added and committed the **Database** and **Tables** folders and the Bookstore.sql file, which was marked as Revision 3. Finally, when he added the table creation scripts, SVN assigned Revision 4 to those files. Essentially, each line represents a commit, i.e. a particular version in the repository.

Of course, this is just how revision numbering works in SVN, but it gives a reasonable feel for how a source control system tracks revision history. Other source control systems might take a different approach to tracking revision numbers, just as they would any other feature.

Adding test or reference data to source control

Often, our database schema will include certain special tables called lookup tables, which store static or reference data, usually for the purpose of displaying data in human-readable form in the application. A typical example would be a lookup table that translates US state codes into state names.

Another type of data we might add to source control is the test data necessary to facilitate integration testing, that is, if we don't instead create scripts that retrieve the data. In any case, if we choose to hard-code any test data, we can add the script files to source control, just like any database code or schema object. To illustrate the point, we'll just add some simple test data to bookstore tables, as shown in Listing 3-3.

```
USE Bookstore;
GO

-- test data
SET IDENTITY_INSERT dbo.Book ON
GO

INSERT  INTO Book
        ( BookID, Title )
VALUES  ( 1, 'Huckleberry Finn' ),
        ( 2, 'Slaughterhouse-Five' ),
        ( 3, 'Beloved' ),
        ( 4, 'Pride and Prejudice' ),
        ( 5, 'Cat''s Cradle' ),
        ( 6, 'Frankenstein' ),
        ( 7, 'Atonement' ),
        ( 8, 'The Razor''s Edge' ),
        ( 9, 'The Age of Innocence' ),
        ( 10, 'Song of Solomon' );

SET IDENTITY_INSERT dbo.Book OFF
GO

SET IDENTITY_INSERT dbo.Author ON
GO
```

```
INSERT   INTO Author
         ( AuthorID, FirstName, MiddleName, LastName )
VALUES   ( 1, 'Kurt', '', 'Vonnegut' ),
         ( 2, 'Edith', '', 'Wharton' ),
         ( 3, 'Mary', '', 'Shelley' ),
         ( 4, 'W', 'Somerset', 'Maugham' ),
         ( 5, 'Ian', '', 'McEwan' ),
         ( 6, 'Toni', '', 'Morrison' ),
         ( 7, 'Jane', '', 'Austen' ),
         ( 8, 'Mark', '', 'Twain' );

SET IDENTITY_INSERT dbo.Author OFF
GO

INSERT   INTO AuthorBook
VALUES   ( 8, 1 ),
         ( 1, 2 ),
         ( 6, 3 ),
         ( 7, 4 ),
         ( 1, 5 ),
         ( 3, 6 ),
         ( 5, 7 ),
         ( 4, 8 ),
         ( 2, 9 ),
         ( 6, 10 );
GO
```

Listing 3-3:   Some test data.

Generally speaking, every script we store in the VCS will describe a change to a single object. Of course, here we have a script that modifies the data of several objects at once. We could, certainly, split this into three separate data loading scripts, but because of the **FOREIGN KEY** dependencies, and because it's such a small amount of test data, it seems an unnecessary complication in this case.

We add this script to source control in exactly the same manner as described previously. In brief:

- In **TortoiseSVN**, create a new folder called **TestData**, as a subfolder of **Bookstore**.

- Save Listing 3-3 to the **TestData** folder as `TestData.sql`.

- Add the **TestData** folder to the working directory – this will add both the folder and the file.

- Right-click **BookstoreDatabases** and perform a commit to the repository – again, this will commit both the **TestData** folder and the file (remember to include a meaningful commit message).

Once again, if we right-click the **BookstoreDatabases** folder, and navigate **TortoiseSVN | Repo-Browser**, we will see that the **Databases** folder in the repository contains the new **TestData** subfolder and file.

Updating the working folder

Up to this point, we've demonstrated two users (Jane and Fred) accessing the repository through their working folders. We performed an add operation to register new folders and files in our working directory, and then a commit to copy those files over to the central repository.

When we perform a commit, we move data in one direction, from the working folder to the repository. If another user adds new files to the repository, there is no mechanism that will alert us automatically and then auto-update our working folder.

In Chapter 2, our second database developer, Barb, also performed the initial repository check-out at the same time Fred did, but she has done no further work on the bookstore project. When Barb next opens her working folder, it will look exactly as she left it, at Revision 2, reflecting none of the work that Fred committed to the repository, adding files to define the `Bookstore` database, plus three tables.

Figure 3-8:   Barb's working folder is still at Revision 2.

Barb can rectify this situation easily by performing an update of her working folder. From TortoiseSVN, she simply right-clicks the **BookstoreProject** folder and selects **SVN Update**. TortoiseSVN displays an **Update Finished** dialog box that shows the files and folders being updated in the target folder.

Action	Path
Command	Update
Updating	C:\SVNBarb\BookstoreProject\BookstoreDatabases
Added	C:\SVNBarb\BookstoreProject\BookstoreDatabases\Bookstore\Database
Added	C:\SVNBarb\BookstoreProject\BookstoreDatabases\Bookstore\Database\Bookstore.sql
Added	C:\SVNBarb\BookstoreProject\BookstoreDatabases\Bookstore\TestData
Added	C:\SVNBarb\BookstoreProject\BookstoreDatabases\Bookstore\TestData\TestData.sql
Added	C:\SVNBarb\BookstoreProject\BookstoreDatabases\Bookstore\Tables
Added	C:\SVNBarb\BookstoreProject\BookstoreDatabases\Bookstore\Tables\Author.sql
Added	C:\SVNBarb\BookstoreProject\BookstoreDatabases\Bookstore\Tables\Book.sql
Added	C:\SVNBarb\BookstoreProject\BookstoreDatabases\Bookstore\Tables\AuthorBook.sql
Completed	**At revision: 5**

Figure 3-9:   Barb's update of her working folder.

Although this dialog box is specific to TortoiseSVN, most source control systems will provide details about what's being updated in our working folder. This will include all updates made by other users and committed to the repository.

Barb's working folder is now up to date, as shown in Figure 3-10.

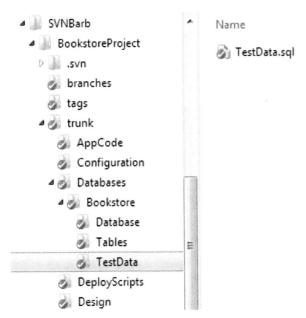

Figure 3-10:   Barb's working folder now has the latest revision in the repository.

A word of caution, though: systems such as SVN let us specify which folder to update. It will update the specified folder with any files or subfolders that have changed within that folder, but not any changes that fall outside the folder, even if related. For example, if Fred subsequently performs an update on the **Database** folder, then this will get any changes to Bookstore.sql, but not to any of the table files.

This can sometimes cause issues, such as another user or an administrator moving a file. For example, we have a **TestData.sql** file, originally committed to the **Bookstore\TestData** folder, and reflected as such in our current working folder.

However, let's say another user subsequently moves the file into the **Database** folder. If we then update only the **Database** folder, the file will show up there but will also be retained in the **TestData** folder because we did not update that folder. If we then edit the file in the **TestData** folder and try to commit our changes, we'll receive an error saying that the commit operation failed and we'll have to try to perform a merge operation to resolve the problem (more on this in Chapter 6). To avoid any potential issues, it is best to update the folder at the highest level of the hierarchy. In Fred's case, that would be the **BookstoreDatabases** folder.

Whenever we edit a file in our working folder, and commit the change to the repository in a multi-user system, we "optimistically" assume that no one else modified the file in the repository since we last performed an update. If a user forgets to perform an update for a substantial period and then blindly edits a file, the risk is high that the user is editing an invalid version of the file, because there is a more recent version of the file in the repository. When the user tries to commit the change, it will reject the commit and again, the user will need to attempt to perform a merge to resolve the conflict.

Whenever we're about to edit a file, we can perform an update first to make sure we have the most recent version. In general, we should update our working folder as often as necessary to ensure we're working with up-to-date files, and try to hit the right balance between too few and too many updates. The exact frequency will depend on the project and the existing state of the development effort. In Chapters 5 and 6, when we get into the topics of merging and branching, it will become clearer why striking the right balance is important.

In addition, most source control systems provide a way to view details about the history of revisions made to the files and folders. TortoiseSVN provides the Repository Browser, as we saw briefly in the previous chapter. In addition, we can use the SVN log to review in detail what SVN committed at each revision. We can access the log whenever we update our working folder (there is a **Show Log** button at the bottom right of the **Update Finished** dialog), or at any other time by right-clicking a file or folder, and navigating **TortoiseSVN | Show Log**.

Summary

We now have our database files and a small amount of test data in source control! Granted, this is an extremely small database, but from these files we can assemble our complete schema at any time, without worrying that the files will be lost or overwritten.

Using SQL script files for database development is nothing new. Most database developers use them at least to some extent, even if their organization's approach to database development is, at best, a lackadaisical one. The challenge for many database developers, in terms of embracing source control as part of their development efforts, is not so much the capabilities of the source control systems themselves, but rather a willingness on the part of the developers to embrace a different development methodology and change-management strategy.

A source control solution represents an important component of effective database development but, more importantly, it is a mindset that understands the importance of scripting all database development, implementing versioned builds, and committing 100 percent to the source control system.

The key to all of this, in practical terms, is to make certain that all developers script every database object to an individual script file, and commit it to source control. If someone needs to change that object, then they should update their working folder with the appropriate script, modify it as necessary, and commit it. No one should be making changes directly to the database schema.

In Chapter 4, we move on to editing, and versioning our source-controlled files.

Chapter 4: Editing and Versioning

By now, you should have a good sense of what source control is and how it works, at least at a high level. We've discussed how the repository, whether distributed or centralized, is the heart of any source control solution. It manages our files and maintains a history of every change to those files since they entered the source control system. Most of our interaction with the repository is through a working folder on our local computer. From there, we can access and edit the files stored in the repository and view the history of their changes.

The previous chapter discussed many of the factors that can influence the way in which a team stores database and application files within the repository; how we work with these files during team-based development; and how we assemble a particular revision in the repository into a build for deployment to a target database.

In this chapter, we delve into the mechanisms and mechanics of modifying database files in the VCS during development. We'll discuss the main strategies for versioning database scripts, distinguishing between code modules that we can simply re-create and later deploy to the target database, and tables where we will need to preserve the business data during any modifications.

We'll also see how the repository keeps an "audit trail" of our modifications, and how we can access and compare the various file revisions to identify the differences between them.

Once again, we'll be using SVN, a centralized repository, to demonstrate the various source control concepts; see Chapters 2 and 3 to ensure you're using the same setup that we use here. However, the tasks we'll perform are common to all source control solutions, including distributed systems, although each product has its own methods for delivering specific functionality. In this book we're more concerned with possibilities than we are with absolutes.

Database Versioning Strategies

Before we begin modifying existing database files, we need to consider exactly how we want to track those changes, as this will affect what we store in the repository and how the repository can track the change history for the database as a whole.

During the development phase, it's often permissible to simply tear down the existing version of a development database, and replace it with the latest revision in the VCS. However, when it comes time to deploy what's in the VCS to a target environment, upgrading the existing database, we have two major challenges to consider:

- **Maintaining state** – How to deploy the necessary table changes to a live database in a way that preserves existing data. We can't simply recompile the database and roll it out. We often have to provide scripts to modify the schema, migrate and update data, or take other steps to protect and archive data.

- **Avoiding downtime** – Many databases are subject to rigorous Service Level Agreements (SLAs) regarding their availability. We can't simply take the database down each time we want to make a change. We often have to find a way to modify the live database with minimal user disruption.

Over the following sections, we'll consider how we modify both code modules and tables in our database schema, in light of these challenges.

Versioning code modules

A common scheme when working with modules in source control is simply to modify the object code and replace the existing file with the new one. Usually, the **CREATE** script will start with an "if exists" clause, such that when we run it the script will drop the object, if it exists, and replace it with the new one.

However, this approach can be problematic down the line, when it comes time to update an object that users may be accessing in a live system. With this approach, there is always a short period, between dropping and re-creating the object, when it will be unavailable. Also, after re-creating the object, we must reapply the appropriate permissions so that users can access it.

Instead (see HTTP://TINYURL.COM/MA7U6A3) we adopt the pattern used by Alexander Karmanov, whereby our script turns the NOEXEC option ON if the object already exists, then creates a "stub" for the object (which SQL Server will compile and not run, if NOEXEC is ON), and then turns NOEXEC OFF and defines the object logic in an ALTER statement.

When working with this script, we simply modify the logic in the ALTER statement, as required, and resave the file. This approach minimizes user interruption when deploying to a live database, and leaves any permissions unchanged. We'll see an example a little later in the chapter.

Versioning tables

So far in this book, we've created only new tables, saving each one to its own .sql file in the repository. What happens, however, if we wish to modify one of those tables, such as adding a new column to the Author table, or changing a data type? We have to choose between several possible approaches to versioning our database.

1. **Save the modified CREATE script** – We store one file per object and edit each file as appropriate to reflect each schema modification. In this approach, we are effectively versioning the current state of the schema.

2. **Save a new upgrade script** – For each schema object, we store the string of upgrade scripts (one change per script) required to advance the object from one defined state to the next.

3. **Save both the CREATE and the upgrade scripts** – Store both the modified CREATE script and the new ALTER file to different folders, so we can either create the current schema directly or upgrade the existing schema.

There are advantages and disadvantages to any of these approaches, and the choice is not necessarily straightforward. In the coming sections, we'll consider each in turn.

Database versioning via an ORM

Of course, you'll likely encounter other approaches too. For example, modern Object Relational Mapping (ORM) tools, such as Entity Framework, will automatically generate database changes from code changes. However, we won't discuss this sort of approach further in this book.

Whichever approach we choose, we have to factor in the need to preserve data when deploying these changes to an existing database. For example, suppose we move a column from one table to another and delete a column from a third table. We need to provide the scripts necessary to alter the three table definitions. We also need a script to migrate the data from the first table to the second table, a process that might require that we store the data temporarily during the migration and update processes or even beyond, until we can verify the changes. In addition, we might need a script to archive the data in the column we're deleting from the third table. And this is just a simple example! Imagine the complexities involved in a large database with lots of data and lots of changes.

On top of that, we have to consider how to make all these changes with minimal downtime and user disruption. This usually involves progressing in small, well-defined steps, each step verified with a suite of automated tests, and only switching users over to the new version once we're certain of the correctness and their impact on overall application performance (see for example HTTP://TINYURL.COM/KL8A3DD). With all these considerations in mind, we must decide which of our three approaches to take when versioning our database. So let's take a closer look at our options.

Approach #1: Version the current state of the table

Each time we modify a table, we commit the latest table creation script to source control. If we need to add a new column to a table, for example, we might update our working folder with the latest version of the table file, create the table, add the new column, regenerate the **CREATE** script, save it back to the **Tables** folder, and then commit it to the repository.

In other words, we save each **CREATE** script to the repository, one table per file, and change each file as necessary to reflect each schema modification. Any user performing an update to their working folder will simply get the latest version of the table's creation script.

There are obvious advantages to this scheme for the development team. It makes it easy for each developer to create a new environment, with the current state of the database schema, by simply running each **CREATE** script in dependency order. It's an approach that works naturally with a VCS, making it very easy to perform a diff (see later) to find out exactly how each object changed between revisions; and this, in turn, makes it relatively easy to perform a merge into a separate branch of the development project.

Another advantage with this approach is that it makes it easy to audit the change history and quickly identify who added or removed a line of code, and when. SVN, for example, offers this capability via the blame command, often used to blame and shame the "developer who broke the build."

Of course, there is an apparent underlying assumption to this approach that we can simply drop any existing table and re-create it, in order to get the latest version. While this may be possible in the development environment, we cannot extend this approach to any environment where we must retain the data. This is why it's reasonably common for a development team to adopt this "version the current state of the table" model during development, but then adopt the "upgrade script" approach once a database has been built and deployed (we use this approach in Chapter 7).

Approach #2: Version the upgrade scripts

In this approach, we store in the VCS an upgrade script to describe each schema modification, with one change (i.e. one `ALTER` command) per script file. In this case, every script is an upgrade script (also called a **migration** script). The team create a build script to `CREATE`, `ALTER` and `DROP` objects as required, in the right order, in order to advance a database from one defined database state, such as an empty database or a specific database build, to the next defined state or build. In other words, when developers update their working folders, they don't retrieve the latest versions of each object, but instead a series of scripts that they must run, in the right order, to progress the database from one state to the next.

> *One change per script versus all changes in one script*
>
> *Creating one script file per `ALTER` command is generally considered best practice because it provides for flexible deployment and management strategies and more granular control over your operations. If we need to change the order in which we apply the modifications, we simply tweak the build script. However, another method sometimes used is to create one script file that includes all the `ALTER` commands. Certain automation tools, such as Red Gate's SQL Source Control Migrations, take this approach. Of course, if we need to change the order, we have to edit the T-SQL script manually. We adopt the one-script-per-upgrade approach in this book.*

This approach works across all environments, from development through to production. To build a new database, we generate a creation script that includes all the migration scripts, applied in the correct order (and we must be certain to include *all* the scripts, which is not always an easy task). To upgrade an existing database, we run all the upgrade scripts not previously applied. This technique relies on the team knowing exactly which scripts they previously applied to an environment, and then applying those upgrade scripts in source control that they've yet to run. It can also mean keeping track of any scripts we *don't* want to run. For example, let's say in one revision someone deleted a table, but in a later revision we spot it as a mistake and restore the table. We would not want to run the script that deleted the table as part of a deployment, or we'd risk losing data.

The problem of version drift

It is vital that nobody modifies a database directly, outside of the source control process. If a target database has drifted from the expected starting state, then running the upgrade scripts may not work as expected. Chapter 7 discusses version drift in more detail.

In a basic implementation of this approach, we might save our upgrade scripts to a specific folder associated with the build to which they apply, with each file named according to the action, the date, and an "index number" indicating the sequence. In our bookstore project, it could look something like Figure 4-1, where Fred has created an **UpdateScripts** subfolder in his working folder, and then within that several version-specific folders containing the scripts for each version.

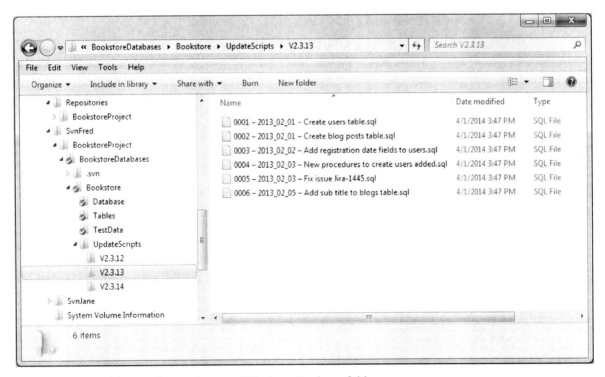

Figure 4-1: Adding update scripts to a Windows Explorer folder.

Of course, this is only an illustration of the types of update files we might create. Our build mechanism would also have to track the individual update operations in some way, through version numbers, timestamps, or some other mechanism (we get to this in Chapters 7 and 8).

There are several advantages to the upgrade scripts approach. As noted, it works for development as well as deployment environments. It provides an audit trail of every modification. It's repeatable; as long as we apply every upgrade script to every environment, in the right order, we will create the same database each time. Since every script is a migration script, we can exert precise granular control over exactly how we wish an upgrade to proceed. If we need to perform a data load or other manipulation in order to support a schema change, we simply add it to the indexed list of files.

There are some obvious downsides too. Since every change is a separate script, we can't simply do a diff to compare the current version of an object with a previous version, to work out what changed. If someone's change introduces a problem, we may need to search through all recent upgrade scripts to find the offending change. Likewise, it's much harder to work out what the schema as a whole looked like at any point in history. It's a method best suited to "one developer at a time," to avoid the likelihood that two developers submit a script with the same index and then need to resolve the conflict. Since every change is a new script, it's also much harder to know if one change might conflict with another. Again, we often resort to searching through all recent upgrade scripts to reassure ourselves that a proposed change is compatible. For similar reasons, branching and merging are hard in this scheme, and developers often avoid them as far as possible.

To make this approach work, we need some automated way of storing and applying the upgrade scripts in a consistent fashion. Chapter 7 of this book will demonstrate a simple approach that relies on build tables and a PowerShell script to run the upgrade scripts in the correct order.

Alexander Karmanov demonstrates a more rigorous and automated approach in his incremental database development and deployment framework (HTTP://TINYURL.COM/ PTA9BCS). He associates every set of upgrade scripts with a database build number. For example, when we first create an empty database, we associate it with a build number (say, "0.0.0.1"), saved in the deployed database in an extended property (or a table valued function). Thereafter every set of changes increments the build number, so the upgrade scripts folder for build 0.0.0.2 contains the scripts necessary to progress the database from build 0.0.0.1 to 0.0.0.2. A configuration file, called a **change log**, stored in source control, associates each build number with the correct set of upgrade scripts, and establishes the order in which we must apply them. If we always know the build of the database that currently exists in an environment, and we have a change log, then we use a deployment tool (in this case a VB script, but equally well a PowerShell script) that will always apply the correct set of upgrade scripts to advance from one build to any other.

Finally, several tools help support the upgrade script approach, such as dbdeploy (HTTP://DBDEPLOY.COM/) or migratordotnet (HTTP://TINYURL.COM/PC8HQJH).

Approach #3: Save both the modified CREATE script and the upgrade script

There are many advantages to having the latest state of the database schema in source control, and it's a natural fit for the core source control processes. However, it relies on schema synchronization scripts to apply a set of changes to an existing database, and there will always be certain types of changes with which these tools will be unable to cope.

With the upgrade scripts approach, we exert granular control over our database upgrades, but it can be painstaking and slow, and works against some of the natural source control processes. In essence, this approach is optimized to deal with the edge cases, i.e. those changes that required very strict control, rather than the common cases, those changes we could apply by simply comparing the source and target schemas and having a tool generate a script to synchronize them.

Some teams opt for a "bit of both" approach, storing both the latest creation scripts and, in a separate source control directory, the upgrade scripts. It sounds tempting, but without the right tools and a strict control process, *there be dragons here*. What if someone updates one but not the other? Which one is right? What if creating the object according to the latest CREATE script doesn't give the same result as running the specified set of ALTER scripts on the existing build?

However, tools exist that allows us to adopt this "both ways" approach but remove some of the associated danger, and move us more towards the best of both worlds. Most development teams would like to optimize their source control processes around Approach #1. However, because we can't drop and re-create the tables when upgrading an existing database, we use schema comparison tools instead to compare the source database as described by the script in the working folder, to the target database as it exists in the environment, and generate automatically the upgrade script necessary to bring them into alignment.

We can even extend this approach to upgrading existing databases in environments such as **Test**, **Staging** and even **Production**. Of course, such an approach requires extreme care. While we can rely on a synchronization tool for 95% of database modifications, there will always be the other 5% that require manual intervention. For example, there is no way for a tool to know that we renamed a table, rather than dropped one table and created a new one. In such cases, we still need to write a migration script to specify exactly how we wish the synchronization to proceed. Likewise, we'll also need migration scripts to perform any data load and manipulation operations that might be necessary to incorporate our schema changes. An example might be trying to deploy a change that adds a NOT NULL constraint to a column that contains existing data, including NULL values. In order to deploy such a change successfully, we'd need to write a migration script that loaded a default value to any NULL columns in the table, stored that script in source control, and incorporated it in the deployment process.

> *Migration scripts in SQL Source Control*
>
> *Chapter 8 will review a technique that allows us to adopt this "version the current state" method but also store migration scripts in source control and incorporate them in a database deployment, as required.*

Source Control Versioning Mechanisms

Regardless of how we choose to version the objects in our database, we can rest assured that our VCS will store all of these files, and preserve the history of any changes we make to them over time. There is a good reason why we've referred interchangeably to a source control system as a version control system or VCS. As soon as we commit a file or folder, the source control repository maintains a full history of revisions to that object. It means, for example, that we have access to every file as it existed at every version in the repository (although, as discussed, if we're versioning only upgrade scripts, there is notionally only one version of every file).

To track all these changes and provide access to their histories, source control systems assign some form of **revision number** to each set of changes that comprise a single commit. Some systems refer to these revision numbers as **changeset numbers**.

Most source control systems will also provide a way to view revision history, revealing what changed, who made the change, and when, for each version in the repository.

Version numbering and history

Different source control systems approach versioning in different ways. SVN's versioning takes the form of global sequential revision numbers, an incremental numbering system. It assigns a number to each changeset (committed revision), incrementing the number for each new revision. The more recent the revision, the higher the revision number.

As discussed in Chapter 2, SVN tracks changes within every file, on a file-by-file basis. In contrast, a distributed system such as Git uses **Git hashes** to ensure that it can identify changesets uniquely across all files, across multiple peer repositories.

Among VCSs that use an incremental numbering system, each will likely differ in implementation. Some will apply sequential numbering at the folder or file level, so the sequence of revision numbers for a specific folder, for example, will be "unbroken" by changes made to other folders. Other repositories will increment revision numbers across the entire repository, so any change to any structure in the repository will increment the revision number.

Regardless of implementation details, every VCS can identify every changeset, such that it can present a full change history for each file and structure, and can reproduce the repository as it existed at any particular revision. Each time we commit a set of changes, the VCS will increment the revision number and we'll subsequently have access to both versions of the changed file and be able to compare different versions (most source control systems don't store both versions, but rather the "delta" between the two versions, as we'll discuss shortly).

Older source control systems maintained histories for files only, which could result in a fair amount of confusion if someone changed the directory structure itself. These days many source control systems, including SVN, store the directory structure as well as the files, thus maintaining a history of changes to the directory structure resulting from moving, renaming, or deleting folders. Git and Mercurial work slightly differently in that they don't store the directory, only the file path, so we can't commit an empty folder. However, the net effect to users is the same, and the working directory's folder structure is as they expect.

Deltas and diffs

Although, from a user's perspective, the repository maintains each version of every file, that's not how it works internally. Given all the data that a repository stores, particularly if we consider that every version of every file is accessible through the source control system, a repository has the potential to grow enormous, up to many terabytes if it includes lots of binary files. Even if it stores mostly text files, we still have the potential for extremely large repositories when we take into the account the number of files and the number of revisions for each file. Add to that the metadata that tracks information about each version, and you could end up with a repository so large that backup and maintenance operations become enormous tasks and performance starts to degrade.

A modern VCS doesn't actually save each version, but instead saves the differences (deltas) between versions so that it can *reassemble* a particular file version. A delta is a record of the differences between two files or trees. The VCS compares one or more of these records to a baseline version to construct the requested version.

The evolution of deltas

When source control systems first began using deltas to maintain change histories, the deltas applied only to the files themselves, or more precisely, to the text files. But as source control systems have evolved, delta calculations have incorporated binary files, as well as tree structures. In other words, many modern source control systems can now record every change that occurs within the repository.

How deltas work

Once again, different source control systems calculate deltas in different ways. For instance, solutions that can calculate deltas only on text files tend to do line-by-line comparisons between those files to arrive at the delta. On the other hand, systems that support binary deltas use a byte-oriented algorithm to calculate the differences between files.

Regardless of the exact approach, the end result is that the repository stores each file version as either the entire file or a delta that specifies what changed in the file since the previous revision.

For example, let's say that in an idle moment a Hunter S. Thomson fan among our developers wants to add the book "Hell's Angels" to the test data. He modifies the `TestData.sql` file appropriately, and commits the change (this will create a new revision in the repository if you go ahead and do it).

We can represent the associated delta that the repository stores for the `TestData.sql` file as follows (assuming the original data load was a multi-row `INSERT INTO...VALUES` rather than separate `INSERT`s for each row):

```
+ ,(9, 'Hunter', 'S', 'Thomson')
+ ,(11, 'Hell''s Angels')
+ ,(9, 11)
```

The "+" signs represent the fact that we've added three rows to the file. Of course, this is only a rough representation of the delta, as it must also take into account where to insert the data, along with other information, but it should give you a sense of how deltas work and how they can save space in the repository.

Deltas work in much the same way for changes to the directory tree. For example, if we were to rename the **TestData** folder to **Data**, we would represent the delta as follows:

```
- /trunk/BookstoreProject/Databases/BookstoreDB/TestData
+ /trunk/BookstoreProject/Databases/BookstoreDB/Data
```

This looks like two actions, deleting the **TestData** folder and adding the **Data** folder. However, internally, if we rename or move a file or folder, the SVN repository will not store a new copy, but rather store the delta, in this case the file path.

"Move" versus "delete then add"

Some systems treat a move or rename, whether to a file or folder, as a deletion from one location and an addition to another location, and will therefore actually store two copies. Even so, the final result is the same from the user perspective.

When a repository stores deltas for each revision rather than the actual files, the source control system must often "build" a file when we request a particular version, starting with the last stored file and applying the deltas in the order they were committed.

For example, let's say our `TestData.sql` file entered the repository as Revision 7, and the latest version is at Revision 15, when we added the Hunter S. Thomson book. The VCS may retrieve the original stored file (Revision 7) and then apply any subsequent deltas to reconstruct the latest version.

Not surprisingly, as the number of revisions grows, so too does the number of deltas. In fact, sometimes that number gets to be so great that performance degrades significantly when we try to retrieve a version. For example, Revision 30 might require the repository to apply 21 deltas to the first version! For this reason, a source control system might periodically store the full version of a file. For example, it might, depending on how it is configured, store every tenth file as its full version. As a result, it need never apply more than nine deltas to a single version.

Some VCSs, such as Microsoft's Team Foundation Server (TFS), use reverse deltas to store different versions of a file. In that case, the repository stores the most recent version in its entirety and applies reverse deltas to rebuild earlier versions. This makes sense when we consider that most users are interested in the most recent version.

The exact method that the VCS uses to store and maintain versions in a repository is not nearly as important as its ability to retrieve specific versions as we request them. In addition, the VCS must provide some mechanism to allow users to easily view information about different versions and compare them in order to see their differences. And that's where the **diff** comes in.

Performing diffs

A delta is a recording of the differences between file versions, and the repository uses it to construct a file when we request a particular version. In other words, a delta is systemic and integral to the repository storage process. Related in concept, but distinct, is a diff, which is a function available to allow users to compare files visually. Although some of the mechanisms used to calculate deltas and calculate diffs may be the same, the functions themselves are different.

In essence, a diff is a visual tool, separate from the repository, which provides a line-by-line comparison between two files. By performing a diff, we can see exactly what changed between one version of a file and another (or even compare two different files). For example, we can perform a diff between Revision 20 of a file and Revision 30, and see exactly what is different. This process can be particularly useful when trying to troubleshoot a database issue and needing to find out, for example, when someone changed a column from nullable to non-nullable.

File encoding

*If creating script files in SQL Server Management Studio and saving them to SVN, you might run into file encoding issues when trying to perform a diff between file versions. In some cases, SVN incorrectly infers that such a file is not text but is binary. If this occurs, right-click the file, point to **TortoiseSVN**, and then click **Properties**. In the **Properties** dialog box, check whether a **mime-type** property is listed. If so, delete the property and click **OK**. You'll then have to commit your change to source control. Check the TortoiseSVN documentation for more information.*

Source control systems let us run a variety of diff operations in order to compare specific file and folder revisions. The types of diffs we can perform vary from one system to the next, so refer to the product documentation for specifics. That said, some common types of diff allow us to compare:

- the working folder to the repository

- any two revisions of the same file, in the repository

- any two revisions of the same folder, in the repository to produce a unified diff that shows, in a single view, the changes to all files in the folder

- two file revisions to determine not only their differences but also to identify "blame," that is, to include details about who revised which lines of code, and when

- specified revisions of two different files

- the trunk to a branch or two branches

- folder hierarchies

- revisions

- the working folder or the repository to the index (the staging area between the working folder and repository in products like Git).

When we use a GUI to perform the diff, we see a graphical side-by-side comparison of the two file versions, as you'll see later in this chapter. If a source control system doesn't support a specific diff operation, you'll often find a third-party tool that you can use to augment the built-in features. For example, TortoiseSVN doesn't include built-in tools to view the differences between folder hierarchies, but tools such as WinMerge or Beyond Compare will.

Modifying the Bookstore Database

It's time once again to convert theory into practice, and see how database versioning and investigating that version history in the repository, work in SVN. We'll walk through some examples of modifying some code modules and tables in our `Bookstore` database, as follows:

- create a new view, `AuthorsBooks`, to view a list of books and their authors

- alter the `Book` table to add a new column, `YearOfPublication`

- update the test data to populate this new column

- alter the `AuthorsBooks` view to return the new `YearOfPublication` column.

In each case, we'll adopt Approach #1, versioning the latest version of the creation script for the object.

We'll edit these files from within SSMS "optimistically," updating our working folder just before the change to ensure we have the latest versions, but then making the change and committing it to the repository, hoping that no other user changed that file in the meantime. If they did, we'll need to resolve any potential conflict with a merge operation (see Chapter 6).

Some centralized source control systems, including SVN, still allow us to lock a file explicitly, to prevent someone else trying to edit it at the same time as us. In SVN, to place a lock on a file, right-click the file in the working folder, and navigate **TortoiseSVN | Get lock**. When we commit the change, SVN will release the lock automatically (or we can release the lock manually at any point). This pessimistic approach can occasionally be useful for very high-priority changes, but the use of locks should be the exception not the rule in most teams, and we won't cover this approach in detail. Third-generation, distributed source control systems do not even support such a locking mechanism.

Once we've made all our changes, we'll see how the repository allows us to view them, who made them, and when, and how the current file versions differ from the previous ones.

Create a new view

So far, we've only created three tables, plus some test data, so our first task is going to be to create a code module, namely a view. Listing 4-1 creates the AuthorsBooks view. As discussed earlier, the script is such that any modification further down the line, when this view is "live" and we need to change its structure, incurs minimal interruption to end-users.

```
USE Bookstore;
GO
IF OBJECT_ID('dbo.AuthorsBooks') IS NOT NULL
    SET NOEXEC ON
 -- if the object exists, SQL Server will compile, but not run, the
 -- subsequent CREATE VIEW batch
GO
PRINT 'dbo.AuthorsBooks: creating initial stub';
GO
CREATE VIEW dbo.AuthorsBooks
AS
    SELECT  'A code stub, which will be replaced by an ALTER Statement'
            AS [stub]
GO
SET NOEXEC OFF
 -- the ALTER VIEW batch will always run
GO
PRINT 'dbo.AuthorsBooks: view code is updated';
GO
ALTER VIEW AuthorsBooks
AS
    SELECT  ( a.FirstName + ' ' + a.MiddleName + ' ' + a.LastName )
                                            AS FullName ,
            b.Title
    FROM    Author a
            INNER JOIN AuthorBook ab ON a.AuthorID = ab.AuthorID
            INNER JOIN Book b ON ab.BookID = b.BookID;
GO
PRINT 'dbo.AuthorsBooks: view creation script finished';
```

Listing 4-1:   Creating the AuthorsBooks view in the Bookstore database.

In Fred's working folder, create a new folder called **Views**, as a child of **Bookstore**, and then save Listing 4-1 to this folder, as `AuthorsBooks.sql`. Right-click on the **BookstoreDatabases** folder and **Add** the new folder and file to the working folder, then right-click to reset the authentication data if necessary, then right-click again and commit the changes to the repository.

Alter the Book table

Let's now assume that a little later we receive a request to store the year of publication for each book. We need to add a new column to our `Book` table. Listing 4-2 shows the `ALTER TABLE` statement.

```
ALTER TABLE dbo.Book
ADD YearOfPublication INT;
```

Listing 4-2:   Altering the `Book` table in the `Bookstore` database.

For the sake of simplicity, we've assumed we'll only ever want to store the year, and we've used an `INT` data type for the `YearOfPublication` column. In reality, we'd be more likely to use a `DATETIME` data type, and store dates that are more accurate.

As discussed in the previous sections, we have the choice to save this to source control as a new upgrade script, or we can simply regenerate the new `CREATE` statement after adding the column, and save to the repository a modified version of the `Book.sql` creation script.

In this example, we'll modify the existing `Book.sql` file. In my case, I altered the Book table in my sandbox database, as per Listing 4-2 and then used **Script Table As | CREATE To | File** to replace the existing `Book.sql` file in my working folder (having first performed an **Update** of my working folder, to ensure no one had altered the file in the meantime).

As a result of the modification, Fred's working folder now contains changes that we need to commit to the repository, as shown in Figure 4-2.

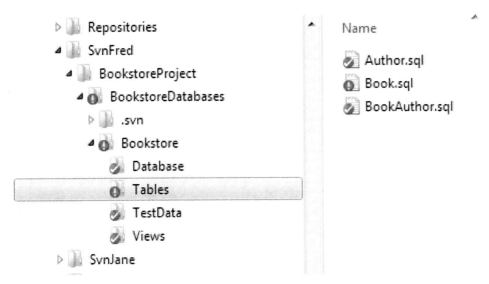

Figure 4-2: Edited file waiting to be committed to the repository.

Finally, right-click on **BookstoreDatabases** and commit the change (be sure to add a comment to the **Commit** dialog box).

Update the test data

We may also need to generate some test data for the new `YearOfPublication` column.

```
UPDATE    [dbo].[Book]
SET       [YearOfPublication] = 1884
WHERE     BookID = 1;
GO
UPDATE    [dbo].[Book]
SET       [YearOfPublication] = 1969
WHERE     BookID = 2;
GO
```

```
UPDATE   [dbo].[Book]
SET      [YearOfPublication] = 1987
WHERE    BookID = 3;
GO
UPDATE   [dbo].[Book]
SET      [YearOfPublication] = 1813
WHERE    BookID = 4;
GO
UPDATE   [dbo].[Book]
SET      [YearOfPublication] = 1963
WHERE    BookID = 5;
GO
UPDATE   [dbo].[Book]
SET      [YearOfPublication] = 1818
WHERE    BookID = 6;
GO
UPDATE   [dbo].[Book]
SET      [YearOfPublication] = 2001
WHERE    BookID = 7;
GO
UPDATE   [dbo].[Book]
SET      [YearOfPublication] = 1944
WHERE    BookID = 8;
GO
UPDATE   [dbo].[Book]
SET      [YearOfPublication] = 1920
WHERE    BookID = 9;
GO
UPDATE   [dbo].[Book]
SET      [YearOfPublication] = 1977
WHERE    BookID = 10;
GO
```

Listing 4-3:   Adding new test data to the Book table.

Again, we have the option to save Listing 4-3 as a new upgrade script, or we can modify the existing `TestData.sql` file, which is the option we'll choose here. In order to do this, first run the code in Listing 4-3 to add the new data to your development database, then follow the steps below.

1. In SSMS, right-click the **Bookstore** in Object Explorer, point to **Tasks**, and then click **Generate Scripts**.

2. In the **Generate and Publish Scripts** wizard, click **Next** if the **Introduction** page appears.

3. On the **Choose Objects** page, select the option **Select specific database objects**, select the **Tables** check box so that all tables are selected, and then click **Next**.

4. On the **Set scripting options** page, click the **Advanced** button and in the **Advanced Scripting Options** dialog box, navigate to the **Type of data to script** option in the **General** category and select **Data only**. Click **OK** to close the dialog box.

5. Back on the **Set scripting options** page, save the script to the **TestData** subfolder in the working folder, replacing the existing file (or save it to a query window to review it first). Then click **Next**.

6. On the **Summary** page, review your chosen options and then click **Next**. The **Save or Publish Scripts** page will appear and display the status of the script generation process. When that has completed, click **Finish**.

Once again, commit the change to the repository, as for the `Book` table.

Alter the view

Finally, we want to modify our view definition to return the new `YearOfPublication` column. This time, we can simply update the `AuthorsBooks.sql` file in our working folder by opening it in SSMS and modifying the `ALTER VIEW` statement, as highlighted in Listing 4-4. After you've made the change, save the file back to Fred's working folder.

```
ALTER VIEW AuthorsBooks
AS
    SELECT  ( a.FirstName + ' ' + a.MiddleName + ' ' + a.LastName )
                                                 AS FullName ,
            b.Title,
            b.YearOfPublication
    FROM    Author a
            INNER JOIN AuthorBook ab ON a.AuthorID = ab.AuthorID
            INNER JOIN Book b ON ab.BookID = b.BookID;
```

Listing 4-4:   Modifying the AuthorsBooks view to return YearOfPublication.

Finally, commit the change to the repository, as for all the other changes.

Investigating Bookstore Revision History

Now that we've made changes to our Bookstore database, we can view the history of these revisions and compare what changed between one revision and the next. Although SVN approaches versioning differently from other source control systems, the concepts behind versioning are consistent among the various products: the repository can identify each changeset uniquely, allowing us access to the histories associated with every file and folder.

SVN maintains revision numbers at the repository level. Whenever we commit a set of changes, which may involve, for example, moving folders, editing files, adding files or deleting files or folders, SVN assigns a revision number to the changeset. It increments the number by one with each commit, based on the last assigned revision number, which is the last changeset we committed to the repository.

Figure 4-4 depicts the revision history as it might look for a typical set of database revisions. In fact, it's the revision history for our Bookstore database, specifically the view from the SVN log. To access the log, right-click the **BookstoreDatabases** folder, point to **TortoiseSVN**, and click **Show Log**. This launches the **Log Messages** dialog box, which lists the most recent revisions associated with the file or folder from which we launched the log. If we launch the log from a folder, the information includes revisions to any of the files or subfolders within that folder. Of course, a different VCS will display this sort of information differently, but it will always be available in some form. For example, in Git and Mercurial, we would see all changesets regardless of the folder we used to launch the log, rather than only the changesets "from here down."

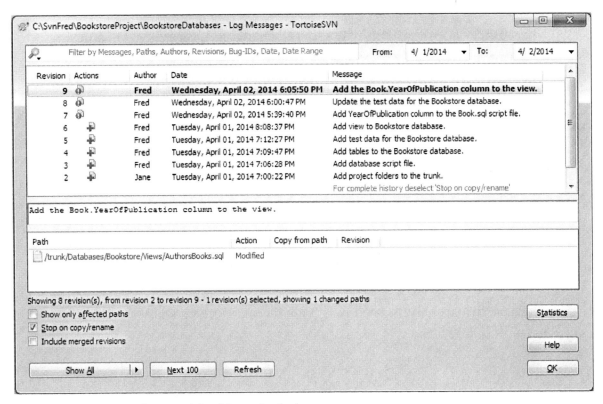

Figure 4-3:   Viewing basic revision history in the log.

For every commit to the repository, SVN increments the revision number. For each revision, we see:

- **The revision number** – in this case, we see Revisions 2 through 9.

  - We do not see Revision 1, since this change, which established the initial repository structure, is out of the scope of the repository's **Databases** folder, which is the folder to which we linked Fred's **BookstoreDatabases** folder.

  - If we launch the log from the **TestData** folder, we see only Revisions 8 and 5.

  - Other source control systems may show all changesets, regardless of from where we launch the log.

- **A symbol that indicates the action** associated with the commit.

  - For Revisions 2 through 6, each action adds either a new file or folder.

  - For Revisions 7 through 9, each action modifies an existing file.

- The **author** of the change – here, we see Jane associated with Revision 2 and Fred with all other revisions.

- A **timestamp** indicating when the author made the change.

- The associated **Commit message**.

If we select a particular revision, the lower pane reveals more details about the actions associated with that revision.

The revision number not only identifies a specific set of changes, but we can also use it to access a snapshot of the repository at a specific point in time. When we open the Repository Browser (shown in Figure 4-4), we're viewing the most recent revisions of all the files and folders stored in the repository. Collectively, these files form the project's current version, which SVN refers to as the head (notice the **HEAD** button in the upper-right corner). You'll find that other source control solutions use the term *head* in different ways. In Git, for example, the term refers to the location of the working directory.

When we select the **Databases** folder, it will show the latest revision for the project as a whole (Revision 9), since that was the last revision to affect the contents of this folder. In Figure 4-4, we've drilled down to the **Bookstore** subfolder, and we can see the latest revisions to affect each folder and its contents.

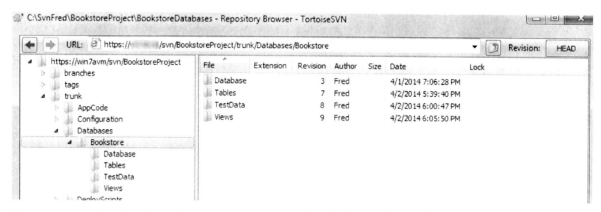

Figure 4-4: Viewing the revision number associated with the **Bookstore** folder.

SVN will also let us view the repository as it existed at a previous version. Click the **HEAD** button, and in the **Select Revision** dialog box we can specify the revision we would like the repository to display. In this case, we'll go back in time to see the repository as it existed when we committed Revision 5, as shown in Figure 4-5.

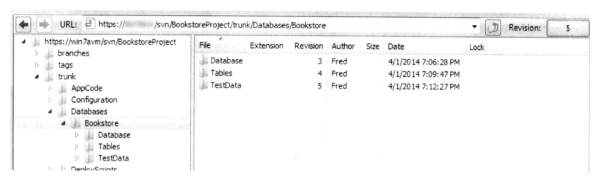

Figure 4-5: Viewing the repository at Revision 5.

The **Bookstore** folder no longer contains the **Views** subfolder, which we did not commit till Revision 6. It does contain the **TestData** subfolder, and the `TestData.sql` file, since these formed the **Commit** for Revision 5. However, the `TestData.sql` file will not have data for the `YearOfPublication` column, nor will the `Book.sql` file include this column.

Although we're viewing the repository as it appeared at Revision 5, the repository still retains all versions. Viewing by revision number acts simply as a filter that excludes any changes that occurred after the specified revision number; it does not delete any data. We can return to the head version at any time.

Diffing files in Bookstore

In the following sections we'll look at some of the types of diff operations we can perform using TortoiseSVN, but most source control systems support similar operations.

Diffing non-text files

In many source control systems, diffs are limited to text files. Even systems that support binary deltas do not necessarily support binary diffs. In such cases, users will need external tools to perform certain types of diffs. SVN provides the built-in TortoiseIDiff to compare image files, though we won't cover its use here. As discussed earlier, if you need more extensive features than are available in TortoiseSVN, you can turn to third-party tools such as WinMerge and Beyond Compare.

The important point to take out of all this is not how SVN works, but rather how a source control system provides a number of ways to track information about a file throughout its history. That is what source control is all about.

Diffs from TortoiseSVN

The most basic diff operation in TortoiseSVN, and the easiest to perform, is to compare a current version of a file in the working folder with the version that preceded it. Note that, with TortoiseSVN, we can diff only files, not folders, meaning that we can't, for example, perform a diff between two folder hierarchies.

Diff with previous version

To compare the last two versions of the `AuthorsBooks.sql` file, right-click the file in Fred's working folder, point to **TortoiseSVN**, and then click **Diff with previous version**. This launches TortoiseMerge, with the two versions of the file opened side by side, as shown in Figure 4-6.

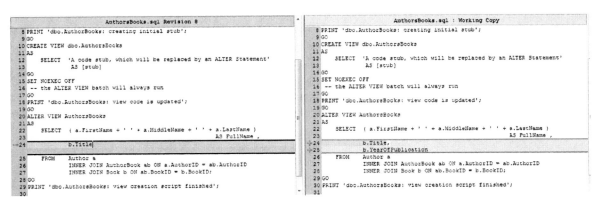

Figure 4-6:   Viewing a diff between file versions.

The version on the right is the current version (the working copy, which is Revision 9) and the version on the left is the file as it existed at the previous revision (Revision 8). TortoiseMerge performs a line-by-line comparison, highlighting the differences and using plus and minus signs to indicate what changed between the two versions.

In this case, we are comparing two commits. However, our current working copy may contain uncommitted changes, in which case we'll get to see the differences between the file version we want to commit and the file version with which we started. Remember that this is only a local diff; we'll only see the changes we made locally. If, in the meantime, someone else changed the revision we started with, we won't know about that until we update the working folder.

To demonstrate this, let's make just a small change to the `AuthorsBooks.sql` in the working folder. Move the comments on Lines 5 and 6 down two lines, to after the `GO` command, and modify the text. Save this change to the working folder but don't commit the change.

In Fred's working folder, right-click the file in TortoiseSVN (it will be marked with a red exclamation mark), and navigate to **TortoiseSVN**. We see two options, **Diff** and **Diff with previous version**. Figure 4-9 shows the result of **Diff**. This time, we're comparing our working copy (uncommitted) with the last committed version.

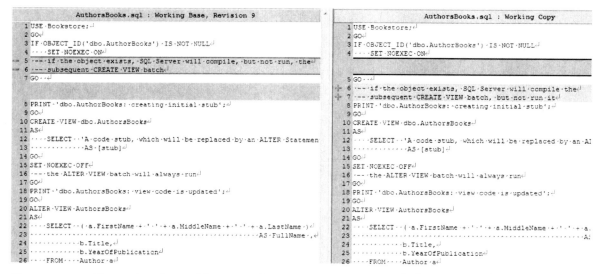

Figure 4-7: Comparing the working copy of `AuthorsBooks.sql` with the committed version.

If we were to pick the **Diff with previous version**, we'd see Revision 8 on the left-hand side, and the diff would also highlight the addition of the `YearOfPublication` column.

If we're happy with our changes, we can commit and create a new revision (Revision 10). If we spot something wrong, we can right-click the file and navigate to **TortoiseSVN | Revert**. The subsequent **Revert** dialog box asks us to confirm that we want to roll back our changes, which will return our working folder to its original state, and our working copy of the file will be back in sync with the most recent version in the repository (Revision 9). Again, however, this does not necessarily mean the working folder is still coordinated with the repository; other users might have committed their changes since our last update.

Diff with URL

TortoiseSVN also offers a **Diff with URL** function. We use it primarily to compare files and folders in a branch with the same file or folder in trunk, which we'll cover in the next chapter. However, we can also use it to compare a file in the working folder with a version of a file in the repository. To try it out, hold down the **Shift** key, right-click the `AuthorsBooks.sql` file and navigate **TortoiseSVN | Diff with URL**. When the **Diff with URL** dialog box appears (shown in Figure 4-8), choose Revision 6 (the revision where we created the view initially) and click **OK**.

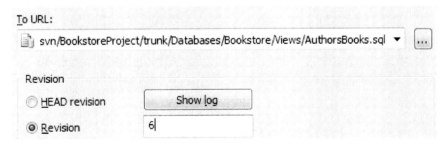

Figure 4-8:   Selecting a revision for viewing differences.

You'll then be presented with a side-by-side comparison of the working copy of the file, as shown in Figure 4-9. In the left window is our working copy and on the right is Revision 6, as it's stored in the repository.

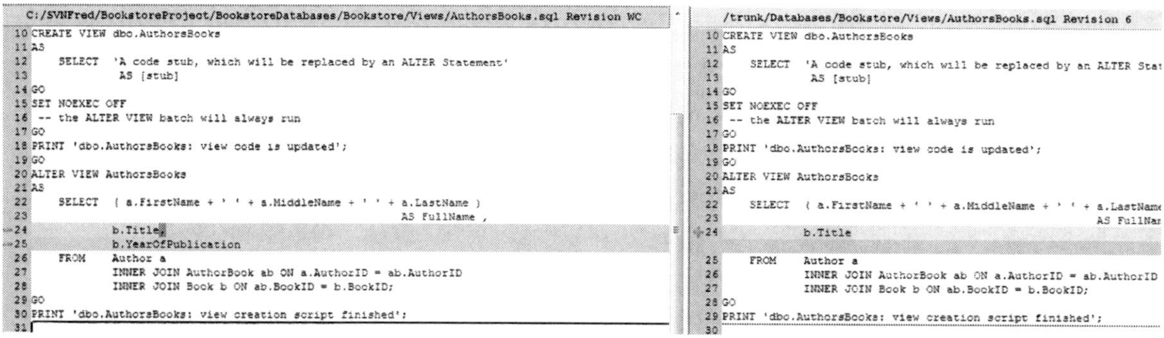

Figure 4-9:   Diff with URL, comparing a working copy of a file to the repository version.

The repository represents the one source of truth, so the plus signs on the repository copy (Revision 6) show what lines we must add to the working copy to bring it into sync with the repository copy, and the minus signs on the working copy indicate what lines must be removed from that copy to bring it into sync with the repository copy. In this case, we don't want to make any changes, but it does provide us with a way to view what has changed over time and perhaps better understand why those changes were made.

We can also launch **Diff with URL** from a folder. For example, launch it from Fred's **Bookstore** folder and compare to Revision 6. We see a **File patches** box containing all the files that changed within that folder between the two revisions, and we can click on each one to compare the individual file versions. Figure 4-10 compares the working copy of `TestData.sql` (on the right) with Revision 6 in the repository (on the left).

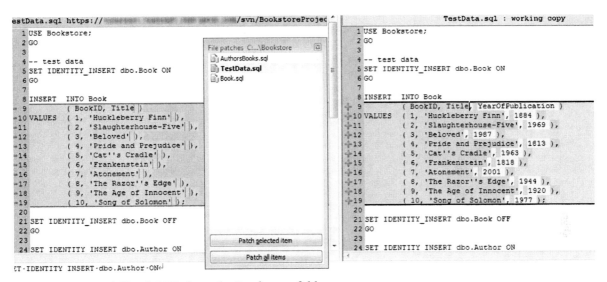

Figure 4-10: A diff with URL from the **Bookstore** folder.

Diff with blame

Many source control systems support a feature called **blame**, which can identify who changed a line of code, and when. In SVN, the blame feature works in conjunction with a type of diff that shows you how a file has changed, and who made those changes.

To perform a blame, right-click a file in Fred's working folder, such as Book.sql, select **TortoiseSVN | Blame**. This launches the **blame** dialog box, shown in Figure 4-11. In this case, the dialog box refers specifically to the file in Fred's working folder. Notice that, in the **From revision** box, I've added the 4, which is the revision number assigned to the file when it was first committed to the repository. The current revision is 7, which was populated automatically.

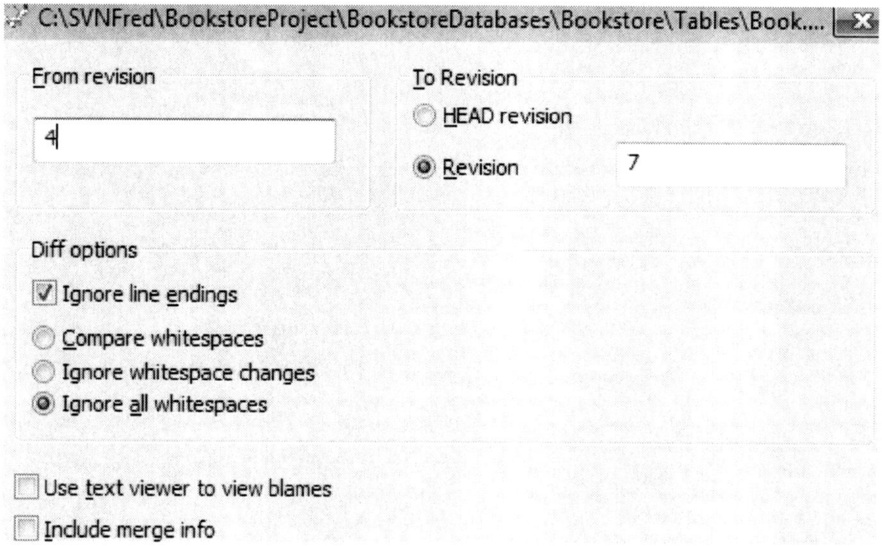
C:\SVNFred\BookstoreProject\BookstoreDatabases\Bookstore\Tables\Book....
From revision
4
To Revision
HEAD revision
Revision
7
Diff options
Ignore line endings
Compare whitespaces
Ignore whitespace changes
Ignore all whitespaces
Use text viewer to view blames
Include merge info

Figure 4-11: Performing a blame and a diff.

Make sure the **Use text viewer to view blames** option is deselected so we get the GUI in **TortoiseBlame**, as shown in Figure 4-12.

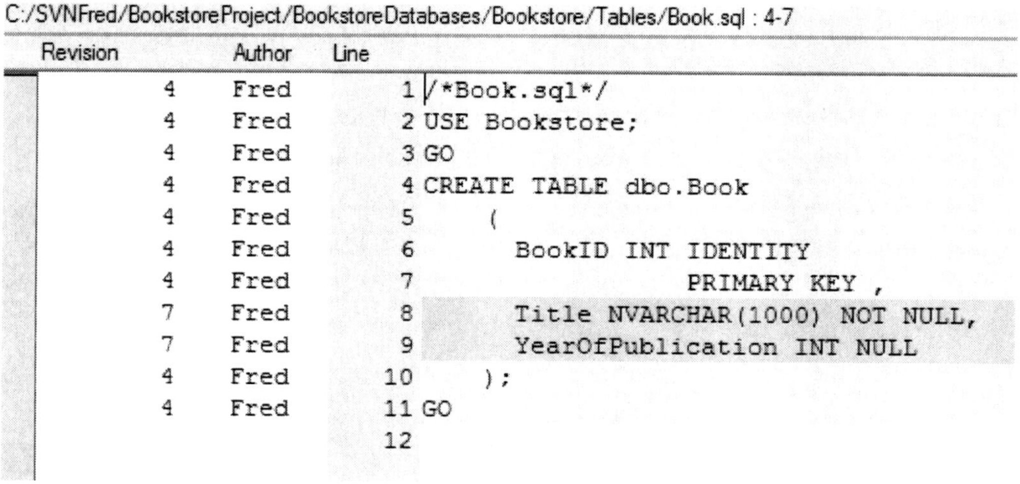
C:/SVNFred/BookstoreProject/BookstoreDatabases/Bookstore/Tables/Book.sql : 4-7
Revision
Author
Line
4 Fred 1 /*Book.sql*/
4 Fred 2 USE Bookstore;
4 Fred 3 GO
4 Fred 4 CREATE TABLE dbo.Book
4 Fred 5 (
4 Fred 6 BookID INT IDENTITY
4 Fred 7 PRIMARY KEY ,
7 Fred 8 Title NVARCHAR(1000) NOT NULL,
7 Fred 9 YearOfPublication INT NULL
4 Fred 10);
4 Fred 11 GO
12

Figure 4-12: Performing a diff and blame on the `Book.sql` file.

Notice that Fred's name is listed next to each line of code, along with the applicable revision number for each line he added or modified. Hovering over the name will also give us the timestamp for that commit and the associated commit message.

If we right-click the user's name, we can select further options. For example, we can open the log, blame the previous revision, or launch TortoiseMerge.

Diffs in the SVN log

We can also perform some diffs via the SVN log. If we launch the log from a file, such as the AuthorsBooks.sql file, we can then right-click a revision within the log, and select the appropriate option from the context menu, as shown in Figure 4-13.

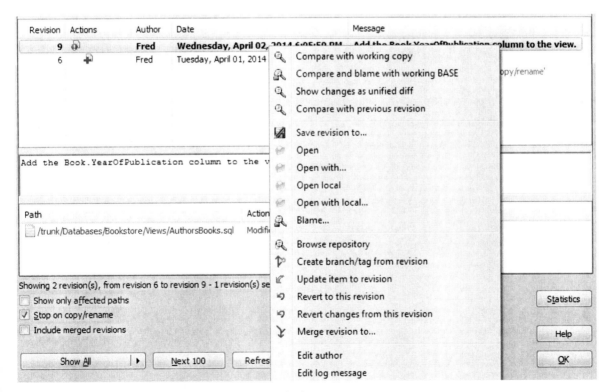

Figure 4-13: Performing a diff on a revision in the log.

For example, to find out simply how a file changed between any two revisions in the repository, click on the first revision and then Ctrl-click on the revision to which you wish to compare. With both selected, right-click and select **Compare revisions** from the context menu. Alternatively, we can also choose to see the blame revisions, as well as a "unified diff," which is like a summary of all the changes in a single file.

If we launch the log from a folder then we can perform similar diff operations, but in this case we get to see a **Changed files** list of all the files that changed between the two selected revisions, and we can click on each to compare them side by side, or perform a unified diff to see all changes to all files in a single view.

We'll see further examples in the next chapter, where we'll perform a diff between a project branch or a specific tag, and the trunk.

What to Do When Things Go Wrong: Revert

Occasionally, when working with files and editing them, we will err and make an unintended change, or a change we regret. If we spot our mistake early, after saving the change to our working folder but before committing it the repository, it is fairly easy to roll back our changes with the **Revert** command, as we discussed earlier in the chapter.

However, if we commit the change to the repository and *then* realize we just stuck something out there that our coworkers will be laughing about for the next five years, what do we do? Not to worry. Source control once again comes to our rescue.

Suppose, for example, Fred is editing the `AuthorsBooks.sql` view and adds the `ISBN` column to the `SELECT` list, in the mistaken assumption that the column exists in the `Book` table. It is such a quick and easy edit, that he uses Notepad to add the column to the script, without verifying his change.

A source control system is, for all practical purposes, indifferent to such mistakes, and lets Fred commit the file to the repository. The database is then deployed to QA, where testers quickly realize that all those failing queries are the result of Fred's flawed view. After receiving an Inbox full of rebukes, Fred immediately returns to his working folder to roll back his changes.

The easiest way to roll back a file is to use the file's log. Right-click the file in the working folder, and navigate **TortoiseSVN | Show log**. The log will reflect all of the file's commits, including the most recent one, which contains the error Fred wants to revert, which is Revision 10 in Figure 4-14.

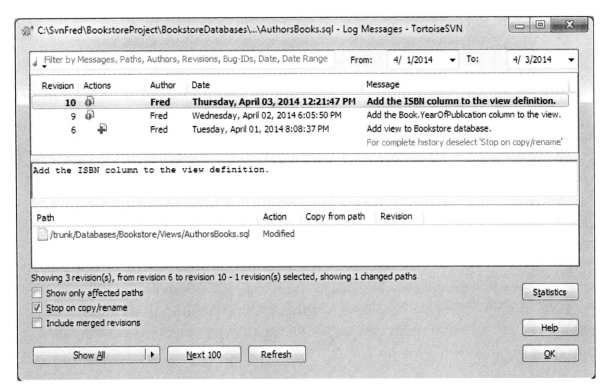

Figure 4-14: Viewing the log for the AuthorsBooks.sql file.

We can roll back a file to any previous revision, as well as roll back sets of files or folders, if necessary. In this case, Fred just wants to roll **AuthorsBooks** back to Revision 9, so right-click the Revision 9 entry, and select **Revert to this revision**. Simply select **Revert** on the **Reverting changes** dialog box, and then wait as SVN reverses our changes and displays the **Merge Finished** dialog box (shown in Figure 4-15), indicating that SVN has essentially performed a reverse merge by comparing Revisions 9 and 10. Again, each source control system will have its own methods for reverting to a previous revision.

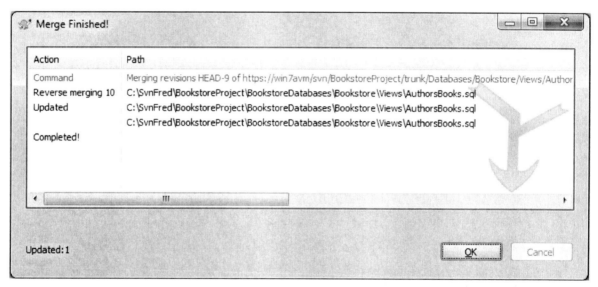

Figure 4-15:   Displaying the results of the reverted changes.

Fred can verify that the code has reverted to its previous state, without the reference to the **ISBN** column, and he can then commit the file to the repository. If we reopen the file's log, we can see results that some might not expect: a new revision has been added to the repository, as shown in Figure 4-16.

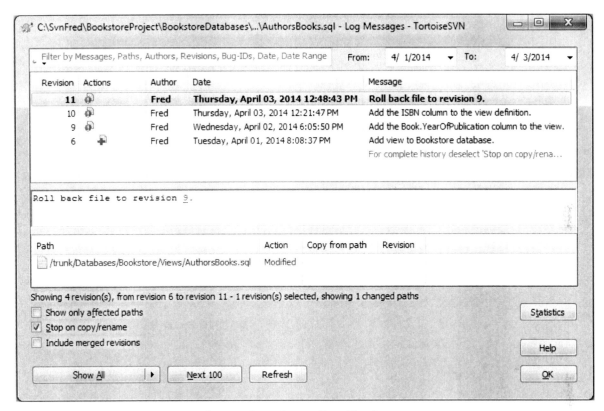

Figure 4-16: A new revision number resulting from a file rollback.

The goal of any source control system is to maintain a record of all changes to a file throughout its history. Although SVN rolled back Fred's changes, the file itself keeps moving forward. Revision 10 still exists, but we now also have Revision 11, which happens to look exactly like Revision 9. What all this means is that Fred's error has not disappeared after all, at least not from the file's history, but at least the most current version of the file is now correct and the QA folks can quit badgering him, at least until he does something like this again.

The World of Source Control

I hope this chapter demonstrates that there's a lot more to source control than simply storing files. A source control system's ability to manage files and folders as well as preserve a history of their changes makes it possible to perform a variety of tasks, including those we've covered in this chapter: managing files and folders in the repository; editing files in the working folder; accessing specific file and folder revisions; and performing diffs that tell exactly what has changed between those revisions.

Yet the tasks we've performed so far have been relatively straightforward, in no small part because only one user has been making all the changes. But that's not how it works in the real world. One of the greatest values that a source control system brings to a development team is its ability to handle multiple users, some of whom are working on the same files at the same time. From here in, we enter the real world with a discussion of how to branch and merge files in order to support concurrent development efforts. As you'll soon see, that's where source control really starts to get interesting.

Chapter 5: Branches and Tags

All our work so far on our **BookstoreProject** and all files relating to that project, has been in a single directory, i.e. the trunk directory (often called "master") of our working folder. Our development work has proceeded in a "straight line" from Revision 1 to the current revision.

At some point in the development process, however, the team will find a need to separate out development efforts, so that two groups can work simultaneously on the same version of the repository, but for different purposes. An example often quoted is one team working on new development (e.g. version 2.0) of a project, while another works on bug fixes for version 1.0. Another example is the need to separate off and stabilize a certain version of the repository for QA testing or customer assessment or similar, while the development effort continues.

To accommodate either case, we need to create a **branch** (or fork) in our repository to allow the growth of our development tree to diverge from the straight and narrow. From the version in the repository at which we create the branch, the growth continues in the original location (trunk or branch), but also sprouts off into one or more new branches. From the users' point of view, each branch represents a distinct copy of the project files on which a team member can work independently, while preserving the fact that each set of files shares the same roots.

Of course, at some point we may need to **merge** the changes from one branch back into the master, or into another branch, or both. We won't cover merging until Chapter 6, but it's worth remembering that branching and merging are flip sides of the same coin. A team's confidence and ability to perform merges, with conflict resolution as necessary, will dictate their policy towards branching.

In this chapter, we'll discuss how branching works conceptually, review briefly some popular branching strategies, and then demonstrate how to create branches in SVN. We'll also cover the related topic of **tags**, where a tag is essentially a branch that the team agree not to modify, and often denotes a fully tested and releasable version of a project.

How Branching Works

The methods used to implement branching vary from one VCS to the next, but the basic branching concepts apply universally. From the point of view of a user accessing the repository through their working folder, branching is similar to copying a folder and its contents from one location in the file system to the other. At that point, we have two distinct versions of the folder, and we can modify the contents of each independently. Figure 5-1 shows our working folder, with the trunk folder, as we've become accustomed, but also a second "copy" of the project, **v1.0BugFixes**, in the **branches** directory.

Figure 5-1:   Creating a branch based on a version in the trunk.

From the VCS's viewpoint, however, the branch is usually not a full copy of the files and their histories, but rather pointers to the files' origins. There are several advantages to creating a branch in a VCS, as opposed to just making a second copy of a set of files in the file system.

1. **The VCS tracks all changes made to the branch files** – it stores the file deltas within the branch, rather than in the trunk where the files originated.

2. **The VCS knows the exact revision in the trunk from which the branch originated** – since the VCS knows the exact point in time when the code paths separated, it knows how far back to look on each path to gather the information it needs to carry out any subsequent merge operation.

Figure 4-1 provides an overview of how the branching process might work.

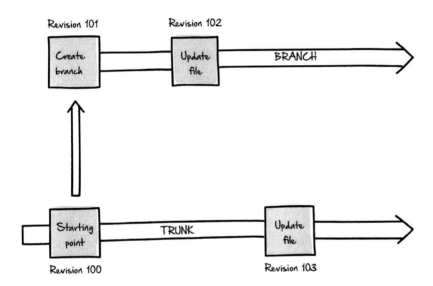

Figure 5-2:   Creating a branch at Revision 100.

In this example, let's assume Revision 100 of our database project occurs when we're nearing a release. As is often the case when working with a second-generation VCS like SVN, we create a branch that we'll use for working with QA and refining our release (v1.0). Within the branch, developers can fix bugs and address problems related to such issues as the need to change lookup data or to modify a stored procedure. At the same time, other developers will move forward with the next new version of the database (v2.0), which will incorporate elements of the v1.0 design, but with significant additions and changes.

Someone on the team creates a branch from the project folder in the trunk, at Revision 100. The set of files and folders in the branch becomes Revision 101 in the repository. From this point, any changes to files in the branch are independent of the trunk. The VCS stores in the branch all changes made to the branch files, with earlier revision histories available only in the trunk, at Revision 100.

When we modify a file within the branch and commit the change, that change becomes Revision 102, with the changeset stored as part of the branch. The corresponding file within the trunk will still show as Revision 100 since, at this point, we've made no changes in the trunk. However, if we now modify the file in the trunk and commit the change, the new file version becomes Revision 103, but that revision has nothing to do with Revision 102, or anything in the branch.

At some stage, the team will produce a fully tested v1.0 release and deploy it to production. However, they will also want to merge some or all of the v1.0 fixes to the v2.0 code base in the trunk. To do this, they'll need to apply to the trunk the changes made to the branch since creation, while taking into account any potentially conflicting changes made to the trunk in the meantime. We'll see how to do this in the next chapter.

Branching Strategies

How a team uses branching is specific to that team and how its source control system ties into its deployment and product lifecycle strategies. Some teams simply don't create branches, some create them only when strictly necessary, and others create them as soon as a development effort starts, to separate out different strands of the development effort.

Understand that it's not the process of branching that is problematic, but the process of merging changes from one branch into the master or another branch, the latter of which has also changed in the meantime. The more branches diverge, the more difficult merging becomes, which is why you should merge early and often. Again, we'll cover merging in Chapter 6.

All modern VCSs include the mechanisms necessary to merge files and resolve any conflicts that should arise, though the process isn't always straightforward. Third-generation distributed VCSs, such as Git and Mercurial in particular, treat branching and merging as a very natural part of the source control process. Let's review briefly this "spectrum" of branching strategies.

No branching

Some development teams rarely stray from the straight and narrow. Users on a first-generation VCS, or even some on second generation, don't support concurrent editing, let alone branching and subsequent merging. Users check out files, placing locks on them to prevent simultaneous update attempts, and check the files back in when they've finished editing them. At no time do multiple developers work on the same file at the same time. They don't really need to create branches to support concurrent development efforts. They do not ever need to merge files and resolve conflicts.

For some development teams, this sort of strategy might work just fine. However, such an approach can result in lower productivity, as team members end up waiting for others to complete their work before they can proceed. It can also result in irregular and delayed deployments. Teams that support concurrent development efforts, whether through branching or concurrent editing, can often achieve more in a shorter space of time. The flip side to this is that they often have to merge files and, in that process, sometimes have to resolve conflicts as a result of that merging.

Branch when needed (release branches)

A common strategy is to create a branch only as required, typically as the team approach a release. Release branches provide a mechanism for more smoothly incorporating source control into the team's quality assurance and deployment processes.

For example, let's say a team uses a very simple approach where they use master for releasable code, and create a branch for development work. During the project development phase, all members of the team work on a single "development" branch. At a defined point, they merge the changes into master, tagged appropriately, and these are then deployed from master to their QA or staging environment. Note that, in our worked examples to this point, we've effectively used trunk as the development branch, so we would create the tag to a different branch, but the principles are exactly the same.

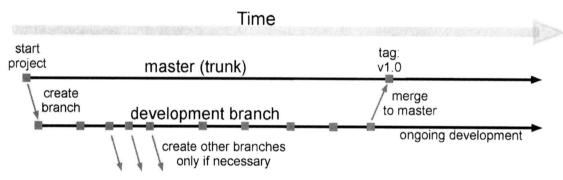

Figure 5-3:   Working with a master and development branch.

Team members might create additional branches under duress, but they essentially adopt a two-prong strategy. They set up the initial project structure as the master and create a branch for development, or they might start with the trunk for development and create a branch for the master (for our discussion here, we'll assume that the trunk is the master).

This approach usually requires complex folder structures to support multiple releases and ongoing maintenance within a single branch. To overcome this difficulty, many teams move to a branching strategy that also includes one or more release branches. A release branch lets a team fix bugs and refine the application in preparation for its final release. Figure 5-4 shows a release branch created for the 1.0 release.

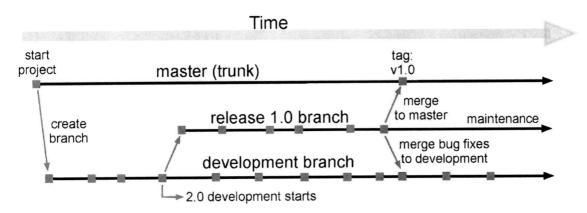

Figure 5-4:   Using a release branch to test and refine an application.

The application and database developers work in the development branch until the code is ready for QA. At that point, someone creates a branch for the 1.0 release. The team deploy to QA from the release branch, fix bugs that QA reports and address any other outstanding issues, and then merge into the master, tagging the release and deploying from there to production. After deployment the team might continue to use the release branch for ongoing maintenance, or create another branch specifically for that purpose.

In the meantime, development continues in the development branch in preparation for the 2.0 release. During the QA process, the team might wish to merge into the development branch some or all of the bug fixes on the release branch, either at regular intervals or when the product is ready for release. It will also be necessary to merge regularly from development to release, to ensure the two branches don't drift too far apart.

Release branches solve certain issues towards the end of a development cycle but, ultimately, having a single branch for development, although it makes the VCS processes rather straightforward, can lead to delays in deployment. Some features take longer to develop than others and the team can notionally deploy only when all planned features for that release are complete. This starts to become a problem if, for example, we fix a serious bug while building a new feature, and would really like to deploy the bug fix immediately to the released version, but have to wait till the feature is complete.

We can get around this problem by "cherry picking" that one commit that fixed the bug, merge it into the release branch and deploy it. We'll discuss this in more detail in Chapter 6, but it's a far from ideal solution.

Another problem that can arise is that all features are ready to go except one which has thrown up unexpected difficulties, and management decides to release the product without the errant feature. One option, although again it's not ideal, is to create a temporary branch that contains all features except the errant one, and deploy from the temporary branch to QA/Staging/Production. Once v2.0 is complete, the team can merge to master and remove the temporary branch. A better option, and the norm in a third-generation VCS, is to have created a specific feature branch for the errant feature (see the next section) and not merge it into master for deployment until it is ready.

Feature flagging instead of branching

One way that some teams remove the concern of delayed deployments, without the need to introduce branching, is to use "feature flags" within the application code, whereby they wrap every feature code that prevents it from running until enabled via configuration. It means the team can deploy all features, even incomplete ones, only enabling each feature for the user as it becomes ready. We won't discuss this approach in detail, as we implement it in application code not in the VCS, but this article and the links in it offer a good overview: HTTP://TINYURL.COM/P8EULMA.

Typically, when the team start "cherry picking" commits or creating temporary branches, it's an indicator of a broader problem in their development process. The team may need to consider refining their branching strategy to separate more cleanly the various strands of development For example, they could create a separate branch for release patching, and a separate branch for major feature. This is a strategy we call "feature and release branching."

Feature branches

A popular approach within development teams who work to shorter, more frequent release cycles, is to create feature braches in addition to release branches. The team creates temporary branches to develop specific product features, rolling out one branch per feature, or "user story," so that they can develop each one in isolation, without causing instability in the development branch, or allowing any single development effort to disrupt the nightly build process.

When that feature is complete and fully tested, the team can merge the feature into the development branch, from where they can incorporate it into the development and QA processes. Figure 5-5 illustrates one example of feature branching with multiple active features, none of which will affect the main line of development.

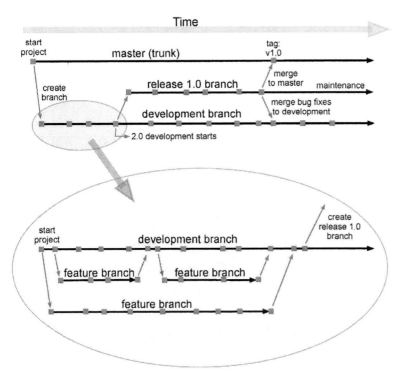

Figure 5-5:   Implementing feature branches to isolate development.

Use of feature branches, with a dedicated purpose for each branch, allows for a consistent deployment strategy for every release, and it allows "maximum concurrency" in the team's development efforts. Ultimately, one may arrive at a rather "freewheeling" branching scheme, such as the one described in Vincent Driessen's excellent article, *A successful Git branching model* (HTTP://TINYURL.COM/39HD87L).

As you can imagine, however, such a strategy also requires very strict discipline with regard to the subsequent merging processes. The last thing you want is for a stored procedure to get updated in the release branch, but never have the update make it back to the development branch. There is also a good reason why frequent branching is a model best suited to a third-generation VCS such as Git, since they offer very strong support for branching and merging.

Branching strategy for database development

The way a team approaches branching is tied to its development and product lifecycle strategies. Every team is different, and no single approach is the absolute *right* way to branch.

What complicates matters for database developers is that teams often plan their product lifecycle strategies around application development, and expect the database team to tag along (excuse the pun). Often the database team has little or no input on when and how to create branches.

However, product groups are trying more than ever to incorporate database development into their development processes, particularly those groups that embrace Agile development methodologies. In such situations, branching often plays a significant role. As a result, it's more likely than ever that at some point, as a database developer, you'll find yourself having to work within one or more branches during a database's development cycle.

For database developers, release branching with a single development branch is relatively painless because the team simply place the database in the VCS in the development branch, alongside the application, and the team are, most of the time, not trying to develop different versions of the same database in two places at once. When the team create a release branch, of course, there will be two different versions of the database but, as long as they merge frequently in both directions, and adhere strictly to the established development and source control procedures, it should not make life too difficult.

In this book, in order to focus on basic database source control concepts, we don't stray too far beyond simple branching of this nature. However, as discussed, some teams will find this limiting, and see the need to use feature branching alongside release branching, to provide a more flexible structure for maximizing development efforts and improving efficiency. For database developers, however, the more branching that occurs, the greater the number of database versions out there. Without careful planning and good database and interface design, this can get dangerously complicated.

At this stage, it becomes important that your database design makes intelligent use of **schemas** (HTTP://TINYURL.COM/5ND8JN), to group together database objects that support each logical area of the application's functionality. That way, if a developer creates a branch to work on a specific feature, any related database changes will be on one specific schema, representing one logical area of the database. This is likely to make the subsequent merging processes less painful.

Regardless of the exact branching strategy, a team that creates an application that makes direct access to base tables in a database will have to put a lot of energy into keeping database and application in sync (to say nothing of having to tackle issues such as security and audit). This issue will only worsen, the more branches we maintain and the more versions of the database we have in the VCS.

A good database development team will, firstly, make considerable efforts to ensure that they understand the application domain as fully as possible, and so get the database design right up-front and minimize the need for substantial refactoring later. Secondly, they will never expose the inner workings of the database to the application.

Each application should have a stable, well-defined interface with the database (one for each application, usually, if more than one application uses a single database). The application development team owns the interface definition, which should be stored in the VCS. The database developers implement the interface, also stored in the VCS. Database developers and application developers must carefully track and negotiate any changes to the interface. Changes in it have to be subject to change-control procedures, as they will require a chain of tests. The database developers will, of course, maintain their own source control for the database "internals," and will be likely to maintain versions for all major releases. However, this will not need to be shared with the associated applications. An application version should be coupled to an application-database interface version, rather than to a database version.

In many respects, a branching strategy for database development is no different from any other application development. Indeed, it's likely that the team will adopt the same strategy for applications as for databases. However, I think it fair to say that, from the database developer's perspective, they would like the branching strategy to be as simple as possible, perhaps adopting a simple "branch-as-needed" approach, at least until the whole team become highly competent at managing database source control processes.

Feature branching should be used judiciously and is best suited to cases where developers can work on discrete parts of the database, and where there exists a well-defined interface between application and database.

Tags

The revision numbers that a source control system uses to track version histories are separate from the types of numbering systems used to identify product builds, versions or releases. They can be specifically associated with one another, but they are separate systems. That's where *tags* come in. Tags provide an easy way to denote a snapshot of your repository at a given point of time, usually based on a particular revision number.

A tag is essentially just a branch, but one that we should not modify, once created. We use tags, generally, to associate a build number with a stable, releasable revision in the repository. As we saw earlier, in Figure 5-3, some teams only ever have tagged versions in master, since they always want master to contain only code that can be, or has been, released.

For instance, suppose we had deployed the `Bookstore` database based on the files in our repository, as they existed at Revision 4. The database deployment is part of the product release 1.0.0.0. We can create a tag named **release 1.0.0.0** and associate it with Revision 4. Thereafter, we'll always know exactly what was in release 1.0.0.0, just by referencing the tag, as long as no one subsequently changes the files and folders associated with the tag.

A deployment strategy might include a process that extracts the most recent revision number from the source control system and incorporates that number into the build number. However, the number structures themselves remain separate. In other words, if our most recent database build is 1.2.5.35, then that build number might or might not somehow reflect the revision number, but the build number has no bearing on how the VCS assigns revision numbers. Tags are usually on the most recent revision, of course, but we can tag any revision in the repository.

Branching in SVN

It's time to see branching in action in SVN. The team have completed v1.0 of the **Bookstore** application. At that point, they created a tag for the release in their **Tags** folder, which effectively forms their "deployment" branch. In other words, they will deploy from this folder to production. We'll see how to create tags shortly, in the *Creating Tags in SVN* section later in this chapter.

Our development duo now want to create a branch off of trunk, containing the whole project for the v1.0 release, where they can perform some bug fixing on the released version, while mainline development continues in the trunk, on the next major release (v2.0).

Since Barb is the only one who checked out the entire repository, she will be the one to create the branch in the repository. Fred can just check out, to his working folder, the bits of the branch he needs, specifically the **Databases** folder. When we create a branch, it must still represent a "single version for the entire project." If Fred were to create a branch off of the **Databases** directory (since he doesn't have trunk checked out), then we defeat this objective. For example, when it comes time to build and deploy the branch, a CI server might check out the branch directory and run the build; if all it had was the **Databases** folder then it wouldn't have all the project files it needed to run the full build.

One way for Fred to create a branch on his own would be to create a second, separate working folder, check out trunk to that folder, and then create the branch from there. With the branch created in the repository, Fred can once again just check out what he needs to his original working folder, and probably delete the second working folder.

However, for simplicity, in these exercises we're simply going to have Barb create a branch called **v1.0BugFixes**, based on the current revision of the **trunk** folder in the trunk.

Before creating the branch, Barb needs to update her working folder with the latest revision in the repository, so right-click **BookstoreProject** and click **SVN Update**. If you've been following along with the exercises up to this point exactly as described, then this should bring Barb's working folder to Revision 11. However, if you've been experimenting with other options or trying side-experiments, then your revision numbers won't match. It doesn't matter; as long as you provided a descriptive commit message, you'll still know which changes you committed at each revision.

Clearing the authentication

As you'll recall from Chapters 2 and 3, if you've set up working folders for Jane, Barb, and Fred on the same computer, you will need to clear the authentication history before signing in as a different user. To clear the settings, right-click a folder in the working directory, point to **TortoiseSVN**, *and then click* **Settings**. *On the* **Saved Data** *node, click* **Clear All** *next to* **Authentication data**.

Create the branch in the repository

To start creating the branch, right-click the **trunk** folder in Barb's working folder, point to **TortoiseSVN**, and then click **Branch/tag**. This launches the **Copy (Branch/Tag)** dialog box, shown in Figure 5-4.

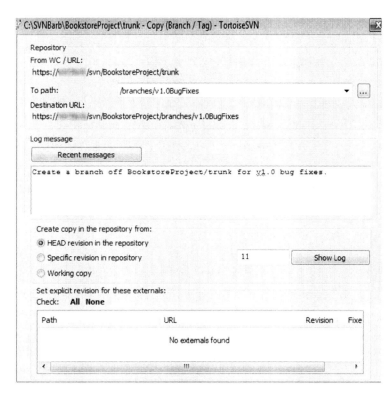

Figure 5-6:   Creating a branch in TortoiseSVN.

The dialog box will automatically display the folder from which it was launched as the source of the branch. Instead, we must specify a folder for our branch, so in the **To path** text box, type in **/branches/v1.0BugFixes**. In the **Create copy in the repository from** section, select the option **HEAD revision in the repository** to ensure that we're creating the branch based on the most recent revision in the repository.

Click **OK**, and a **Copy Finished** dialog box confirms that the new revision is Revision 12. In other words, creating the branch creates a new revision in the repository. You may also see a message regarding your working copy:

> *"Your working copy remains on the previous path. If you want your next changes to be committed to the copy or branch you have just created, then you need to switch your working copy over to the new URL. Use the switch command to do that."*

SVN uses a path (URL) to serve as the pointer from a working folder to the repository. SVN uses that path to keep the working folder and repository in sync. This is simply a reminder to Barb that, despite creating a branch, the path remains unchanged (pointing to **<server>/svn/BookstoreProject**, since Barb checked out the entire project). Therefore, when Barb updates her working folder after creating the branch, she'll get all changes to the branch as well as to the trunk. In other cases, a user that checks out only specific portions of the repository (such as Fred) may need to switch their working folder to tell SVN to use a different path, pointing to different, but related, content in the repository. We'll see how to do this shortly, when we discuss how Fred updates to retrieve the new branch.

That's all we need to do to set up a branch in SVN but, returning to Barb's working folder, you may be surprised *not* to see the new branch in the **branches** folder. When we create a branch, we add it directly to the repository. To verify this, launch Repository Browser by right-clicking the **BookstoreProject** folder, pointing to **TortoiseSVN**, and then clicking **Repo-browser**. Figure 5-7 shows the repository with the new **v1.0BugFixes** branch.

We've created a separate copy of the project, in the branch, from Revision 11 in trunk. However, as noted, on the server the repository has merely created a new branch folder with pointers back to the original content in trunk.

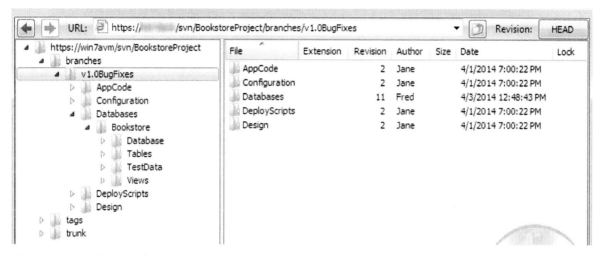

Figure 5-7: The new branch as it appears in the repository.

Update the working folders

For the branch to appear in Barb's working folder, she needs to update her folder, so right-click her **BookstoreProject** folder, perform an **SVN Update**, and verify that the **branches** subfolder now contains the new branch (as shown previously in Figure 5-1).

If Fred needs to work on the new branch, he has two ways to update his working folder. The first, and the one we use here, is to now create a new subfolder of **BookstoreProject** called something like **BookstoreDatabases_v1.0Bugfixes** and from there perform an SVN checkout of the **/branches/v1.0BugFixes/Databases** folder. In effect, Fred is creating a second working folder, one that points to the **Databases** folder in the branch rather than in the trunk.

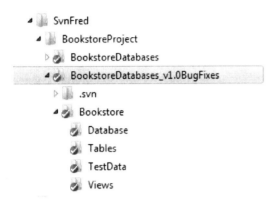

Figure 5-8:   Updating Fred's working folder with the new branch.

Switching the working folder

Fred's other option, when he needs to work on the branch, is to switch his current working folder (**BookstoreDatabases**) to point to the branch, instead of the trunk. To do this, right-click the current root folder in the working folder (in Fred's case, the **BookstoreDatabases** folder), point to **TortoiseSVN**, and then click **Switch**. In the **Switch To Branch/Tag** dialog box, switch the path from **/trunk/Databases** to **/branches/ v1.0BugFixes/**. This will update the working folder with the files from the new target. Any commits Fred makes from that point forward will occur on the branch, until he switches the working folder back to trunk.

Keep in mind, however, that the way we're dealing with working copies here is specific to TortoiseSVN and, by extension, second-generation source control systems. In third-generation systems, our only choice is to check out the entire repository, and switching back and forth between branches is generally much more common.

Modifying the branch

In order to prove that anyone can now work on this branch independently of the **BookstoreProject** in the trunk, let's have Fred make a small modification to the `AuthorsBooks` view in the branch, by adding a comment and a calculated column.

Within Fred's **BookstoreDatabases_v1.0Bugfixes** branch, open the `AuthorsBooks.sql` file, add a comment, and then add the `NewBookID` calculated column, which creates an ID based on the `BookID` value and part of the `LastName` value. Listing 5-1 shows the new code for the `ALTER VIEW` statement, highlighted to make it easier to identify. (Don't dwell on the logic of this column too much; it's only for demonstration purposes.)

```
ALTER VIEW AuthorsBooks
-- retrieves all authors and all their books
AS
   SELECT   ( a.FirstName + ' ' + a.MiddleName + ' ' + a.LastName )
                                          AS FullName ,
            (CAST(b.BookID AS VARCHAR) + '_'
                            + LOWER(LEFT(a.LastName, 2)))
                                          AS NewBookID,
            b.Title,
            b.YearOfPublication
   FROM     Author a
            INNER JOIN AuthorBook ab ON a.AuthorID = ab.AuthorID
            INNER JOIN Book b ON ab.BookID = b.BookID;
GO
```

Listing 5-1:   Modifying the `AuthorsBooks` view definition.

Save and close the modified `AuthorsBooks.sql` file and then, back in TortoiseSVN, right-click **BookstoreDatabases_v1.0Bugfixes** and perform an **SVN Commit**, with a suitable commit message (again, make sure you're connecting to the repository as Fred).

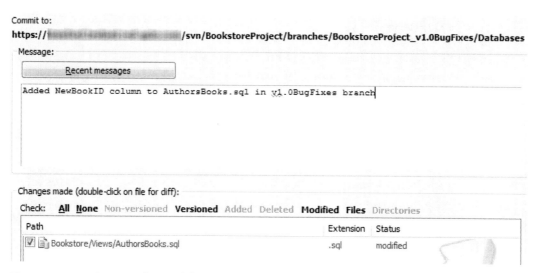

Figure 5-9: Commit the modified `AuthorsBooks` view to the **v1.0BugFixes** branch.

The **Commit Finished** dialog box will appear, showing that we're now at Revision 13 (or whatever the revision number is on your system). Remember, we started with Revision 11, created our branch (Revision 12), and altered the `AuthorsBooks.sql` file (Revision 13).

The **BookstoreDatabases_v1.0Bugfixes** branch in Fred's working folder should now show all green, indicating that there are no current changes that need to be committed to the repository. At this point, the trunk remains unchanged at Revision 11. The changes made in this exercise affect only the branch.

Diffing between branches and the trunk

In Chapter 4, we worked through some examples of performing a diff between different file versions. However, we can also perform diffs between files or folders in the trunk (or a branch) and the corresponding files or folders in another branch (or associated with a tag). Let's look at a few examples.

Comparing folders

We can perform a high-level diff between a folder in the trunk and a corresponding folder in our branch. From Fred's working folder, launch repo-browser, right-click the **trunk** folder, and click **Mark for comparison**. This will turn the folder bold. Next, navigate to the **v1.0Bugfixes** folder, right-click it and select **Compare URLs**. This will launch the **Changed Files** dialog box, which provides a list of differences between the trunk folder and the branch folder, as shown in Figure 5-10.

Figure 5-10:   Viewing differences between the branch and trunk project folders.

The dialog box lists all the objects that have been added or have changed. As expected, it shows only the AuthorsBooks.sql files, which we modified in the branch. Double-click the file to launch TortoiseMerge and see a side-by-side comparison of the file as it exists in our branch (on the left in Figure 5-11) and as it exists in trunk in the repository (on the right).

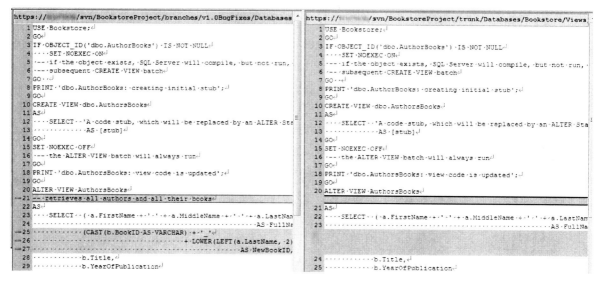

Figure 5-11: Performing a diff between a file in a branch and file in the trunk.

Not surprisingly, the diff shows the column and comment that Fred added.

Unified diffs

Another useful type of diff to perform is a **unified diff**, which shows all the file changes that have occurred between a specific revision, such as the first revision in the new branch, or a tagged revision, and the current revision. To demonstrate this, let's make another simple change to a different database object in the branch. In Barb's branch (for a change!), add a comment of your choice to the `AuthorBook.sql` file, and commit it.

Then, launch the SVN log from **BookstoreProject**, and highlight the two revisions to compare, in this case, Revisions 14 and 12, as shown in Figure 5-12.

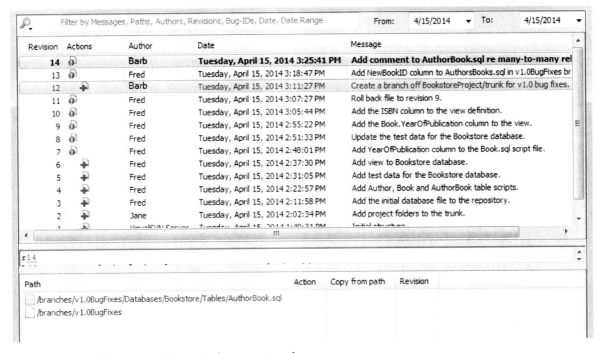

Figure 5-12: Selecting revisions in the repository log.

Having highlighted the two revisions, right-click one of the files and click **Show differences as unified diff**. This launches the TortoiseUDiff utility, which displays all the differences (as additions and deletions) that have occurred between the two versions, as shown in Figure 5-13.

```
revisions 12-14, BookstoreProject - TortoiseUDiff                                    [ □ ] [ ◻ ] [ X ]
File
  1 Index: branches/v1.0BugFixes/Databases/Bookstore/Tables/AuthorBook.sql
  2 ===============================================================================
  3 --- branches/v1.0BugFixes/Databases/Bookstore/Tables/AuthorBook.sql (revision 12)
  4 +++ branches/v1.0BugFixes/Databases/Bookstore/Tables/AuthorBook.sql (revision 14)
  5 @@ -1,3 +1,5 @@
  6 +-- Define the many-to-many relationship between the Author and Book tables.
  7 +
  8  /*AuthorBook.sql*/
  9  USE Bookstore;
 10  GO
 11 Index: branches/v1.0BugFixes/Databases/Bookstore/Views/AuthorsBooks.sql
 12 ===============================================================================
 13 --- branches/v1.0BugFixes/Databases/Bookstore/Views/AuthorsBooks.sql    (revision 12)
 14 +++ branches/v1.0BugFixes/Databases/Bookstore/Views/AuthorsBooks.sql    (revision 14)
 15 @@ -18,9 +18,13 @@
 16  PRINT 'dbo.AuthorsBooks: view code is updated';
 17  GO
 18  ALTER VIEW AuthorsBooks
 19 +-- retrieves all authors and all their books
 20  AS
 21      SELECT  ( a.FirstName + ' ' + a.MiddleName + ' ' + a.LastName )
 22                                                    AS FullName ,
 23 +          (CAST(b.BookID AS VARCHAR) + '_'
 24 +                              + LOWER(LEFT(a.LastName, 2)))
 25 +                                          AS NewBookID,
 26              b.Title,
 27              b.YearOfPublication
 28      FROM    Author a
 29
```

Figure 5-13:   Viewing a unified diff of revisions in the branch.

As the figure shows, the diff reflects Barb's changes to files, with the changes highlighted in green. Notice too, highlighted in yellow, the path and file names, along with the revision numbers.

Revision graphs

TortoiseSVN also lets us generate *revision graphs,* which provide a fast and simple way to view where our branches and tags came from in the trunk. In other words, a revision graph provides a visual aid for seeing the source revision on which we based our branch or tag.

In Barb's working folder, right-click the **v1.0BugFixes** branch folder, point to **TortoiseSVN**, and click **Revision Graph**. This launches the **Revision Graph** dialog box, shown in Figure 5-14.

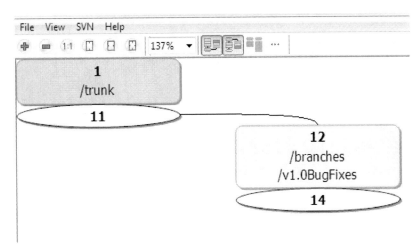

Figure 5-14:   Reviewing a revision graph of the **v1.0BugFixes** branch.

The revision graph shows that we created the branch based on Revision 11 in the trunk and that the newly created branch became Revision 12. It also shows that the branch is now at Revision 14.

We can hover over any of the revision icons to reveal a pop-up message providing additional details about that revision, such as the URL, the author, and the date and time that user committed to the repository. The Revision Graph dialog box also provides options for displaying more information and taking additional actions. For example, we can display all the revisions in which changes were made or mark a revision as the working copy.

Creating Tags in SVN

To demonstrate how tags work, we'll create one for our **Bookstore** project. Conceptually, tags function the same way in other VCSs, but there may be implementation differences.

Creating a tag in TortoiseSVN is nearly identical to creating a branch, except that we specify a different location (in this case, the **tags** folder in **BookstoreProject**).

For this example, we'll create a "retrospective" tag based on Revision 4 and imagine that this related to release 1.0 of our `Bookstore` database. Revision 4 also represents our very first schema, with just our three initial tables, so if we ever want to see everything that changed since, we can compare our current release to this tag.

In Barb's (or Jane's) working folder, right-click the **trunk** folder and navigate **TortoiseSVN | Branch/tag** to launch the **Copy (Branch/Tag)** dialog box that we saw previously, when creating a branch.

To name the tag, we simply type the correct path into the **To path** text box so it reads **/tags/v1.0**. SVN will apply the tag to all content in the trunk as it existed at Revision 4. Next, add a comment, and then specify the revision number in the text box associated with the **Specific revision in repository** option. Figure 5-15 shows the **Copy (Branch/Tag)** dialog box with the configured information.

Once satisfied that the tag is exactly as you want it, click **OK** to close the **Copy (Branch/Tag)** dialog box.

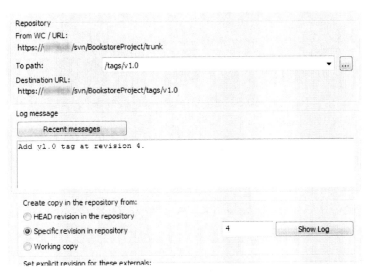

Figure 5-15:   Adding the **v1.0** tag.

As was the case when creating a branch, SVN creates the new tag in the repository, but it does not appear in Barb's working folder until we right-click her working folder and select **SVN Update**. Having done this, it should show the new **v1.0** tag, in the **tags** folder. Notice that the tag contains the folders (and files) as they existed at Revision 4.

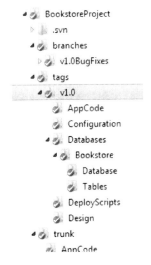

Figure 5-16:   Viewing the **v1.0** tag in Barb's working folder.

If we want to see exactly what has changed since that revision, we can open Repository Browser and compare URLs between the trunk and the **v1.0** tag or between the **v1.0BugFixes** branch and the **v1.0** tag. In either case, the **Changed Files** dialog box will show all added and modified files and folders. We can then click on any one to see exactly how it changed. Alternatively, we can perform a unified diff to see all the changes in a single, shortened view.

Finally, remember that, just as a branch in the repository is really just a new pointer to the same content, so is a tag. That means our new tag is pointing back to the original content, as it existed at Revision 4. Another way to consider it is that the repository stores deltas, as described in the previous chapter, not copies. Here, the delta is just a new path to the same content.

Summary

Branching is an integral feature of any modern source control system. Branching lets teams work on distinct sets of files that share the same roots, without one team overwriting the work of another team. We can create a branch just about as easily as we can copy a folder.

Our approach to branching will depend, at least in part, on our broader management strategies, which determine how files are stored, deployed, implemented, and in other ways managed throughout the product lifecycle process.

Of course, having created a branch and made changes as required, we'll often want to **merge** those changes back into trunk, or into another branch. That's the challenge for the next chapter.

Chapter 6: Merging

If branching is the process of "segregating" the development effort into different streams, then **merging** is the process of bringing these streams back together. Branches allow team members to work on a particular feature or logical area of an application, or a set of bug fixes, without their changes affecting users working on trunk or on other branches. Merging allows team members to incorporate changes made in one location (branch or trunk) into another. In this chapter, we refer to this as "**inter-branch**" merging. For example, when we create a branch for bug fixes of the current database release or for developing a particular feature, then team members working on the branch will, at some point, want to merge those changes into the "ongoing development" branch. To make this process as painless as possible, it's also important that the team perform regular merges in the opposite direction, incorporating into their branch the changes made by the ongoing development team.

In addition to inter-branch merging, we may also need to perform "**intra-branch**" merging, when more than one user makes changes to the same file in the trunk, or in the same branch. For example, let's say Barb and Fred both start work on the same revision of one of our database files. Barb commits her change first. When Fred commits, the operation will fail and Fred will need to perform an update. If Fred's proposed commit does not conflict with Barb's commit, most VCSs will perform an **auto-merge**, as part of the update, producing a third file version that reconciles Barb's change and Fred's proposed change, and which Fred can then commit. If the changes do conflict, Fred will need to assist manually in the merge operation.

While inter-branch and intra-branch merge operations serve different purposes from the team's perspective, conceptually they are similar in nature. If the team adopts good practices, committing small changes often and updating often, then intra-branch merges should be painless, since they will entail merging a single (small) proposed commit with a single existing commit. Inter-branch merge operations can be trickier, since the merge operations may need to reconcile a range of commits in the branch with a range of commits in another branch, manually assisting with any conflicts that arise. The longer users wait between merges, the more painful is the process.

In this chapter, we'll discuss a few best practices to help avoid painful merge operations, then explain conceptually how various varieties of intra-branch and inter-branch merges work, pointing out significant differences between merging in a centralized VCS versus a distributed one. Finally, we'll walk through some simple merge examples in SVN, so you get a feel for how it works in practice.

How to Avoid Painful Merges

The more work you do in your working folder without committing, and without checking what other users have been up to via an update, the more painful you'll find the resulting "big bang" merge. To minimize the potential pain, follow these simple rules:

1. **Update your working copy often** – Before starting work on a file, retrieve the latest version into the working folder to make sure you've got the very latest revision from the repository.

2. **Commit small changes often** – Having made and tested the smallest possible changeset that will leave the database in a consistent working state, commit it.

3. **Always start a merge from a clean working folder** – No uncommitted changes.

4. **Merge often** – By following the first two rules we will, by definition, perform frequent small intra-branch merges. However, we must also apply the spirit of these rules to our inter-branch merging. For example, if we're working on a feature branch that we will need to merge into the mainline development branch, then during development we should:

   a. frequently merge from mainline to branch to "update" the branch with any changes made in mainline development so the two strands don't drift too far apart

   b. frequently merge small, tested changes from branch to mainline.

Even if you follow all of these guidelines, merges can sometime still be tricky and, without due care, can leave your working folder or repository, or both, in a mess.

If a failed merge leaves the working folder in an unstable state, almost every VCS will provide a way to undo changes and get back to the starting revision. In the case of SVN, for example, we can use the **revert** command (see HTTP://TINYURL.COM/86S4SC8). We can also simply take a copy of the current working folder prior to commencing the merge.

For particularly knotty merges, talk to whoever is responsible for maintaining the repository, and consider taking a full backup (assuming the repository is relatively small) or an incremental backup, before starting the merge.

How Merging Works

The basic concept behind merging is universal: we need to merge changes in one location with changes made in another location. However, perhaps more so than for any source control concept discussed previously in this book, different VCSs have different ways to perform the various merge operations, and merging in a centralized VCS is quite different from merging in a distributed one. In this section, we'll try to focus on conceptual descriptions of each variety of merge operation and along the way point out significant differences in how the type of merge works in centralized versus distributed systems.

Intra-branch merges: conflicting changes on the same branch

This type of merging occurs when a potentially conflicting change occurs during concurrent modification of the same file in the same branch of a repository. It results in the need to merge the repository's version of a branch or the trunk, with the local version of the same branch or trunk.

A typical workflow leading up to the need to perform an intra-branch merge in a centralized VCS might look something like this:

1. Barb updates her local working copy – Barb has the latest revision, 29 say (R29 for short).

2. Fred updates his local working copy – Fred also has R29.

3. Fred commits successfully a change to file *x* – the repository generates a delta to describe the change and registers R30.

4. Barb finishes modifying file *x* and either:

    a. **attempts to commit** – the repo can't generate a delta because the "base" for Barb's proposed commit is R29 whereas the repository version is now at R30, so the repository notifies her of the need to update before committing

    b. **performs another update before committing** – and gets notified of Fred's change.

5. Barb needs to perform a merge.

As we discussed, briefly in Chapter 1, in a centralized VCS this intra-branch merging process can become somewhat "dangerous," especially if we forget to employ good practices that help avoid large, complicated merges. The essential problem is that a centralized VCS will "block" a user's attempt to commit a change from their working folder to the central repository if another user has changed that file in the meantime. Instead the VCS invites the user to perform an update, which incorporates a merge operation (auto or manual), *before* committing. Having established a "merged" version of the file, in the working folder, the user will typically have no history of the state of the file when attempting the initial commit, so if the merge goes wrong, the user risks losing work. To avoid this possibility, users have to resort to "pre-VCS versioning" of their working folder, by simply making a copy of the working directory to a folder, named by date, or appended with a letter or number.

Welcome to the Stone Age

It seems ironic that, when using a second-generation system VCS, users often resort to the sort of "copy the folder" version control that would make even a first-generation VCS blush with shame. Fortunately, third-generation systems have figured how to avoid having to make a precautionary backup.

By contrast, intra-branch merging in a distributed VCS is safer, since each user has a local repository. In a DVCS, we can commit locally and then "pull" the latest changes from a remote repo and merge as necessary. The merge operation is safer in that it involves a local commit and a remote commit, and we need to create a third commit that combines the two. We commit the merged version locally and finally push the merged version to the remote repository. If the merge fails, we can simply try it again.

Continuing our example, if Barb's proposed commit does not conflict with Fred's commit, the repository will perform an auto-merge, creating a merged file that contains both sets of changes, which Barb can commit to the repository (as R31). Barb will have the option to review how the VCS achieved the merge, but it does the work automatically. Users of a centralized VCS, such as SVN, typically don't even think of this as a "merge" because they clicked on **Update** to begin the process and the merge was automatic. Distributed VCSs make these two distinct steps, allowing us to separate them, and making it clear that users are merging as they pull.

If Barb's proposed commit does conflict with Fred's commit, Barb must perform a manual merge, and then commit the merged version. The VCS will store some temporary files in Barb's working folder to allow Barb to view various versions of the "conflicted" file, examine each conflict and take steps to resolve them, usually with the help of a merge tool (you'll see this in action shortly).

In most cases, regardless of whether we use a centralized or a distributed VCS, the more complex the merge, the more likelihood there is for conflicts and the more work we will have to do to resolve them.

However, as noted in Chapter 2, a DVCS, which will track changes across all files collectively rather than on a file-by-file basis, does generally offer much stronger support for merging and can more often merge changes without any manual user intervention.

Inter-branch merges: moving changes between branches

For teams that segregate their development efforts into branches, with each branch serving a defined purpose, such as to create a specific feature, there will inevitably be the need to merge changes from the trunk to the branch, from the branch to the trunk, or from one branch to another branch. A user might also decide to merge only specific changes, or all changes since the branch was created.

The team will potentially need to merge in a lot of files that have changed both in the origin (the trunk, say) and in their branch. If the changes don't conflict, the VCS will auto-merge, as described previously. However, if they conflict then the user faces a lot of extra work when trying to merge the changes manually. Fortunately, the previously described danger of intra-branch merging does not apply to inter-branch merges, since the merge operation will always involve two commits, as opposed to a commit and a proposed commit.

Nevertheless, the best way to avoid unnecessary pain is to perform frequent merges. It will make it easier to iron out conflicts before the files in the source and the destination diverge too far.

Don't be afraid of branching, but have a healthy respect for the subsequent merging process, and use branches only when they'll augment the development process. A superfluity of branches can result in a lot of extra work.

Merging from mainline to branch

Let's say that a small team of developers, led by Fred, need to work on a set of complex analytical database functions. They will take some time and testing and, in order not to disrupt other developers, they decide to create a feature branch off of "mainline." Meanwhile, Barb and the rest of the team continue the main development effort, modifying the database schema as required in mainline (which could be in trunk, or a dedicated branch).

The onus is on Fred and his team to periodically merge changes from mainline into the feature branch in order to ensure the two strands of development do not drift too far apart. Every developer should regularly update their working folders with the latest changes by other team members working on the same branch. In addition, the team should periodically pause their feature development to merge the mainline development changes into their feature branch. Typically, one team member will merge in all changes since branch creation, resolving any conflicts, then commit the merged files to the branch project directory in the repository, from where the other team members can update their working folders.

Merging from branch to mainline

At a certain point, Fred's team will finish work on each analytical function and will want to merge the feature into mainline. Fortunately, their task is made less onerous by their periodic merges in the other direction, since now all they need to do is merge into mainline the specific changes relating to their new function.

At this point, it may be that the feature branch is no longer required and the team can delete it. Alternatively, they may want to keep it open to develop the features further.

How to Merge in SVN

Up to this point, we've lived in a conflict-free SVN world, but that is about to change. We're going to walk through both intra- and inter-branch merges for our **Bookstore** project, resolving conflicts as we encounter them.

Intra-branch merges in SVN

The best way to demo how SVN handles "intra-branch" merging, in other words merging that arises from two users committing changes to a single branch, is to walk through a couple of examples, one where the VCS is able to perform an auto-merge, and another that requires user intervention to resolve a merge conflict.

Auto-merge

Fred and Barb are working in trunk (**https://<server>/svn/BookstoreProject/trunk**) and both update their working folders, so each has the latest revision in the repository (Revision 15, in this example). Both users decide to modify the definition of the `Author` table:

1. Barb changes `Author.sql` to add a `Title` column to go along with the name columns.

2. Fred changes `Author.sql` to make the `MiddleName` column nullable.

Fred successfully commits his change, creating Revision 14 in the repository, as shown in Figure 6-1.

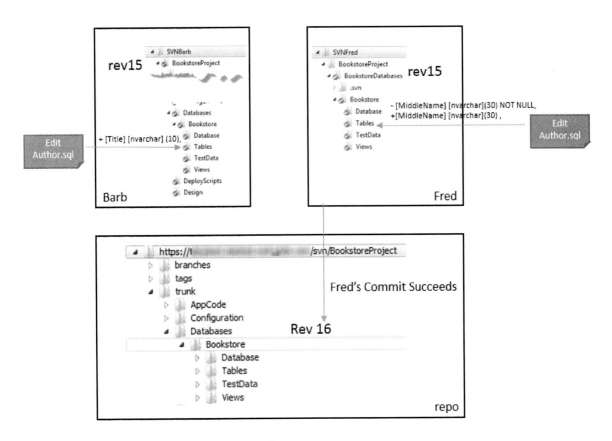

Figure 6-1: Committing Fred's changes to the repository.

Subsequently, Barb tries to commit her change and receives a **Commit failed** message (shown in Figure 6-2), telling her that Author.sql is out of date. If Barb had committed first, then Fred would see this message instead; another reason to commit early and often!

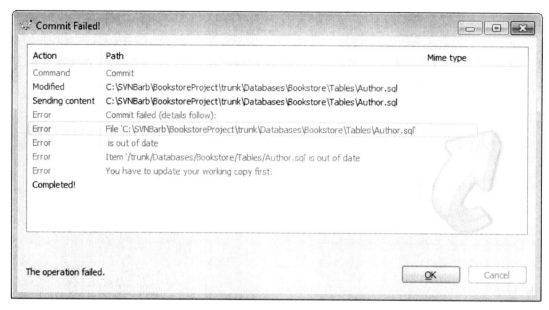

Figure 6-2: Receiving a **Commit Failed** message when trying to commit.

When Barb clicks **OK** on the **Commit Failed** dialog box, SVN automatically suggests that she update her working copy, as shown in Figure 6-3.

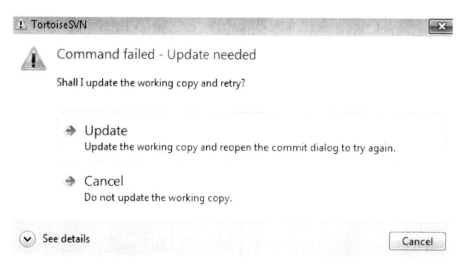

Figure 6-3: TortoiseSVN prompts Barb to update or cancel the operation.

If Barb clicks **Update**, SVN will bring her working folder up to Revision 16 and attempt to automatically merge the Revision 16 version of the file in the repository with her working copy of the file. If it can't do so safely, SVN will request manual help with the merge. If the change was complex, Barb might choose to cancel at this stage so as not to risk losing those changes, save them off somewhere else first, as described earlier, and then perform an update.

Here, however, Barb simply clicks **Update**. In this case, the changes she made do not conflict with those of Fred, so SVN performs an auto-merge and invites Barb to commit the new auto-merged version of the file, which contains both her new `Title` column and the nullable `MiddleName` column. The resulting commit is Revision 17 in the repository.

Remember that Fred will still have Revision 16 of the `Author.sql` file until he performs an update of his working folder.

Things get more interesting, however, when our developers' changes overlap.

Manual merge (dealing with conflicts)

Once again, both Fred and Barb update their respective working folders so that they both have the latest revision (now Revision 17). Fred adds a new `Type` column to the `Book` table and commits the change. Listing 6-1 shows the change that Fred makes to the `Book.sql` file, with his added code highlighted.

```
CREATE TABLE dbo.Book
    (
      BookID INT IDENTITY
              PRIMARY KEY ,
      Title NVARCHAR(1000) NOT NULL,
      YearOfPublication INT NULL ,
      [Type] CHAR(12) NULL
    );
GO
```

Listing 6-1:   Adding the `Type` column to the `Book` table.

This takes the repository to Revision 18. Barb subsequently updates her working folder and retrieves the latest version of the Book.sql file, with the new column.

Then Fred decides that Type was a poor choice of column name. He changes it to BookCategory. In the meantime, Barb, who has a strong preference for using varchar data types, as opposed to char, changes the Type column to a varchar(15). Fred commits his changes first, creating Revision 19 in the repository. Figure 6-4 provides an overview of the changes both Fred and Barb have made and reflects Fred's commit.

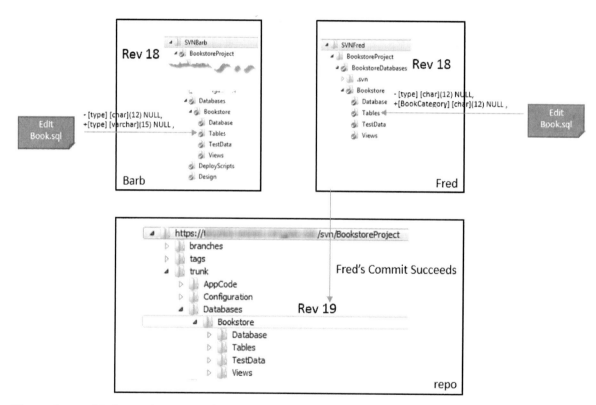

Figure 6-4: Updating the Type column in the Book table.

This time Barb does the right thing and checks the log (shown in Figure 6-5) before attempting her commit.

Revision	Actions	Author	Date	Message
19		Fred	06 May 2014 14:59:30	**Modify book.sql table, renaming type CHAR(12) to BookCategory CHAR(12)**
18		Fred	06 May 2014 14:43:48	Modify Book.sql to add Type CHAR(12) column
17		Barb	06 May 2014 14:35:18	Modify Author.sql to add a Title NVARCHAR(10) column to go along with the name columns (required merge)
16		Fred	06 May 2014 14:24:25	Modify Author.sql in trunk, to make the MiddleName column nullable

Figure 6-5:   Viewing the log to verify the revision history.

She sees that her working folder is out of date and, thanks to Fred's descriptive commit message, understands quickly what has happened. Again, she might at this stage consider saving off her current working folder to a separate location, but in this case she simply updates her working folder and, as she expects, the **Update Finished** dialog contains a "conflict" warning, as shown in Figure 6-6.

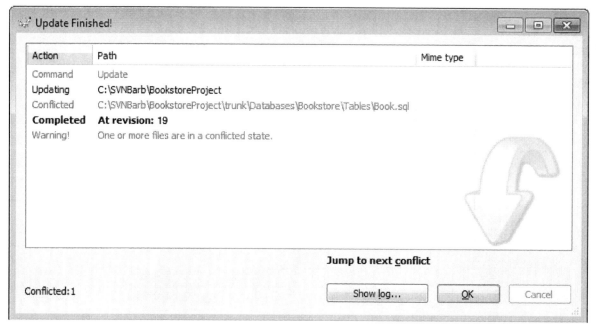

Figure 6-6:   Conflicting versions of the Book.sql file.

193

Barb clicks **OK** to close the dialog box. Her **Tables** sub-directory now looks as shown in Figure 6-7, with multiple copies of the `Book.sql` file.

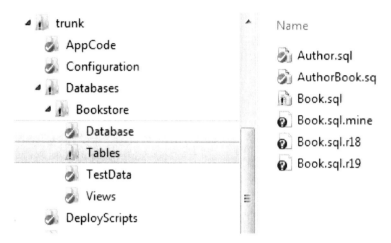

Figure 6-7: Conflicting versions of the `Book.sql` file in Barb's working folder.

When SVN updated Barb's working folder and detected the conflict, it added three temporary files to the **Tables** folder, all of them related to the original `Book.sql` file:

- **Book.sql.mine** – Barb's current working copy of the file before she updated her working folder. The file includes no conflict markers. It contains only her latest changes, and nothing else.

- **Book.sql.r18** – This is a copy of the file as it existed at Revision 18. In other words, it is the "base" revision from which both users started, before making their conflicting changes.

- **Book.sql.r19** – This is the most recent revision of the file, committed to the repository by Fred. Some VCSs refer to this simply as "theirs."

In addition, SVN marked Barb's working copy of the Book.sql file with a yellow exclamation point, indicating that the file is in a "conflicted" state.

If Barb opens the file in a text editor, she'll find the content displayed in a "unified diff" format (see Chapter 5), similar to what is shown in Listing 6-2.

```
CREATE TABLE dbo.Book
    (
        BookID INT IDENTITY
                PRIMARY KEY ,
        Title NVARCHAR(1000) NOT NULL,
        YearOfPublication INT NULL,
<<<<<<< .mine
        [Type] VARCHAR(15) NULL
=======
        BookCategory CHAR(12) NULL
>>>>>>> .r19
    );
GO
```

Listing 6-2:   A unified diff of the Book.sql file.

Barb does not work with any of these files directly. Instead, she closes the Book.sql file and launches a merge tool, in this case TortoiseMerge, to help her perform the merge operation. Her goal is to come up with a new "merged" version of the Book.sql file in her working folder that reflects her change or Fred's, or both, and which she can commit to the repository, as shown in Figure 6-8.

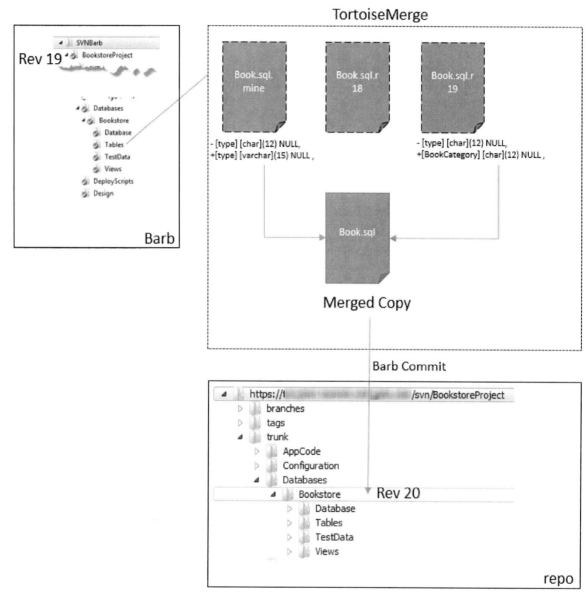

Figure 6-8: Merging file changes in TortoiseMerge.

To open TortoiseMerge, Barb right-clicks the Book.sql file, points to **TortoiseSVN**, and then clicks **Edit Conflicts**. This launches TortoiseMerge, as shown in Figure 6-9.

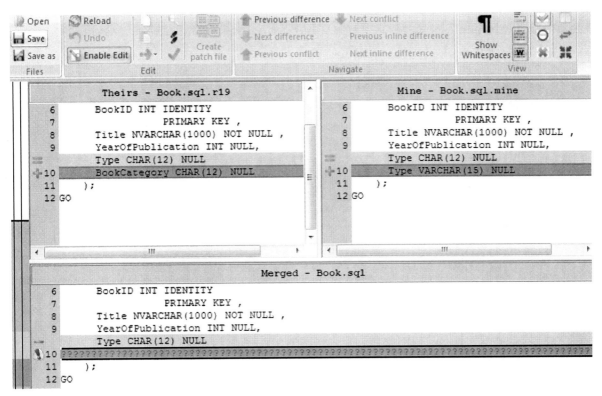

Figure 6-9: Viewing the file conflicts in TortoiseMerge.

What Barb sees on the top screen in TortoiseMerge is the change "they" (Fred, in this case) made. In other words, it shows a comparison of Revision 19 to its base (Revision 18). In the right-hand screen she sees a depiction of how her working copy of Book.sql changed, compared to its base (Revision 18). The bottom half of the screen shows the current state of the "merged" Book.sql file, with the exclamation point and row of question marks denoting where we need to resolve the conflict.

Barb can right-click the exclamation point in the left margin to see a range of options for fixing the conflict. For example, she can choose the **Use text block from 'theirs'** option, **Use text block from 'mine'**, **Use text block from 'mine' before 'theirs'**, or **Use text block from 'theirs' before 'mine'**. She can also type directly into the bottom pane to tweak the resulting output.

In this case, Barb decides that the best option is to combine the two changes, accepting the new column name of BookCategory, but changing its data type to varchar(15), as shown in Figure 6-10.

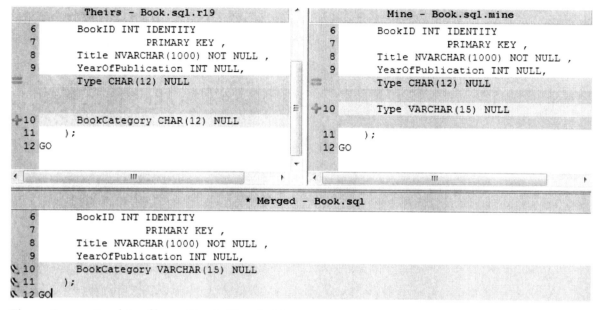

Figure 6-10: Resolving file conflicts in TortoiseMerge.

On the top toolbar of TortoiseMerge, click the **Mark as resolved** button (represented by a green tick), and close the TortoiseMerge window.

Barb can now return to her **Tables** directory of her working folder. Book.sql has the normal white-on-red exclamation mark to denote an uncommitted change. She can commit her change as per usual, creating Revision 20, and Fred, when he updates his working folder, will retrieve Barb's changes.

Inter-branch merging in SVN

Let's now move on to the inter-branch varieties of the merge process, moving changes between branches. The merge operation is similar but the "business case" for performing such a merge is rather different.

In our previous intra-branch merge examples, a user encountered the merge operation via an update or commit command. With inter-branch merges, the user will instigate the merge using the **TortoiseSVN | Merge** command, in order to move changes from the current branch into the originating branch (in other words, the branch or trunk from which the current branch grew) or vice versa. If the operation encounter merge conflicts, due to incompatible changes to the equivalent file in the current branch and originating branch, then SVN may be able to perform an auto-merge, or the user may need to intervene manually, as described for the intra-branch merge examples.

When we define a merge operation, we need to define three key elements: **FROM** (the source), **TO** (the destination) and **WHAT** (the specific revisions we wish to merge):

```
WHAT <revisions> FROM <Source URL or path> TO <Destination URL or
path>
```

In TortoiseSVN, we start the merge by right-clicking the **TO** directory in our working folder and selecting **TortoiseSVN | Merge**, to bring up the **Merge type** page of the **Merge** wizard appears, as shown in Figure 6-11.

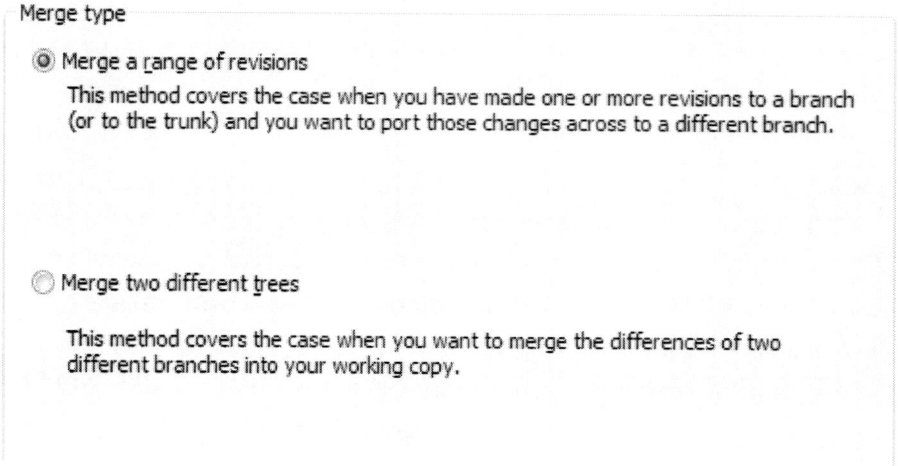

Merge type

◉ Merge a range of revisions

This method covers the case when you have made one or more revisions to a branch (or to the trunk) and you want to port those changes across to a different branch.

◯ Merge two different trees

This method covers the case when you want to merge the differences of two different branches into your working copy.

Figure 6-11:   Choosing the type of merge you want to perform.

The current version of TortoiseSVN supports two possible merge options:

- **Merge a range of revisions** – Copy one or more changes from a branch or the trunk to another branch (or trunk).

- **Merge two different trees** – Reintegrate a branch (source) into the trunk or into another branch (destination). You can merge a specific revision from the source into a specific revision of the target. By default, the **HEAD** revisions are merged. After the merge, the target will look exactly like the source. This option is commonly used to reintegrate a feature branch into the trunk.

Note that previous versions of TortoiseSVN offered a third option, **Reintegrate a branch/ automate merge**, used for the specific case of doing a final merge from a branch back to its source (either the trunk or another branch). However, we now simply use the **Merge two different trees** option, with the assumption then being that we will be doing no more development on the branch and can remove it.

SVN merging precautions

When SVN encounters a formal conflict during inter-branch merging, where SVN cannot reconcile one user's changes to a file in the source branch with another user's changes to the same file in the target branch, it will ask the user to intervene. Earlier in the chapter, we've seen how conflict resolution works for intra-branch merging, and the same principles apply to dealing with such conflicts in inter-branch merging.

However, in the absence of these formal conflicts during inter-branch merging, the extent to which SVN will simply "do exactly as it's told" can surprise new users. It will happily make quite drastic changes during a merge, such as overwriting one column with another, without a murmur. After all, it performs what is simply a textual comparison; the VCS has no "context" to understand whether or not a change is potentially dangerous, or what the user really intends.

Let's say Fred is working on our `AuthorsBooks` view in a branch (and has not yet merged the changes to mainline development in the trunk). In the meantime, the team working in trunk have deleted the view and implemented the same functionality in a stored procedure. If Fred were to blindly merge all revisions from trunk to branch, one might expect these changes to raise a conflict, but in fact there is a good chance they won't; Fred will lose his view, and any work he did on it, and gain a stored procedure.

All this is a longhand way of saying that we must proceed with caution when approaching a potentially troublesome merge. Follow good merging practices and take necessary precautions, as described earlier in the *How to Avoid Painful Merges* section.

In SVN, it is relatively easy to use the log to **revert** back to a specific revision, That is, we can roll back to the previous revision before we commit, and after we commit.

In addition, SVN offers a variety of repository backup mechanisms, including "hot" backups (`svnadmin hotcopy`) and full and incremental backups (`svnadmin dump`).

We won't discuss repository maintenance in any detail (see HTTP://TINYURL.COM/O5JR7XG for full details), but if you do need to back up our small **Bookstore** repository, while working through the examples in this book, or create a repository "clone," perhaps to perform some of your own experiments, then the following simple steps will do the trick:

1. In VisualSVN Server Manager, at the SVN Server level, select **Action | All Tasks | Start Command Prompt**.

2. Back up the repository:

    a. Either a full backup of all revisions, e.g.:
        ```
        svnadmin dump D:\Repositories\BookstoreProject > D:\
        SVNBackups\BookstoreProject.bak
        ```

    b. Or a full backup of a revision range, e.g.:
        ```
        svnadmin dump D:\Repositories\BookstoreProject > D:\
        SVNBackups\BookstoreProject_r26.bak -r 1:26
        ```

3. Create a new *empty* repository (not with the trunk/branch/tag structure) e.g. called **BookstoreProject_2**.

4. Restore the backup to the new repository:
    ```
    svnadmin load D:\Repositories\BookstoreProject_2 < D:\
    SVNBackups\BookstoreProject_r26.bak
    ```

5. Check out the cloned repository to a new working folder, as described previously in the book.

Merging a range of revisions

Within this type of merge, we can specify either an:

1. **All revisions** merge – for example:

    a. Calculate all changes made to the trunk (**FROM**), since we created Branch *x*, and apply them **TO** the working folder of Branch *x*, or

    b. Calculate all changes made to Branch *x* (**FROM**), since branch creation, and apply them **TO** the working folder of trunk.

2. **Specific range** or **cherry pick** merge – specify one or more specific revisions, a range of revisions, or a combination of both.

Try to use the cherry pick merge sparingly, and only when strictly necessary. It can quickly get confusing keeping track of what specific changes you've merged where. Generally, it is better to make small regular merges of all revisions. If you find yourself reaching for a cherry pick merge regularly, examine your development workflow, work out why and try to fix the problem.

In order to see each type of merge in action, we'll return to our **Bookstore** example. Back in Chapter 5, our team created a new branch of the Bookstore project, called **v1.0BugFixes**. In this branch, Fred made some improvements to the `AuthorsBooks` view, adding a calculated `NewBookID` column. Let's continue that development effort and see how to move changes from branch to mainline, and vice versa.

Let's say that Fred is continuing development work on the **v1.0BugFixes** branch, but is aware of the continuing work on mainline development, in the trunk, and doesn't want his bug-fixing branch to drift too far apart from the trunk.

From clean working folders (no uncommitted changes), he updates both his trunk and branch directories and then performs a diff between the two to find out the extent of the changes.

In Fred's working folder:

- Launch the repository browser.

- Right-click the **Bookstore** folder in the **v1.0BugFixes** branch, select **Mark for comparison**.

- Right-click the **Bookstore** folder in the **trunk** and select **Compare URLs**.

The resulting **Changed Files** dialog box, shown in Figure 6-12, summarizes the differences between the two locations.

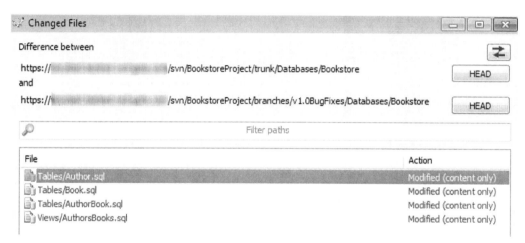

Figure 6-12:   A diff comparing the **Bookstore** directory in branch and trunk.

Double-click each change file to review exactly what changed in each case. The `Author` and `Book` files represent changes made in the trunk, not yet applied to the bug fixes branch, and vice versa for the other two files.

Fred doesn't feel any of the changes to the trunk will conflict with his changes in branch so, after discussion with Barb, they decide that Barb will merge into the bug fixes branch the changes made in trunk, since branch creation.

All revisions merge

In this merge operation, we're merging mainline to branch. We want SVN to calculate the changes necessary to advance the trunk from the revision at which we created the branch to the current revision (the **HEAD**), and apply that change set to the working folder in the **v1.0BugFixes** branch.

As discussed previously, we begin the merge operation from the **TO** directory (the destination for the merge), so in Barb's working folder, right-click the **branches\v1.0BugFixes** folder and select **TortoiseSVN | Merge**, to bring up the **Merge type** page (refer back to Figure 6-11). Select **Merge a range of revisions** and click **Next**. In the **URL to Merge from** text-box, use the ellipsis button to navigate to the **trunk** folder.

By default, we'll see the **specific range** radio button activated, but the range left blank, meaning we'll merge all revisions (alternatively we can explicitly select **all revisions**).

Figure 6-13: Determining what revisions to merge.

Reverse merge

We can also specify a reverse merge, which is essentially a way to undo a commit.

Triple-check that the **merge from** URL is correct, and then click **Next**. The **Merge options** page appears, as shown in Figure 6-14, providing several options for how to perform the merge. A full discussion of these options is beyond the scope of this chapter, but you can find more information in the TortoiseSVN documentation, as well as the SVN "red book" (HTTP://SVNBOOK.RED-BEAN.COM/).

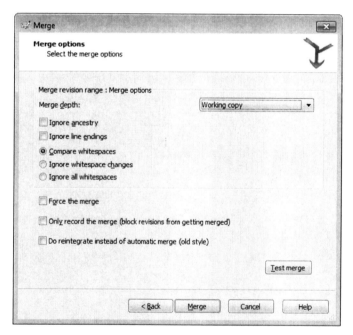

Figure 6-14:   Reviewing merging option before testing or performing the merge.

Accept all the default selections in the screen, and click **Test merge** to verify that the merge will work exactly as expected. The **Merge Test Only** dialog box, shown in Figure 6-15, reports that it will merge in all changes for Revision 12 (the revision that created the branch) through to the latest revision (20), and that it will entail changes to the Author and Book tables in the branch.

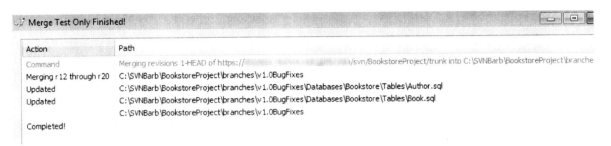

Action	Path
Command	Merging revisions 1-HEAD of https:// ... /svn/BookstoreProject/trunk into C:\SVNBarb\BookstoreProject\branche
Merging r12 through r20	C:\SVNBarb\BookstoreProject\branches\v1.0BugFixes
Updated	C:\SVNBarb\BookstoreProject\branches\v1.0BugFixes\Databases\Bookstore\Tables\Author.sql
Updated	C:\SVNBarb\BookstoreProject\branches\v1.0BugFixes\Databases\Bookstore\Tables\Book.sql
	C:\SVNBarb\BookstoreProject\branches\v1.0BugFixes
Completed!	

Figure 6-15: Verifying that the merge will perform as expected.

This is exactly what we expect, so click **OK** and return to the **Merge** wizard. There, we can click **Merge** to begin the actual merge operation. We should see a **Merge Finished** screen, indicating success. Since there were no conflicting changes, TortoiseMerge has auto-merged into branch the changes made to the `Author` and `Book` tables in trunk, since branch creation.

Back in Barb's working folder, we should see red exclamation marks indicating that we need to commit to the repository these changes to the **v1.0BugFixes** branch project folder.

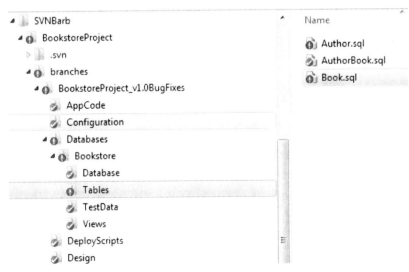

Figure 6-16: The working folder showing changes to be committed.

In Barb's working folder, right-click **BookstoreProject** and commit the changes in the normal way. Figure 6-17 shows the **Commit** dialog box, listing the details of the merge. In this case, the merge operation creates Revision 21 in the repository.

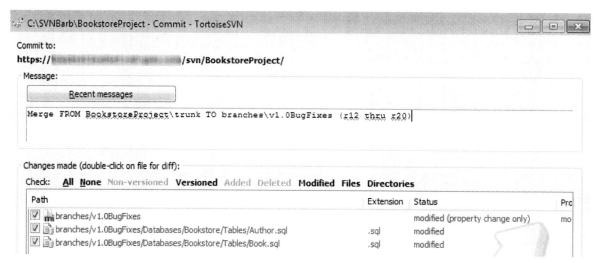

Figure 6-17:   Committing a merge to the repository.

Notice in Figure 6-17 that the folder listing shows **modified (property change only)**. This refers to the fact that SVN notes in the folder's metadata that a merge occurred (the folder structure itself has not changed).

Fred can now update his **BookstoreDatabase_v1.0BugFixes** working folder to capture the changes.

Work would continue on branch, with the team regularly merging the latest changes to trunk into their **v1.0BugFixes** branch. At a certain point, however, the team may want to transfer the bug fixes into mainline development.

For the sake of this example, we can stick with the branch changes already applied in Chapter 5 (which added a comment to the AuthorBook table and adding the NewBookID calculated column to the AuthorsBooks views). These changes do not conflict with any changes in the trunk, so we can simply perform an all-revisions auto-merge in the opposite direction (branch to trunk). In this case, we want SVN to calculate the changes necessary to advance the branch from the revision at which we created the branch (R12) to the current revision in the branch (R21), and apply that change set to the working folder in the trunk.

After ensuring that working folders are up to date and contain no uncommitted changes, we start the merge operation from Barb's trunk folder (**C:\SVNBarb\BookstoreProject\ trunk**) since we want to merge the changes **TO** this folder. The URL to merge **FROM** is **//<server>/svn/BookstoreProject/branches/v1.0BugFixes**. The test merge confirms that we're merging into the trunk the effects of Revisions 12 through 21 in the branch, and that it involved modification of the `AuthorBook` and `AuthorsBooks` files, in the trunk.

Action	Path
Command	Merging revisions 1-HEAD of https://1_____ /svn/BookstoreProject/branches/v1.0BugFixes into C:\SVNBarb\BookstoreProject\trunk,
Merging r12 through r21	C:\SVNBarb\BookstoreProject\trunk
Updated	C:\SVNBarb\BookstoreProject\trunk\Databases\Bookstore\Tables\AuthorBook.sql
Updated	C:\SVNBarb\BookstoreProject\trunk\Databases\Bookstore\Views\AuthorsBooks.sql
	C:\SVNBarb\BookstoreProject\trunk
Completed!	

Figure 6-18: Verifying our merge operation into the trunk.

Once the merge completes, Barb commits the changes to create Revision 22. Fred can then perform an update of his **BookstoreDatabases** working folder to capture the changes.

Cherry pick merge

The second type of "range of revisions" merge is what we call the "cherry pick," where we want only to move a specific change, or a specific range of changes, from one location to another.

The cherry pick works very similarly to the **all-revisions** merge we just saw, so we'll work through this example very quickly. In one of our developers' **v1.0BugFixes** branch folder (for example, **C:\SVNBarb\BookstoreProject\branches\v1.0BugFixes\Databases\Bookstore**), we'll make three separate changes to our `Bookstore` database (three separate commits), as follows:

- R23 – Create a new `BookCategory` table to define the categories in the `Book` table, rather than supporting arbitrary category names:

  - Save the new `BookCategory.sql` to **Tables** and commit.

- R24 – Populate the `BookCategory` table with lookup data:

  - Create a new **LookupData** folder, save the new `INSERT` script, `BookCategoryData.sql`, to this folder, and commit.

- R25 – Update the `Book` table to reference the `BookCategory` table

  - Edit the existing `Book.sql` script and commit.

Listing 6-3 shows all three changes in a single script (purely to save space). Save `BookCategory.sql` and `BookCategoryData.sql` to separate files, as described above, and then edit the existing `Book.sql` file, as described in the listing.

```
/*BookCategory.sql*/
USE Bookstore;
GO
CREATE TABLE dbo.BookCategory
    (
      BookCategoryID INT PRIMARY KEY ,
      CategoryName NVARCHAR(50) NOT NULL
    );
GO

/*BookCategoryData.sql*/
USE Bookstore;
GO
INSERT INTO dbo.BookCategory VALUES (101, 'Art & Architecture');
INSERT INTO dbo.BookCategory VALUES (102, 'Children');
INSERT INTO dbo.BookCategory VALUES (104, 'Fiction');
INSERT INTO dbo.BookCategory VALUES (103, 'Food & Beverage');
INSERT INTO dbo.BookCategory VALUES (105, 'History');
INSERT INTO dbo.BookCategory VALUES (106, 'Mind & Body');
INSERT INTO dbo.BookCategory VALUES (107, 'Religion & Spirituality');
INSERT INTO dbo.BookCategory VALUES (108, 'Sports & Recreation');
INSERT INTO dbo.BookCategory VALUES (109, 'Technology');
INSERT INTO dbo.BookCategory VALUES (110, 'Travel');
GO

/*Book.sql*/
USE Bookstore;
GO
CREATE TABLE dbo.Book
    (
      BookID INT IDENTITY
                PRIMARY KEY ,
      Title NVARCHAR(1000) NOT NULL ,
      YearOfPublication INT ,
      BookCategoryID INT , -- replaces BookCategory VARCHAR(15)
      CONSTRAINT fk_bookcategory FOREIGN KEY ( BookCategoryID )
                    REFERENCES BookCategory ( BookCategoryID )
    );
GO
```

Listing 6-3: Changes relating to the new BookCategory table and lookup data.

For the `Book` table, notice that we're changing the existing `BookCategory` `VARCHAR(15)` column to `BookCategoryID INT` and adding a `FOREIGN KEY` constraint that references the new `BookCategoryID` column in the `BookCategory` table. In our development environment, the existing `BookCategory` column contains no data, so we can get away with applying this upgrade to our "live" `Bookstore` database by simply altering the `Book` table to remove that column and adding the new column definition, and constraint (the code download for this chapter provides an `ALTER TABLE` script that does this). However, this is a classic example of an upgrade that would require a lot of care in any environment where the `BookCategory` column contained data. We'd need to be sure to make the upgrade in a way that preserved the integrity of any existing data. We'll discuss this sort of issue in more detail in Chapter 8.

Now comes the fun part. The powers that be decide that we should add only the `BookCategory` table to the trunk for version 2.0, as well as update the `Book` table. As a result, Barb plans to merge to the trunk Revisions 23 and 25, but not Revision 24, because it is as yet undecided how to handle the lookup data in v2.0. For this situation, we need the cherry pick merge.

We start the merge operation in Barb's trunk folder (**C:\SVNBarb\BookstoreProject\ trunk**) since we want to merge the changes **TO** this folder. Again, we choose the **Merge a range of revisions** option, and the URL to merge **FROM** is **//<server>/svn/ BookstoreProject/branches/v1.0BugFixes**.

This time however, instead of leaving the specific range blank (indicating all revisions), we specify just two specific revisions by entering **23,25** (or use **Show log** to locate the correct revision numbers on your system). Figure 6-19 shows how the **Merge revision range** page of the Merge wizard should look.

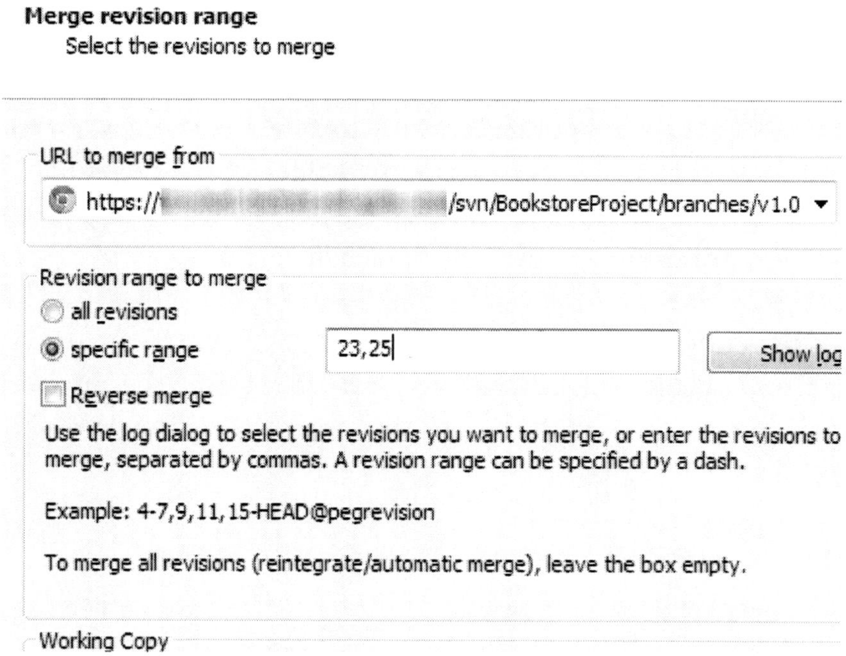

Merge revision range
Select the revisions to merge

URL to merge from

https://▓▓▓▓▓▓▓▓▓▓▓▓/svn/BookstoreProject/branches/v1.0 ▾

Revision range to merge
○ all revisions
◉ specific range   23,25| Show log
☐ Reverse merge
Use the log dialog to select the revisions you want to merge, or enter the revisions to merge, separated by commas. A revision range can be specified by a dash.

Example: 4-7,9,11,15-HEAD@pegrevision

To merge all revisions (reintegrate/automatic merge), leave the box empty.

Working Copy

Figure 6-19:   Merging specific revisions from the branch to the trunk.

A **Test merge** will verify that the merge will successfully perform the changes you expect. If everything looks good, we can execute the merge and return to Barb's folder where we'll see in the trunk the new `BookCategory.sql` file (R23), and the modified `Book.sql` file (R25), but not the **LookupData** folder or file.

We can have Barb commit the merge at this point, and it should go fairly smoothly. We know no one has been working in the trunk since our last merge, so SVN should perform an auto-merge with no conflicts, and designate the commit as Revision 26.

Merge two different trees

In the "range of revisions" merge, SVN calculates the change set to describe a string of revisions to one branch and applies them to another branch. The "merge two trees" merge is somewhat different. In this type of merge, SVN compares two different trees with the goal of making them identical. Let's say we've made our final bug fix to our **v1.0BugFixes** branch and want to merge it into trunk and close off the branch (delete it).

If we perform a "merge two trees" merge, from branch to mainline, SVN will compare the two trees (trunk and branch) and calculate the changes necessary to get from the current revision in the trunk to the current revision in the branch, and apply those changes to the trunk of the user's working folder.

This type of merge requires a lot of care. We need to be certain that no one has committed further changes to the trunk since we last merged all revisions from trunk to branch, otherwise we risk losing those changes to the trunk (we'll discuss this in a little more detail in the *Inter-branch merges with conflicts* section).

With this note of caution in mind, let's walk through an example.

Step 1: Modify AuthorsBooks view in the branch

Let's make some final changes to our **v1.0BugFixes** branch in Barb's working folder. Listing 6-4 shows an updated definition for our AuthorsBooks view, with the changes highlighted. We remove the NewBookID computed column, add an alias to the Title column, add another inner join to the BookCategory table, include the CategoryName column in the SELECT list, and define a CASE expression to handle the author names.

```
ALTER VIEW AuthorsBooks
-- retrieves all authors and all their books
AS
    SELECT  ( CASE WHEN MiddleName IS NULL
                    OR MiddleName = '' THEN a.FirstName + ' ' + a.LastName
                ELSE a.FirstName + ' ' + a.MiddleName + ' ' + a.LastName
            END ) AS FullName ,
            b.Title AS BookTitle ,
            bc.CategoryName AS BookCategory ,
            b.YearOfPublication AS YearPublished
    FROM    Author a
            INNER JOIN AuthorBook ab ON a.AuthorID = ab.AuthorID
            INNER JOIN Book b ON ab.BookID = b.BookID
            INNER JOIN BookCategory bc
                ON b.BookCategoryID = bc.BookCategoryID;
GO
PRINT 'dbo.AuthorsBooks: view creation script finished';
```

Listing 6-4:   Updating the `AuthorsBooks` view in the v1.0BugFixes branch.

Update the copy of `AuthorsBooks.sql`, in **C:\SVNBarb\BookstoreProject\branches\ v1.0BugFixes\Databases\Bookstore\Views**, as described in Listing 6-4, and then commit the change, which creates Revision 27 in the repository.

In order to test the view, we can populate the `BookCategoryID` column of all rows in the **Book** table with the value **104**, which points to the **Fiction** category in the **BookCategory** table. The relevant portion of the new `TestData.sql` file will look as shown in Listing 6-5.

```
INSERT  INTO Book
        ( BookID, Title, YearOfPublication, BookCategoryID )
VALUES  ( 1, 'Huckleberry Finn', 1884, 104 ),
        ( 2, 'Slaughterhouse-Five', 1969, 104 ),
        (...etc...)
```

Listing 6-5:   Loading test data for the `BookCategoryID` column.

Commit the changes to the repository to create Revision 28.

Step 2: Merge two trees (branch to trunk)

We're going to merge the branch into the trunk, but this time around we're going to do a tree merge, which merges all the files. The assumption is that the team have decided to use the lookup data in 2.0, so everything can now be merged. In other words, all changes in the branch will be incorporated into the trunk.

Barb should be sure to perform a final update of her working folder before going ahead with the merge. To perform a tree merge, navigate to the **trunk** folder in Barb's working folder and launch the **Merge** wizard. When the **Merge type** page appears, select the **Merge two different trees** option.

Next comes the confusing part. On the **Tree merge** page, make sure the URL displayed in the **From** text-box points to the *trunk*, and the URL in the **To** text-box points to the *branch*, as shown in Figure 6-20. This might seem rather odd at first, and it is, but TortoiseSVN thinks in terms of where the roots of the branch come from (the **From** text-box) and where they have ended (the **To** text-box).

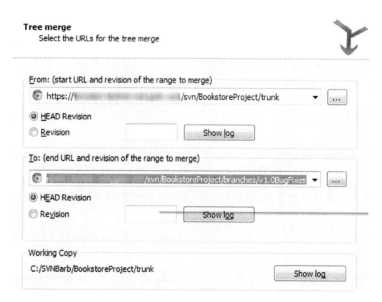

Figure 6-20: Performing a tree merge from the branch to the trunk.

Those are the only options we need to set to perform a tree merge. To recap, we're expecting to merge the new **LookupData** folder and `BookCategoryData.sql` file into trunk, since we skipped those in the previous cherry pick merge, plus our new changes to the `AuthorsBooks` view, and to `TestData.sql`. We can confirm this with a test merge.

Action	Path
Merging differences between repository URLs	C:\SVNBarb\BookstoreProject\trunk
Added	C:\SVNBarb\BookstoreProject\trunk\Databases\Bookstore\LookupData
Added	C:\SVNBarb\BookstoreProject\trunk\Databases\Bookstore\LookupData\BookstoreCategoryData.sql
Updated	C:\SVNBarb\BookstoreProject\trunk\Databases\Bookstore\TestData\TestData.sql
Updated	C:\SVNBarb\BookstoreProject\trunk\Databases\Bookstore\Views\AuthorsBooks.sql
	C:\SVNBarb\BookstoreProject\trunk
Recording mergeinfo for merge between URLs	C:\SVNBarb\BookstoreProject\trunk
	C:\SVNBarb\BookstoreProject\trunk
	C:\SVNBarb\BookstoreProject\trunk
Updated	C:\SVNBarb\BookstoreProject\trunk
Completed!	

Figure 6-21: Viewing the results of the tree merge.

If it all looks good, execute the merge operation.

Step 3: Commit the effect of the merge to the repository

With the merge complete, the trunk in Barb's working folder should show that it has changes ready to commit to the repository. Go ahead and commit those changes. This creates Revision 29 in the repository.

Given all the changes that Barb made to the `AuthorsBooks` view, you might have expected SVN to baulk at the merge, but it automatically incorporates all Barb's changes, overwriting anything that gets in the way. We can confirm this with a diff between the most current revision and the preceding revision. Right-click the `AuthorsBooks.sql` file in the trunk, point to TortoiseSVN, and then click **Diff with previous version**.

This launches TortoiseMerge and compares the two versions of the file, as shown in Figure 6-22.

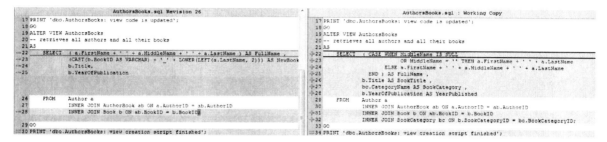

Figure 6-22: Comparing revisions of the merged `AuthorsBooks.sql` file.

When we did the merge, SVN treated the revised copy of the file in the branch as the correct version of the file and incorporated all changes. The assumption in this case is that Barb knew what she was doing and, by merging the files, she was essentially giving her blessing to these changes, in both the branch and the trunk.

Inter-branch merges with conflicts: down the SVN merge rabbit hole

As we've tried to stress throughout this chapter, merge operations of all types require extreme care, or you can very quickly end up in a mess. So far, we haven't run into any formal "conflicts" from SVN's point of view; as we've seen, it's pretty ruthless about the sort of changes it will make without complaint during inter-branch merges.

However, it's very easy to merge in changes that SVN won't complain about, but your team members will. It's also possible to run into what SVN regards as a formal conflict. We're not going to offer fully worked examples here, as it's a deep rabbit hole, but we will offer some idea of what can go wrong so that you can practice and experiment on your own systems.

In our previous merge to trees example, we stressed the importance of no one else making changes to the trunk, after merging trunk to branch and before performing the tree merge (branch to trunk).However, what if someone did make a change? Let's say that, after our cherry pick merge to trunk (of the `BookCategory.sql` file and modified `Book.sql` file), but before we merged the two trees, Fred made a further change to the `Book.sql` file in trunk.

Cloning the repository

If you want to follow along from here in, you may want to create a clone of the `BookstoreProject` repository. I created a backup of the repository as it existed after the cherry pick merge (Revision 26, in my case) and restored it to a new copy of the repository, exactly as described in Steps 1-5 in the previous SVN merging precautions section.

So, let's rewind in time and pick up on our previous example straight after the cherry pick merge. The new sequence of events from this point might be as follows:

1. FRED: Edits the `Book` table in **trunk**. For example, changes the `Title` column to `BookTitle`, adds a `BookPageCount NVARCHAR(5)` column, and commits the changes.

2. BARB: In the **v1.0BugFixes** branch, she modifies `AuthorsBooks` view as described in Listing 6-4 and commits the change.

3. BARB: Performs an update of her working folder.

4. BARB: Performs the "merge two trees" as described in the *Step 2: Merge two trees* section of the previous example.

When we have Barb execute Step 4, SVN will see no problem. It will simply report that, as part of the "merge two trees" merge, it plans to update `Book.sql` in trunk, as well as add Barb's new **LookupData** folder and file, and her update to the `AuthorsBooks` view, as shown in Figure 6-23.

Action	Path
Command	Merging from https://tonytest.testnet.red-gate.com/svn/Test_Bookstore2/trunk, revision HEAD to https://tonytest.testnet.red-gate.c
Merging differences between repository URLs	C:\Test_SvnJane\Test_Bookstore2\trunk
Added	C:\Test_SvnJane\Test_Bookstore2\trunk\Databases\Bookstore\LookupData
Added	C:\Test_SvnJane\Test_Bookstore2\trunk\Databases\Bookstore\LookupData\BookstoreCategoryData.sql
Updated	C:\Test_SvnJane\Test_Bookstore2\trunk\Databases\Bookstore\Tables\Book.sql
Updated	C:\Test_SvnJane\Test_Bookstore2\trunk\Databases\Bookstore\Views\AuthorsBooks.sql
	C:\Test_SvnJane\Test_Bookstore2\trunk
Completed!	

Figure 6-23: A potentially problematic "merge two trees" operation from the branch into the trunk.

If Barb doesn't have her wits about her, and simply performs the merge and commits the changes to trunk, the net result is that Fred's changes are simply lost. Fred might consider this a conflict, even though SVN doesn't!

Alternatively, let's imagine that Barb is eagle-eyed enough to spot this problem before committing, and so **reverts** the effects of the merge. How does she resolve this problem? Let's say she tries an "all revisions" range merge from trunk to branch, to capture Fred's changes into the branch. Figure 6-24 shows the error messages Barb receives when she tries this type of merge. The problem she has here is that she can now only merge all revisions from trunk to branch, if the branch hasn't changed since the last time she merged all revisions from branch to trunk.

Action	Path	Mime type
Command	Auto-merge https:// svn/Test_Bookstore2/trunk into C:\ \Test_Bookstore2\branches\v1.0BugFixes	
Error	Reintegrate can only be used if revisions 12 through 28 were previously merged	
Error	from	
Error	https://tonytest.testnet.red-gate.com/svn/Test_Bookstore2/branches/v1.0BugFixes	
Error	to the reintegrate source, but this is not the case:	
Error	trunk	
Error	Missing ranges: /trunk:22	
Completed!		

Figure 6-24: A failed "all revisions" range merge from the branch to the trunk.

Instead, she'll need to make sure no one is working on trunk, and cherry pick from trunk to branch just the revision relating to Fred's `Book.sql` edit, and commit it.

Now that her working folder in branch has Fred's latest change to the trunk, she can perform a "merge two trees" merge safely. The net result should be that Fred's change is preserved and the branch and trunk trees are now identical.

As you can tell, the situation can get complicated quickly, and it can get even worse.

Let's rewind in time again, back to just after the original cherry pick merge (Revision 26, if your revision numbers exactly match those in the books), and consider this new workflow, containing an extra change by Fred:

1. FRED: Edits the `Book` table in **trunk**. For example, changes the `Title` column to `BookTitle`, adds a `BookPageCount NVARCHAR(5)` column, and commits the changes.

2. BARB: In the **v1.0BugFixes** branch, she modifies `AuthorsBooks` view as described in Listing 6-4 and commits the change.

3. BARB: Performs an update of her working folder.

4. **FRED**: edits the `AuthorsBooks` view in trunk to reflect his changes to the `Book` table.

5. BARB: Performs the "merge two trees" as described in the **Step 2: Merge Two trees** section of the previous example.

Now, when Barb attempts the "merge two trees", not only does she have the problem of potentially overwriting Fred's changes to the Book table, in trunk, but also an out-of-date copy of the `AuthorsBooks` view. Figure 6-25 shows the formal conflict, although SVN lists even this as a "maybe."

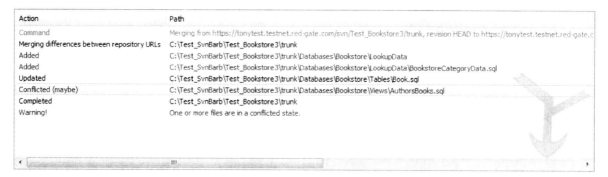

Figure 6-25: A very problematic "merge two trees" operation with conflict.

If Barb decides to press ahead with the merge anyway (we hope she wouldn't do this!) she would be invited to try to resolve the conflict, as shown in Figure 6-26.

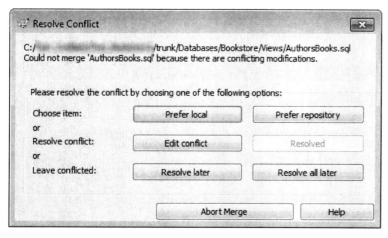

Figure 6-26: Taking steps to resolve conflicts in the `AuthorsBooks.sql` file.

Normally, of course, Barb will want to view each conflict and attempt to resolve it with the help of TortoiseMerge, as described earlier in this chapter, in which case she would choose **Edit conflict**. However, she also has the options to **Prefer local** or **Prefer repository**. These options are not self-explanatory. In short, **Prefer local** means "in the case of a conflict prefer what is there already over the incoming change" and **Prefer repository** means the opposite. SVN will auto-merge all other changes

So, for example, if Barb selects **Prefer local**, SVN will prefer Fred's local changes to the working folder in the destination (trunk) over the changes Barb is attempting to merge into trunk. In general, it's worth avoiding these options unless you're absolutely positive it's what you want. Likewise, it will be rare to simply opt to let SVN auto-merge what it can and leave everything else in a conflicted state for you to resolve later."

Barb's situation is getter rather dire here. Her merge is still going to update Book.sql and so will remove the changes Fred made to that file. So, she's trying to edit a conflict on a view that she changed in the branch and that Fred changed in trunk, while another part of the merge will remove the reason for Fred's change to the view! At this stage, the best choice is probably to abort the whole sorry mess of a merge, have a word with Fred and try to sort the mess out manually.

Merge with caution!

Summary

Merging can be the scariest of all source control functions. Working with revisions, updating your working folder, committing changes to the repository, even creating a branch, are all easy operations in comparison. But merging calls for a different awareness altogether. You're trying to join together two different, but related, lines of development into a single structure. Depending on your circumstances, you might need to perform inter-branch merges or intra-branch, and the merge might occur automatically or you might have to step in to decide how the merge is carried out. In most cases, however, as long as you update your working copy often, commit small changes often, and merge often, you should be okay. Certainly, merging (and the branching that goes with it) should be used carefully and judiciously, but they can both be valuable tools in helping to streamline and maximize your development efforts.

In Chapter 7, we'll move on to take a look at the bigger picture, in terms of deploying a database from what we have in source control. There, you'll get a better sense of how source control is just one piece in a much larger puzzle.

Chapter 7: Manually Deploying Databases from Source Control

We've covered a lot of ground since Chapter 3, when we first discussed all of the planning considerations that help determine how we create, organize and modify database files in source control. Over the course of Chapters 4 through 6, we discussed how to manage concurrent editing of our database files, and how the VCS maintains every version of every file, allowing us to see an audit history of every item that comprises our database. We also looked at how to use branching and merging to streamline the development efforts of the team.

It's time now to pull all the pieces together and build and deploy a database. Our stated goal, right from the start, has been that, once the development effort was finished, we would have in source control a single source of "truth" for defining precisely the database we wish to deploy to our users, along with the ability to deploy that database to any given environment (such as the test, staging or production environments), either to create the database from scratch or to upgrade an existing database.

This chapter will start by taking a closer look at some of the potential issues surrounding database deployment, specifically as they relate to deploying new databases, and deploying upgrades to our existing databases. We'll then walk through an example of each type of deployment for our `Bookstore` database.

- **Building a new `Bookstore` database from scratch** – from the latest version of all the `CREATE` scripts in the VCS.

- **Upgrading an existing `Bookstore` database** – we'll store in the VCS the migration scripts necessary to describe a series of changes, and then string them together into an upgrade script.

In terms of tools, we'll rely on nothing more than a build table to track which build we've deployed to which environment, and a PowerShell script to string together in the correct order the scripts that comprise the build. As such, this chapter provides only a solid but basic and rather manual way to deploy our databases. It's a good starting point but we'll soon want to introduce further automation. Chapter 8 will describe a more automated and tool-based approach, and will explore how to work with **migration scripts**, which will allow us to deploy more complex changes, ones that we need to map out carefully and precisely, in order to ensure we preserve the integrity of existing data.

Database Deployment Pitfalls

Regardless of the approach we take to deploy a database, the main obstacles to database deployment are often the same. Back in Chapters 3 and 4, we discussed a few of the major challenges, including:

- **The vast array of object and configuration files** that comprise a database and its environment – all of which, potentially, we need to script and maintain in the VCS, and include in the build.

- **The need to maintain a table's "state"** when we upgrade an existing database – a database is all about data persistence. We can't simply recompile a database and roll it out over the top of the existing one. We often have to provide scripts to modify the schema, migrate and update data, or take other steps to protect and archive data.

- **The need to minimize downtime and user disruption** during database upgrades – if the database is down, a large part of the business is down.

In this section, we'll consider three more potential obstacles in the path to smooth database deployments, in the form of version drift, improperly tested upgrade scripts, and failure to consider how to roll back problematic deployments. Each of these can, and frequently does, cause failed deployments, or deployments that introduce problems.

Version drift

Some organizations, even those that perform due diligence when it comes to their application files, make most or all their production database changes directly to the database, on an ad hoc basis. Such changes are often at the expense of lost data or broken applications, and can even threaten the integrity of the database itself. When this happens, it is a very difficult task to work out what change caused the problems, and when. The original script files, if they still exist, might be spread across multiple file servers or developers' desktops – duplicated, overwritten, out of sync. It's a mess.

Even with database source control practices in place, it can be tempting for users to make small, "quick fixes" directly to a live database, rather than going to the trouble of making the change in source control, retesting everything, and requesting a new deployment. It's particularly hard to resist when users and managers are clamoring for an urgent fix to go live "yesterday."

Suppose the latest database build (2.4.6) in production reflects exactly the most recent version of your schema in source control. However, QA discovers a bug, in the form of a malfunctioning stored procedure, that's affecting online users. A manager calls the DBA in the middle of the night and demands that she fix the bug immediately. She tracks the problem to a data type mismatch. Either she alters the stored procedure directly in the production database now, or she follows the change control procedures and alters it in source control and requests a new deployment. In the latter case, the bug won't get fixed till sometime the next day. She opts for keeping her job and so modifies the appropriate stored procedure parameter, in the production database, goes back to bed, and promptly forgets all about it.

At this point, although the DBA has fixed the immediate problem, she's introduced **version drift**, and likely stored up bigger problems for down the line. The production database is out of sync with the build 2.4.6 files in source control. Any further changes in the VCS that assume the original data type may no longer work correctly when deployed to production.

At that moment, the fun really begins, as everyone tries to figure out what went wrong and how everything got out sync. Let's hope the DBA isn't still catching up on her sleep.

A VCS is effective only if all database developers and DBAs, and anyone else with their hands on the database, make all changes through the VCS, and use official deployment processes. If even one person fails to follow protocol, it will inevitably lead to problems.

Unfortunately, it's nearly impossible to prevent direct changes to a database, but we can take steps to "encourage" our developers to follow the straight and narrow. For example, we can implement DDL triggers to catch database modifications, or include in our deployment process a verification step that compares schemas in order to ensure that the target database is in the state we expect.

Lack of upgrade script testing

Many development teams will automate the testing of their application code, but not apply the same rigor to testing database changes. Ideally, each time we make a database change we should, for both database and dependent application:

1. Perform some basic tests locally to ensure the new functionality works as expected.

2. Commit the change (and any new tests) to the VCS.

3. Automatically deploy the change from the VCS to the integration environment, to which all other developers' changes are also deployed, and run the team's full suite of tests.

4. Periodically deploy to a production-like environment (such as QA) and perform a further range of tests, including performance testing under a full workload.

Development testing

When a developer makes a database change, he or she should verify the change locally, using some basic unit tests, and then commit the change and any new tests to the VCS.

Unit testing databases

It is out of scope to cover this topic in any detail, but we recommend Alex Kuznetsov's series of articles as a good starting point for what's required. See HTTP://TINYURL.COM/OXU6TNZ.

Each and every commit will, ideally, trigger an automated build process, which "continually integrates" each change with the changes of others, and tests it. In other words, a process that automatically deploys every commit to an integration (or "CI") server, loads test data and runs the team's growing suite of tests.

Loading test data into development databases in order to perform testing is not necessarily a trivial issue. It's often unrealistic for developers, or even the QA team, to work with the full set of production data in their sandbox or test environments, simply because the database is too big, contains sensitive data, or both This is one reason why some teams work on a shared database server during development (see Chapter 3).

One way to do it, assuming data sensitivity is not an issue, is to pull a *subset* of data from the production database. However, the new database might have enough schema changes that such a migration becomes a significant task. An alternative is to script out a subset of data or create a staging database from which to pull test data that is safe to use. In either case, preparing the test data for a large database can turn into a time-consuming process. Even so, it's better to spend the time up front preparing test data that everyone can use, rather than everyone trying to create their own data sets on the fly.

Generating test data

Hugo Kornelis offers a detailed description of how to generate test data in T-SQL: HTTP://TINYURL. COM/QYN8Q3B. *If time is in shorter supply, as is almost always the case during a development effort, you might consider a tool that automatically generates test data, such as SQL Data Generator from Red Gate Software. See Phil Factor's article for some tips:* HTTP://TINYURL.COM/OKTJH8D.

By carrying out this form of basic integration testing, we verify that all dependent applications communicate correctly with the database and behave as expected. In other words, integration tests ensure that a change doesn't introduce any new problems (regressions), and that the application code and database can properly exchange data.

Production-readiness testing

At some point in the development process, ideally as early as possible, the team must verify that the database (and application) builds and works in a production environment just like it does in development. Often, QA testing in an environment that mimics that of the production server is missing, or happens in a rush just prior to the deployment deadline. It is often at this late stage, when problems are hard to fix without causing substantial delays, that DBAs discover problems, for example with security and configuration settings, or find that the updates have badly degraded database performance.

DevOps and early deployments

One of the drives behind the "DevOps" movement is to promote the ideas, tools and automation that will allow developers to refine their deployment processes to the point where they can deliver early and often to a "production-like" environment. From here, DBAs and operations staff can review deployments and advise on possible issues much earlier in the project lifecycle.

Briefly, the team need to plan in time and establish the appropriate environments to perform several different types of database testing. For example:

- **QA/regression testing** – Verifies whether the latest changes introduced any new problems into the production environment. Regression testing a database can include testing data load and extract operations, as well as the application's access and transactional operations.

- **Load testing** – Verifies that the database can perform as expected when handling a realistic data load and production-level workload.

No rollback plan

Many deployments to production, application or database, lack a "get-out clause." What if we're halfway through a database upgrade and our deployment fails? What if we upgrade the database and we or worse, our customers, discover that we've introduced a serious bug?

How do we back out, or roll back, our changes and return the database to its previous consistent state? Rolling back database changes is a tricky business. Again, we're up against the issue of data. Schema changes are easy to roll back, but not changes to data.

Still, we have to start somewhere. At the very least, before starting any sort of deployment, we should back up the target database. This provides an immediate restore point to the moment before the deployment process started. Unfortunately, this approach doesn't account for data that might have changed during deployment, such as a new sales order or an update to a medical record. Important information could be lost.

Some deployment processes, in addition to creating a backup, also create database scripts that reverse schema and data changes. This requires the deployment plan to include a specific rollback component that defines how to handle each operation that we potentially need to roll back. The component also records the order of the operations to ensure that rollback can occur in the correct order.

Database Migration Scripts: Getting from place A to place B

Phil Factor's post illustrates the sort of thing that's required. See: HTTP://TINYURL.COM/OE63CTA.

Even with rollback scripts, however, rolling back a database is no small task, and the possibility of lost data still exists. A deployment strategy that includes a rollback component requires carefully considered procedures and scripts to carry out the operations. If we could lock the database against write operations during the deployment process, we could save a lot of trouble, but such an approach is often not possible because there's usually only one database and when it is offline the business is offline. Of course, we'll want to deploy a production database when traffic is at its lowest, but we might still have to keep our database online and available to users during the deployment process. In such cases, our rollback solution may depend not only on our tools and scripts but on other SQL Server tools and components, such as replication or the transaction log.

Building and Deploying Databases

A VCS should be integral to any development effort, but it remains only one piece of a much larger puzzle. As we discussed in Chapter 3, most well run product teams have in place Application Lifecycle Management (ALM) strategies to handle all aspects of application and database development, from inception and planning to maintenance and support. All these strategies and tools need to fit together smoothly in order to ensure successful releases. One of these pieces is the structure that defines how we build and deploy our applications and databases to their target environments.

Having all the correct files checked into source control is only the first step in a build and deployment process. After that, we need in place a build-and-deploy system, usually a set of policies, processes, and automated tools, which know the files to retrieve from source control, how to use those files to build the applications and databases, what steps to take and in what order to take them. Overall, this system must put in place all the necessary processes to ensure that we build the correct versions of the correct components in the correct order on the correct systems.

The build and deployment processes vary greatly from one organization to the next and, to add confusion to the mix, an organization likely deploys applications very differently from how it deploys databases, using different tools and procedures for each. For example, the degree of automation can vary, despite that fact that the more manual the process, the more time it consumes and the more it is prone to error.

All that said, Figure 7-1 attempts to provide a high-level, conceptual overview of how we might deploy a database. It represents only one of many possible ways to approach database deployment but it should, at least, provide you with a good sense of the issues our deployment system needs to address.

Not surprisingly, the build process starts with source control. The build engine then performs the following steps:

1. **Retrieves the files from the repository** and copies them to the build share, a network share created specifically to support build operations.

2. **Connects to the target database** and, optionally, creates a backup; whether it takes a backup depends on the size and purpose of the particular database, but we do need some way to ensure that we can restore the database to its original state should something go wrong.

3. **Prepares for the build** – this might entail creating build packages or taking some other action to prepare the source files and any supporting files for the build process.

   a. If replacing the target database with a clean build, the engine deletes that database and creates the new one by using the files it retrieved from source control.

   b. If updating the target database, the engine instead applies the update scripts to the existing database.

4. **Verifies** the database creation or update.

5. **Inserts the current build number.** The build is then complete and the database deployed to its target environment.

Again, this is a very simple overview of the deployment process as a whole, and in particular of the area enclosed in the dotted lines in Figure 7-1. Preparing the source files, coordinating the various tasks, handling errors, rolling back changes, verifying each step, and the assortment of other tasks, represent a series of sophisticated operations, different for each deployment solution, with no one way being definitively the *right way* to approach any of it.

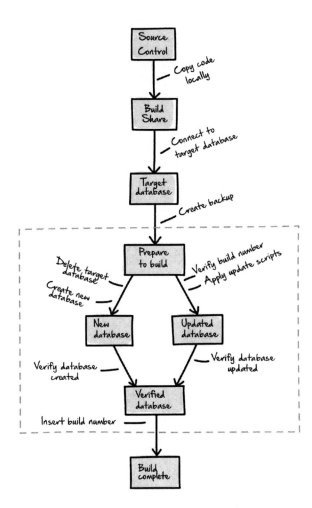

Figure 7-1: Building or updating a database.

Database build numbers

Build numbers provide a way to easily identify a particular application or database build. Build numbers are especially important in database development. They make it possible to distinguish the structure of one database version from another. If the build numbers are different, we should assume that the schemas are different. If the build numbers are the same, we should be able to assume that the databases share the same schema, unless the team permit changes directly to the database. However, if you do then, as discussed in the previous section on *Version drift*, it's difficult to trust anything you see because direct changes essentially undermine the advantages of assigning build numbers, as well as many of the advantages of source control. For example, if a developer and tester are working against different SQL Server instances, but the same database build is installed on both instances, the assumption would be that the databases are the same. However, if someone were to directly modify the developer's database, the tester could run into unexpected results when running a stored procedure because of unknown differences in the schema.

The bottom line?

Don't permit direct changes to a database unless you can confirm with absolute certainly that every one of those changes will be properly scripted and added to source control. Even then, we'd recommend against it. Direct changes make it difficult to know which version of the database is the correct one.

Build numbers also help to ensure that when we update a database, we're updating the correct build. For example, a set of upgrade scripts developed for build 2.0.33 will fail, or lead to unexpected results, if we run them against build 1.3.7. The build number serves as the universal identifier that all users, applications, and processes can reference to verify procedures and carry out tasks.

Our database deployment process must include a mechanism to assign a new build number to a database build. Most tools that automate the database deployment process include this capability. Even if they don't, it's easy to add the script file necessary to assign that number (we'll see an example of how to do this later in the chapter).

The question then becomes how to store the build number. Many teams, and some third-party deployment tools, use the database's extended properties for the build number. This approach is fine if all your database systems support extended properties, but many don't, such as Windows Azure SQL Database (formerly SQL Azure). To get around this, we can, for example, store the build number in a table-valued function instead.

Rather than support multiple systems for assigning build numbers, it's better to devise a single solution that works for any environment. One safe, cross-platform solution is to add a table to your database that tracks build numbers. Its structure is completely customizable, as long as we can query the table to retrieve the current build. Unfortunately, some organizations have restrictions against adding tables, which is why teams and tools often turn to extended properties or table-valued functions.

Of course, whenever we rebuild the database, we'll also rebuild this table so it will only ever contain one row, the current build. However, whenever we update the database, it will track each new build. Later in this section, we provide an example of a table that tracks build numbers.

We can assign build numbers based on whatever numbering system works best for the team. Many teams opt to mirror the application's build number for the database build number. Another common approach is to leverage the build number assigned to a revision in source control, via a tag. Often the application and VCS number are one and the same. Either of these approaches is usually fairly easy to implement and maintain.

Build numbers are often sequential for ease of tracking (though they don't have to be) but other than that, a build number can be a single number, have multiple parts, or be a mix of alphanumeric characters. We can, if desired, tie all or part of the number to our product version number. For example, we might have a three-part build number in which the first part reflects the product version.

The exact build numbering scheme is flexible, as long as each build number can identify uniquely a single database build, and any two databases that share that number also share the exact schema.

Deploying a new database build

In Figure 7-1, only the left portion of the area enclosed in the dotted lines refers to building a database from scratch, and yet many steps can go into building a database, and the larger and more complex that database, the more steps involved.

Above all, we must create the database objects in the correct order. We cannot, for example, create a foreign key that references a column that does not yet exist, and we cannot create views that reference tables that don't exist. Our build process must account for all dependencies, not only among the database objects, but also those outside the database, such as login accounts and server configurations, with an assurance that no objects, configuration settings, variable values, security principals, or any other components are missed.

Although the methods used to build a database will vary from one team to the next, we can separate them into three broad categories:

1. Uncontrolled, ad hoc deployments.

2. Manual deployments from source control, via scripting.

3. Automated deployments from source control.

Ad hoc database deployments

This is database deployment at its most basic. We use a tool such as SSMS to build and test our database. When we're done, we script it out and run those scripts, in the right order, to create the database on the target environment, and then we add the necessary lookup data. Alternatively, we might use a schema comparison tool to compare our development database to the database as it exists in the target environment and let the tool generate and run the necessary deployment script to synchronize the two environments (and use a data comparison tool to synchronize the reference data).

At the very least, we should save to source control the individual script files for each object, and the reference data, along with the deployment script. However, even if we do this, the essential problem remains that we are deploying from a moving target – a database running on a SQL Server instance – rather than from a known version in source control.

It quickly becomes very difficult to track which changes are deployed where, and very easy for what's in source control to become out of sync with what's in development or in each of the deployment environments.

Its obvious shortcomings make it an approach suited only to very small databases and usually only for testing or development purposes. Sadly, it is surprisingly common, not only for development and test databases, but also for ones in production. Hopefully, this far through the book, it's not an approach you'll consider for long.

Scripting database deployments from source control

This is still a manual deployment method, but its cornerstone is that we save to our VCS all scripts and all changes to those scripts, and we only ever deploy to any environment from a known revision in the VCS.

Rather than define manually the order in which we must run the script to deploy the new database, we create a deployment script file, such as a batch or PowerShell file, which serves as a master file that runs the SQL script files for us, in the prescribed order. Whenever we want to create or recreate the database, we run the master script, which must spell out each and every task that's required in order to build each database. Whenever we make a change to the database that affects how the object creation and data load scripts should be run, we must carefully (and manually) update the master file.

Of course, the more tasks we can include in the master file, the better we can automate the process. We can use the master file, not only to call SQL script files, but also for other types of files, such as additional batch or PowerShell files.

We can even set up the master file to accept arguments so that, when we call it, we can specify the instance on which to create the database and create it on as many instances as we like.

It's a much better approach, and one we demonstrate in this chapter, but still subject to the failing of any manual approach. It's easy to make a mistake. For example, if we forget to include an object creation script in the master file then it won't be deployed. If it's a code object, or a table without dependencies, the database will build correctly, but the object will be missing and so will cause application errors.

Automating database deployments

Not surprisingly, the most effective strategy for ensuring reliable, repeatable builds is to automate every step of the build and deployment process, from accessing the correct files in source control to assigning a build number, to deploying it to specified target environments.

The next step for a team that already works from VCS, and has scripting in place to semi-automate builds, is to start using available tools to automate as many aspects of the build process as possible. An organization might develop its own tools for automating deployment, but most will use tools available with the database management system or their VCS, or commercially available tools that plug smoothly into their broader ALM strategy (see the *Planning for Database Source Control* section of Chapter 3).

As noted earlier, in many organizations there is a disparity between deployment mechanisms for applications and those for the databases. For applications, it's becoming more common to see fully automated build processes. The application team add their files to source control, and the build mechanism takes over from there. At the end of each day, or even every time a team member commits a change, there is an automated build from source control to the test environment, followed by an automated suite of integration tests, so that the team deal with all problems as soon as they happen.

It's common, however, that the database will deploy by a much less frequent, much less automated process. In Chapter 2 we discussed the technical and cultural reasons for this, such as the difficulties of refactoring a live database while preserving the data but, nevertheless, the drive in many teams is towards a unified deployment process for both the database and the application. The database team add their files to source control right alongside the application files, and the framework incorporates the tools necessary to automate building the database alongside the application.

In this chapter, we only go as far as scripting the database build process, but Chapter 8 demonstrates an automated approach, based on use of the Red Gate's SQL Source Control SSMS plug-in for managing the database development process via a VCS, with integration into a build server for continuous integration (CI).

Upgrading an existing database

Once we've deployed a database to a production environment and it's populated with real data, we're much more likely to upgrade the existing database rather than re-create it from scratch. The scripts we run during an upgrade deployment must account for the need to preserve the table's data from one version of the database to the next.

As discussed in Chapter 4, as the team modify a database during the development process, they can elect to save to the VCS either the latest **CREATE** script for each object (versioning the current state of the database), or the string of upgrade scripts required to advance the object from one defined state to the next. Some teams adopt the former method during development, when it's permissible to tear down and rebuild databases, but switch to storing upgrade scripts after the first deployment to production.

In any event, the choice of how to version the database will, in turn, affect the tools and processes the team use when it comes time to apply these scripts during the database upgrade process. In some teams, the approaches used to upgrade a database can be a bit haphazard, sometimes applying changes directly to the database and sometimes through upgrade scripts, leaving everyone uncertain as to which database includes the correct schema. Again, automating this upgrade process is the best way to ensure consistency and repeatability.

However, whether we implement a semi-automated or fully automated solution, we're likely to take one of three approaches to upgrading an existing database:

1. Rebuild the database from scratch.

2. Apply a set of upgrade scripts.

3. Use a tool to auto-generate a transition script.

Rebuild the database

Once past the development stage, we're much more likely to perform an upgrade, rather than rebuild a database. That said, some teams choose to rebuild, at least on occasion, partly because it's a much simpler process. They will often rebuild, for example, when implementing a significant number of database changes and they want to tie the database to a new product version, or even a new product.

Of course, this means that the team must contend with migrating the existing data from the old database to the new, a task that grows in time and complexity as the amount of data grows. In addition, the team must orchestrate the application's transition from pointing to the old database to pointing to the new one in a way that minimizes the impact on the application's users.

In most cases, rebuilding databases as an ongoing strategy, is suited only to the early development phase.

Apply upgrade scripts

A common way to upgrade a database is to create a set of upgrade scripts, often called change scripts, which we then apply to a specific database build to transition it to the next defined state.

In this approach, every script we store in the VCS is a new upgrade script. Typically, each script will define a single change to a single object, whether to create that object, alter it, or even drop it. Alternatively, we might create one upgrade script that updates all objects, or create upgrade scripts for each object type (one for tables, one for views, and so on). Some teams store upgrade scripts only for tables, where each change must preserve the data, but use creation scripts for objects such as views and stored procedures, which are not dependent on the data.

The versioning process requires a lot of thought and effort. The upgrade scripts should include any and all of the SQL needed to move a database from one version to the next. The team need to consider exactly how they wish *every* individual database modification to proceed, whether it's a straightforward update to a code object, or a table refactoring that requires a complex and intricate number of steps in order to preserve the existing data. They will run data definition language (DDL) statements, modify security and configuration settings, update reference data, or perform any other action necessary to upgrade the database. It is a time-consuming process and each step in the upgrade process will require rigorous testing. The other challenge with upgrade script versioning is that because every modification creates a new file in the VCS, it works against the VCS's natural diff and blame mechanisms. Developers often resort to opening every upgrade script, one by one, until finding the one that contains a "rogue" change.

On the plus side, with all this work done, the deployment process becomes simple (in theory, at least), since it's merely a case of running the tested upgrade scripts in the right order. However, it still requires considerable care. As discussed in Chapter 4, the team need to ensure that that the right version of every script is in the VCS, that the build script executes each script in a precise order, that no change attempts fail or negatively impact other objects, that we don't miss any scripts or run any twice, and so on.

Also, of course, we need to verify that we apply the upgrade scripts to the right database build number.

In the scheme illustrated below, we start with a clean build, which we've tagged in source control as v1.0. In the VCS, we create a subfolder for our upgrade scripts, and segregate them according to build. So we create a folder called v1.1 in which we store all the upgrade scripts needed to transition the database from build 1.0 to 1.1. When we apply the next set of upgrade scripts, we increment the build number to 1.2, and so on.

- Build database 1.0

  - Apply 1.1 upgrade scripts to build 1.0.

  - Apply 1.2 upgrade scripts to build 1.1.

  - Apply 1.3 upgrade scripts to build 1.2.

- Build database 2.0

  - Apply 2.1 upgrade scripts to build 2.0.

  - Apply 2.2 upgrade scripts to build 2.1.

  - Apply 2.3 upgrade scripts to build 2.2.

Since each set of upgrade scripts targets a specific build, it means that if we need to deploy a new version of build 1.3, starting from scratch, we would first build the 1.0 database, then apply the 1.1 upgrade scripts, next the 1.2 upgrade scripts, and finally the 1.3 upgrade scripts. However, when we implement build 2.0 (the revision tagged v2.0 in source control), we're essentially starting over. We apply the 2.1 upgrade scripts to 2.0, the 2.2 upgrade scripts to 2.1, and so on.

The upgrade scripts should include any of the SQL needed to move a database from one version to the next. They can run data definition language (DDL) statements, modify security and configuration settings, update reference data, or perform any action related to updating the database.

The key is to run them in the correct order. Some teams actually include a number in the names of the upgrade scripts. Other teams create a master batch or PowerShell script that specifies which files to run and in what order. The approach we take depends on the methods we have in place to organize and run our files.

Auto-generate a transition script

An alternative to manually creating and maintaining a string of upgrade scripts for each database build is to store in the VCS only the latest **CREATE** script for each object. Each time we modify a database during development, we simply modify the existing **CREATE** script for that object and commit it to the VCS. For example, if we add a column to a table, we modify the table definition script file and check it into the VCS, rather than create a new upgrade script that alters the table.

Running the latest **CREATE** script to get the latest version of an object implies that we can drop the existing object first, which is not possible outside the early development stages. Instead, teams can automate this process, both in development and when deploying to other environments, using a tool that compares the schema creation files in source control with the database that is to be upgraded. From this comparison, the tool generates one or more transition scripts to run against the target database, to synchronize it with the definition of the database in the VCS.

In this way, we can compare any version of a database schema in source control with any database version. As a result, you can skip from build 1.0 to 1.3 without having to walk through the intermediate steps. If the database doesn't exist, the tool will create a new database. If it does exist, it will calculate the differences and apply the changes. We can also exert some manual control over exactly how the migration takes place. We cover this approach in detail in the next chapter.

Deploying a New Build of the Bookstore Database

It's theory-to-practice time once again, and we're going to use a manual process to deploy the current version of our `Bookstore` database, which entails creating a master script file that runs the various SQL scripts necessary to build our database. Up to this point in the book, we've followed the approach of versioning the `CREATE` scripts for each object, so our master script will simply need to assemble and run these `CREATE` scripts in the right order, and then load any test/reference data.

One of our database developers, Barb, will create our master script in PowerShell, after first adding a table that tracks build numbers.

Saving database backup files

Before starting the build and deployment process, create or designate a folder on the database server or network share for the database backup files. For the examples here, we'll use **C:\DataFiles\Backups**.

Create the build table

We'll have Barb create a build table, `DbBuild`, as described in Listing 7-1. It records a three-part build number and includes a column that tracks the name of the master script file used to orchestrate the build process and a column that records the date we ran the build.

```
USE Bookstore;
GO


CREATE TABLE dbo.DbBuild
    (
        MajorNumber CHAR(2) NOT NULL ,
        MinorNumber CHAR(2) NOT NULL ,
        BuildNumber CHAR(3) NOT NULL ,
        ScriptFile VARCHAR(50) NOT NULL ,
        DateApplied DATETIME DEFAULT ( GETDATE() ) ,
        CONSTRAINT pk_dbbuilds PRIMARY KEY
            ( MajorNumber, MinorNumber, BuildNumber )
    );
GO
```

Listing 7-1: The DbBuild table definition script.

In SSMS, run the script to create the build table, and then save the DbBuild.sql script file to Barb's **Tables** folder in trunk (**\BookstoreProject\trunk\Databases\Bookstore\Tables**), and commit it to the VCS in the usual fashion.

Create a tag for the latest Bookstore revision

The next step is to create a tag that identifies the most current files as part of build v2.0. Make sure Barb's working folder is "clean" (updated and with no uncommitted changes) and then create the tag as follows:

1. Right-click the **trunk** folder, navigate **TortoiseSVN | Branch/Tag**.

2. Name the new tag **v2.0** (in **To path:** enter **/tags/v2.0**).

3. Create the tag from the **HEAD** revision in the repository.

Having created the new tag in the repository, update Barb's working folder to retrieve it.

The tag identifies which files to use for the build. Going forward, any time the team want to build this database version, they need only reference the tag.

Create the build script

We're going to use PowerShell 3.0 to create the build script file, which will encapsulate the logic that assembles v2.0 of our `Bookstore` database. Of course, we could encapsulate similar logic in any number of alternative forms, such as a batch file. However, we chose PowerShell because of its varied language elements, the ease with which we can incorporate flow control, and its capacity for error handling (although we don't include error handling in the example code). Listing 7-2 shows the PowerShell build script.

```
# define variables
# modify server instance and folder paths as necessary
$instance = "localhost\SqlSrv2012"
$db = "Bookstore"
$date = Get-Date -Format yyyyMMddHHmmss
$file = "C:\DataFiles\Backups\$($db)_$($date).bak"
$folder = "C:\SvnBarb\BookstoreProject\tags\v2.0\Databases\Bookstore\"

# variable to verify existence of database
$id = Invoke-SqlCmd `
  -ServerInstance $instance `
  -Database "master" `
  -Query "SELECT database_id FROM sys.databases WHERE name = '$db'"

#check if database exists on server
if ($id.database_id -gt 0)
{
  # back up target database
  Backup-SqlDatabase `
  -ServerInstance $instance `
  -Database $db `
  -BackupFile $file `
  -Initialize
  # drop target database
  Invoke-SqlCmd `
  -ServerInstance $instance `
  -Database "master" `
  -Query "DROP DATABASE $db"
}
```

```
# create database
Invoke-Sqlcmd `
-ServerInstance $instance `
-Database "master" `
-InputFile "$($folder)Database\Bookstore.sql"

# create tables
Invoke-Sqlcmd `
-ServerInstance $instance `
-Database $db `
-InputFile "$($folder)Tables\Author.sql"

Invoke-Sqlcmd `
-ServerInstance $instance `
-Database $db `
-InputFile "$($folder)Tables\BookCategory.sql"

Invoke-Sqlcmd `
-ServerInstance $instance `
-Database $db `
-InputFile "$($folder)Tables\Book.sql"

Invoke-Sqlcmd `
-ServerInstance $instance `
-Database $db `
-InputFile "$($folder)Tables\AuthorBook.sql"

Invoke-Sqlcmd `
-ServerInstance $instance `
-Database $db `
-InputFile "$($folder)Tables\DbBuild.sql"

# create view
Invoke-Sqlcmd `
-ServerInstance $instance `
-Database $db `
-InputFile "$($folder)Views\AuthorsBooks.sql"

# populate tables with test data
Invoke-Sqlcmd `
-ServerInstance $instance `
-Database $db `
-InputFile "$($folder)LookupData\BookCategoryData.sql"
```

```
Invoke-Sqlcmd `
-ServerInstance $instance `
-Database $db `
-InputFile "$($folder)TestData\TestData.sql"

# insert build number into DbBuild table
Invoke-Sqlcmd `
-ServerInstance $instance `
-Database $db `
-Query "INSERT INTO DbBuild
  (MajorNumber, MinorNumber, BuildNumber, ScriptFile)
  VALUES ('2', '0', '0', 'BuildDatabase_2.0.0.ps1')"
```

Listing 7-2:   Creating the PowerShell database build script.

The script contains a number of components, so let's walk through each one. The opening portion of the script creates a number of variables, as follows:

- **$instance** and **$db** point to the SQL Server instance and the target database, respectively. Modify the former as appropriate for your instance.

- **$date** and **$file** generate a file name for the database backup file.

- **$folder** points to the **v2.0** tags folder.

Next, we create the **$id** variable. We use the Invoke-SqlCmd PowerShell cmdlet to populate $id with the target database ID from the **master** database. We're using the variable merely to test the existence of our target database, so we could have returned any column from the sys.databases view.

If the database ID is greater than 0, we assume the database exists and the script backs up the database and then drops it. To back up the database, we use the Backup-SqlDatabase cmdlet and we use the Invoke-SqlCmd cmdlet to issue a DROP DATABASE statement.

Of course, dropping and recreating a database destroys the data, even if we do back it up first, and it's not a technique we'd use in production. We use it simply as a convenience, in case you don't have a SQL Server instance where `Bookstore` does not already exist. We discuss the right way to upgrade an existing database in the next section.

The last half of the script is where all the action takes place, since it's where we build our database. The key is to run the SQL scripts in the correct order to ensure that the database builds correctly. In this case, we first run the database creation script, followed by the table creation scripts, in their proper order. Keep in mind that your script will create the database as specified in that script, in terms of the location and other properties of the data and log files. If deploying to an environment in which these or other properties need to be different, be sure to modify your database creation script as appropriate.

The master script then creates the view and populates the tables (using the lookup and test data). For every command, we use the `Invoke-SqlCmd` cmdlet to run the appropriate script file.

Run the new build

It's time to save our build script and test it out! First, save the script to Barb's **DeployScripts** folder in trunk as **BuildDatabase_2.0.0.ps1**, and commit it to the VCS as usual.

PowerShell supports a number of ways to run a script. The simplest is to right-click the file and then click **Run with PowerShell**. This will launch the PowerShell console, run the script, and close the window. The only challenge with this approach is that, if informational messages are being displayed in the console window, you'll likely not see them, unless you're a very fast reader.

Another easy way to run the script is to open the PowerShell console and drag the file from Barb's working folder to the console. Then press **Enter** to launch the file. Or, if you actually want to edit the script, you can right right-click the file in the working folder and then click **Edit** to open the file in PowerShell ISE. PowerShell ISE gives you more options for testing and debugging the script and working with the file in general.

If you need help getting started with PowerShell, a good place to begin is with Laerte Junior's article *Getting Airborne with PowerShell* (HTTP://TINYURL.COM/P92HSLS). In the article, one of the issues that Junior discusses is how to set the execution policy in order to run a script file. However, to set the policy, we must run PowerShell as an administrator. As you start PowerShell, right-click the PowerShell link, and then click **Run as administrator.**

Once over these small logistical hurdles, the PowerShell script should run fairly quickly, creating the backup, dropping the database, and building the new one.

We can view the database properties in SSMS to verify the creation date. Also be sure to check the `DbBuild` table to ensure that it exists and contains our new build number. In addition, you can run the `AuthorsBooks` view to see whether it returns the expected data.

The build script used in this example is simple, and lacks the normal error handling and control flow logic that defines the conditions under which to exit the script. However, it does demonstrate the basics of how to build and run a script that creates a new database at a particular version.

Upgrading the Bookstore Database

Having deployed v2.0 of the Bookstore database to production, Barb and Fred continue working on the database in their development environment, making improvements that they will ultimately want to release as v2.0.1. This means that at some point they will want to apply these upgrades to the live v2.0 database.

Up to now the team have versioned the latest **CREATE** script for each object. At this stage, they can either:

1. Continue this policy, and at deployment time use a schema comparison tool to generate a upgrade script that they can apply to the target database, or

2. Switch to saving each change as a separate upgrade script and then use a master build script that runs against v2.0 and applies all the upgrade scripts, in the right order, to v2.0.

In this case, the team will adopt the second approach (Chapter 8 will cover the first one).

Preparing the environment

Before we get started with the database upgrade process, we need to set up a folder to store our upgrade scripts. Make sure Fred's working folder is fully updated with all previous changes, and then within **C:\SVNFred\BookstoreProject\BookstoreDatabases\ Bookstore**, create a new subfolder called **ChangeScripts** and within that add a subfolder called **ChangeScripts_2.0.1**. Add and commit these new folders in the usual way.

Creating the upgrade scripts

We'll have Fred make a number of changes to the `Bookstore` database in the development environment:

1. Add the `BookType` table, which provides lookup data for the `Book` table (`AddBookTypeTable.sql`).

2. Add lookup data to that table (`AddDataToBookTypeTable.sql`).

3. Add a `BookTypeID` column to the `Book` table to point to the new table (`AddColumnToBookTable.sql`).

4. Update the test data for the Book table (`AddDataToBookTypeIDColumn.sql`).

5. Add the `BookTypeID` column to our `AuthorsBooks` view (`AddColumnToAuthorsBooksView.sql`).

Listing 7-3 shows, in a single listing, the scripts for all five changes, but we need to save each of these five changes as a separate upgrade script, in the **ChangeScripts_2.0.1** folder.

```
/*AddBookTypeTable.sql*/
USE Bookstore;
GO

CREATE TABLE dbo.BookType
    (
        TypeID INT PRIMARY KEY ,
        TypeName VARCHAR(30) NOT NULL
    );
GO

/*AddDataToBookTypeTable.sql*/
USE Bookstore;
GO
```

```
INSERT   INTO BookType
VALUES  ( 101, 'Paperback' ),
        ( 102, 'Hard cover' ),
        ( 103, 'Electronic book (ebook)' ),
        ( 104, 'Audio' );
GO


/*AddColumnToBookTable.sql*/
USE Bookstore;
GO


ALTER TABLE dbo.Book
ADD BookTypeID INT
CONSTRAINT fk_BookTypeID
REFERENCES BookType(TypeID);
GO


/*AddDataToBookTypeIDColumn.sql */
USE Bookstore;
GO
UPDATE Book SET BookTypeID = 101 WHERE BookID = 1;
UPDATE Book SET BookTypeID = 101 WHERE BookID = 2;
UPDATE Book SET BookTypeID = 103 WHERE BookID = 3;
UPDATE Book SET BookTypeID = 102 WHERE BookID = 4;
UPDATE Book SET BookTypeID = 102 WHERE BookID = 5;
UPDATE Book SET BookTypeID = 101 WHERE BookID = 6;
UPDATE Book SET BookTypeID = 104 WHERE BookID = 7;
UPDATE Book SET BookTypeID = 101 WHERE BookID = 8;
UPDATE Book SET BookTypeID = 103 WHERE BookID = 9;
UPDATE Book SET BookTypeID = 102 WHERE BookID = 10;
UPDATE Book SET BookTypeID = 104 WHERE BookID = 11;
GO
```

```
/*AddColumnToAuthorsBooksView.sql*/
USE Bookstore;
GO
ALTER VIEW dbo.AuthorsBooks
AS
    SELECT  ( CASE WHEN MiddleName IS NULL
                        OR MiddleName = '' THEN a.FirstName + ' '
                                                        + a.LastName
                ELSE a.FirstName + ' ' + a.MiddleName + ' ' + a.LastName
            END ) AS FullName ,
        b.Title AS BookTitle ,
        bc.CategoryName AS BookCategory ,
        ( CAST(b.BookID AS VARCHAR) + '_' + LOWER(LEFT(a.LastName, 2)) )
                                                    AS NewBookID ,
        bt.TypeName AS BookType
    FROM    Author a
        INNER JOIN AuthorBook ab ON a.AuthorID = ab.AuthorID
        INNER JOIN Book b ON ab.BookID = b.BookID
        INNER JOIN BookCategory bc
                ON b.BookCategoryID = bc.BookCategoryID
        INNER JOIN BookType bt ON b.BookTypeID = bt.TypeID;
GO
```

Listing 7-3:   Five upgrade scripts.

Preparing to deploy

Once we have Fred commit all of these upgrade scripts to the VCS, Barb can update her
working folder and then start preparing to deploy the v2.0.1 upgrade.

Create a new tag for the v2.0.1 build

Barb's first step is to create a new tag that identifies all the files that comprise the v2.0.1 build:

1. Right-click the **trunk** folder, navigate **TortoiseSVN | Branch/Tag**.

2. Name the new tag **v2.0.1** (in **To path:** enter **/tags/v2.0.1**).

3. Create the tag from the **HEAD** revision in the repository.

Again, Barb must update the working folder to retrieve the new tag from the repository.

Creating a master upgrade script

We'll again create a master PowerShell script for upgrading the database. The script will target the original build (2.0.0) with updates for the new build (2.0.1). In other words, the script is developed specifically to upgrade 2.0.0 to 2.0.1.

Listing 7-4 shows the master PowerShell upgrade script.

```
# define variables
# modify server instance and folder paths as necessary
$instance = "localhost\SqlSrv2012"
$db = "Bookstore"
$date = Get-Date -Format yyyyMMddHHmmss
$file = "C:\DataFiles\Backups\$($db)_$($date).bak"
$folder = "C:\SvnBarb\BookstoreProject\tags\v2.0.1\Databases\Bookstore\
ChangeScripts
                                            \ChangeScripts_2.0.1\"
[string]$LastBuild = 200

# variable to verify existence of database
$id = Invoke-SqlCmd `
   -ServerInstance $instance `
   -Database "master" `
   -Query "SELECT database_id FROM sys.databases WHERE name = '$db'"
```

```powershell
#check if database exists on server
if ($id.database_id -gt 0)
{
  # retrieve build number
  $CurrentBuild = Invoke-SqlCmd `
  -ServerInstance $instance `
  -Database $db `
  -Query "SELECT (RTRIM(MajorNumber) + RTRIM(MinorNumber) +
    RTRIM(BuildNumber)) AS Build FROM DbBuild
    WHERE DateApplied = (SELECT MAX(DateApplied) FROM DbBuild)"

  # if wrong build, exit script
  if ($LastBuild -ne $CurrentBuild.Build)
  {
    cd c:
    Write-Host "Wrong target build. Update terminated."
  }
  else
  {
    # back up target database
    Backup-SqlDatabase `
    -ServerInstance $instance `
    -Database $db `
    -BackupFile $file `
    -Initialize

    # run update scripts
    Invoke-Sqlcmd `
    -ServerInstance $instance `
    -Database $db `
    -InputFile "$($folder)AddBookTypeTable.sql"

    Invoke-Sqlcmd `
    -ServerInstance $instance `
    -Database $db `
    -InputFile "$($folder)AddDataToBookTypeTable.sql"

    Invoke-Sqlcmd `
    -ServerInstance $instance `
    -Database $db `
    -InputFile "$($folder)AddColumnToBookTable.sql"
```

```
    Invoke-Sqlcmd `
    -ServerInstance $instance `
    -Database $db `
    -InputFile "$($folder)AddDataToBookTypeIDColumn.sql"

    Invoke-Sqlcmd `
    -ServerInstance $instance `
    -Database $db `
    -InputFile "$($folder)AddColumnToAuthorsBooksView.sql"

    # insert build number into DbBuild table
    Invoke-Sqlcmd `
    -ServerInstance $instance `
    -Database $db `
    -Query "INSERT INTO DbBuild
      (MajorNumber, MinorNumber, BuildNumber, ScriptFile)
      VALUES ('2', '0', '1', 'UpdateDatabase_2.0.1.ps1')"

    cd c:
    Write-Host "Database updated to build 2.0.1."
  }
}
else
{
  cd c:
  Write-Host "Database does not exist. Update terminated."
}
```

Listing 7-4:   Creating the PowerShell database master upgrade script.

The script once again begins by defining a number of variables. The only additional variable in this first section is $LastBuild. This contains the build number that our script targets (build 2.0.0, but without the periods). We'll use this to confirm that we're running our upgrade scripts against the correct database version, which we do in the later if statement. First, we define a variable named $CurrentBuild, which retrieves the current build number from the DbBuild table. Next, we compare the $LastBuild and $CurrentBuild values. If they are not equal, we display a message saying that we have the wrong target build and we take no other steps.

If the build numbers do correspond, we back up the database and then run each upgrade script in the appropriate order, accounting for dependencies. Finally, we add our build number and script file name to `DbBuild`.

Deploy the upgrade

It's time to save our upgrade script and test it out! First, save the script as `UpgradeDatabase_2.0.0.ps1` to the **DeployScripts** folder, in trunk, and commit it in the VCS.

Run the script in PowerShell as described earlier. If you want to see the returned messages, then simply drag the file into the PowerShell console and press **Enter**. After you run the script, you should receive a message saying that the database has been updated to the new version. From there, verify that that the backup file has been created and that the `DbBuild` table contains the new build number. Also verify that the `BookType` table was created and populated, the `Book` table includes the new column, and the `AuthorsBooks` view displays the book type.

Run the `UpgradeDatabase_2.0.0.ps1` script again. This time through, it should display a message that you've run the script against the wrong target build. As you'll recall, the script will run correctly only against build 2.0.0, so we are reliant on the build if ever we want to re-create the 2.0.1 database. In other words, if we want to create the 2.0.1 database from scratch, we must first build the 2.0.0 database, and then apply the 2.0.1 upgrade scripts to that database, assuming we rely on upgrade scripts to upgrade the database.

Automating Deployments for Upgrade Script Versioning

In this chapter, we've demonstrated a very basic example of this approach, saving each database modification to a designated folder as an upgrade script, and then using a simple PowerShell script to execute them in the right order during upgrades.

However, it is still an overwhelmingly manual process, and therefore, especially for more complex upgrades than we've demonstrated here, time consuming and potentially error prone.

To introduce better control and a degree of automation into this process, we could, as discussed in Chapter 4, adopt some of the ideas described and implemented in Alexander Karmanov's deployment framework (see HTTP://TINYURL.COM/PTA9BCS). In addition, we can use tools such as dbdeploy (HTTP://DBDEPLOY.COM/) or migrator-dotnet (HTTPS://CODE.GOOGLE.COM/P/MIGRATORDOTNET/) or Octopus deploy (HTTPS://OCTOPUSDEPLOY.COM/) to help us automate deployments.

Alternatively, we can adopt CREATE script versioning through the development and deployment cycle, and again use tools to help automate our processes, as discussed in the next and final chapter.

Source Control and Database Deployment

Source control and database deployment play integral roles in the world of database development. Source control provides the foundation necessary to successfully deploy your databases, yet it is by no means the only mechanism that contributes to an effective deployment strategy. You must have in place whatever policies, procedures and tools are necessary to ensure you can successfully build and upgrade your databases to whatever version you require.

In this chapter, we've looked at several aspects of database deployment and provided exercises to demonstrate a number of concepts. However, this information is meant only to help provide you with a conceptual overview of some of the factors to take into account when deploying a database. Database deployment is a large topic that could easily warrant its own book. In addition, the methods used to deploy databases are as diverse as the teams that deploy them. Our examples, like the information in general, are meant only to reinforce concepts. We are not suggesting that any one way to deploy your databases is the right way. The goal is to be able to deploy consistent, repeatable builds as efficiently as possible. How you achieve that goal is up to you.

Chapter 8: Automating Database Versioning and Deployment from Source Control

Chapter 7 demonstrated a rather nuts-and-bolts approach to deploying a new database and upgrading an existing database from the VCS. Relying on nothing more than a build table and a master script, in PowerShell, we deployed a new version, v2.0, of the `Bookstore` database from the VCS. At this point the team continued development work, but switched from versioning the latest `CREATE` script for each database object to storing each individual database modification as a separate upgrade script. We then used a second PowerShell script to apply the changes to v2.0 of the deployed database, and transition it to v2.0.1.

This upgrade script approach allows very precise control over each change we need to deploy to our databases, but we could regard this as both its strength and its weakness. It requires the developer to describe manually *every* single upgrade, whereas professional grade schema comparison tools are more than capable of automating the vast majority of our upgrades, while still allowing the developer to exert manual control over the harder ones.

In this chapter, we'll discuss ways to streamline our database versioning and deployment processes to make them more reliable and less time consuming, using a set of automation tools. It will allow the team to adopt a unified, more integrated approach to database development and deployment, based solely around `CREATE` script versioning.

Once again the chapter breaks down into theory and practice sections. The theory section takes a broader look at database versioning options and challenges, and how to choose the right versioning approach, and the tools and techniques that will allow us to start automating `CREATE` script versioning and deployment. The practice section demonstrates a particular automation approach, with the examples using tools from the Red Gate stable, such as SQL Source Control and SQL Compare.

Versioning the Database

Our ultimate goal in versioning the database is to preserve a complete history of the database so that we can audit its evolution and, if need be, return to a past known state. In order to achieve this we need to version, primarily (but amongst many other things):

- **the database schema** – every database object (table, view, function, procedure and so on)

- **static data** – any "lookup" data that the application will assume exists (such as a list of all the states and provinces).

When it comes time to build and deploy our database, the build tool must have available the correct version of every object, and all static data. Ideally, the tools or scripts we use to build and deploy the database will allow us to deploy together the required schema objects and tables of lookup data. This allows all the database content to be deployed within one transaction, and sequenced and validated together as a single unit. Simple tools will either not version the data at all or require you to launch a separate process to version data. More advanced tools allow you to select both.

CREATE scripts versus upgrade scripts

In the book so far, we've discussed two basic approaches to versioning a database in our VCS:

1. **Save the modified CREATE script** – We store one file per object and edit each file as appropriate to reflect each schema modification. In this approach, we are effectively versioning the current state of the schema.

2. **Save a new upgrade script** – For each object, we store the string of upgrade, or *transformation*, scripts (one change per script) that describe how to transition a database from an existing schema to the desired schema.

Table 8-1 summarizes some of the pros and cons of each approach.

Technique	Summary	Pros	Cons
CREATE scripts evolve over time	Store CREATE scripts, modify these scripts over time	Auditability – easy to see file evolution (what changed, and who changed it) using VCS diff and blame commands	Harder to deploy upgrades, must infer differences Generally requires tools
Upgrade scripts alter the schema in each script	Store the commands necessary to transform schema to the desired state	Easily deploy changes by running all scripts not run previously	Does not account for version drift May not take the most efficient deployment path Much harder to track changes

Table 8-1:   Comparing database versioning strategies.

When using the upgrade scripts versioning, developers store a new script for every change. If a developer wishes to make an "atomic" change to the database, such as adding a new table column and then making that column available in a view, he or she creates the necessary ALTER TABLE and ALTER VIEW scripts, verifies through testing that they transition the database to the correct new state, and then commits the two new upgrade scripts to the VCS.

The same atomic change with **CREATE** script versioning follows more or less the same path, except that after testing the developer will script out the **CREATE** script for each modified object, and save it to the VCS. In effect, the developer edits two existing scripts in the VCS, rather than creating two new ones.

Either approach is viable, but the real differences between the two emerge when it comes time to deploy the versioned scripts.

Deployment challenges

When using the upgrades script approach, other developers deploy these upgrades to their environment, or a build server applies them to a test environment, simply by running the scripts in the right order. It is a simple technique and allows fine-grained control over exactly how each upgrade should proceed. It can work well, as long as there are rigorous controls in place to determine exactly which scripts do and don't need to run in a particular deployment environment, and to prevent any direct modification of a deployed database.

Deploying changes to a new environment is trickier with **CREATE** script versioning, since the developer (or build server) needs either to drop the existing object and run the **CREATE** script in the VCS, which is not recommended, or find a way to "infer" the alterations required to *transition* the existing object definition, in the target environment, so that it matches its definition in the VCS, while preserving any data. However, assuming the development team can overcome the deployment challenges (we'll discuss how in much more detail shortly), **CREATE** script versioning offers some major benefits, particularly in terms of improved auditing of project changes, and therefore easier team communication and project management.

In either approach, if the process of packaging up all of the required files and deploying them is a manual one, then it is likely to be error prone and time consuming, especially for database deployments, where creating new objects and retiring old columns and tables must be done in a very specific order.

If this will quickly become tiresome for our developers, it could become catastrophic when the time comes to deploy to production servers. The live application can become quite unstable during the database deployment period, as both the new product version and the old product version presume very specific schema states. During the deployment, neither of these exist. We often just take the product out of service during this time. Imagine the panic-stricken DBA who is manually, urgently, carefully, quickly making all these changes while the business is at a stand-still, waiting for word of completion. It isn't long before we start reaching for a new solution, an automation solution, which both reduces the risk and speeds up deployment time.

Choosing a versioning approach

If the development team has a free hand in choosing a database versioning strategy, it is likely to be **CREATE** script versioning, especially if they have an easy and trusted way to generate the transition scripts that will enable sharing changes between developers' environments, and deploying them to testing. It is the approach that can best support their need to develop, test and deploy features quickly, while offering full change auditing through the VCS.

However, it is unwise to make this choice without considering the needs of other relevant users and functions. For example, we ought to consider then needs of:

- **the build server** – collects all project assets from the VCS to build and configure them and then package and deploy the product to a test server
- **operations staff** – are responsible for the stability and performance of the product in the production environment
- **the product owner** – manages the features and priorities of the product.

Table 8-2 summarizes the main users and functions that have a stake in the VCS system and its versioning mechanism, and what needs they have.

User/function	Primary need	Primary tool	Ideal workflow
Developer	Easily publish and consume schema changes	SQL Management Studio	Publish changes from SQL Management Studio, apply others' changes when updating the codebase
Build server	Test schema and code changes	TeamCity, Jenkins, Team Foundation Server, Cruise Control	A build step applies the database migrations, testing the eventual deployment path
Operations	Minimize risk	SQL Management Studio, database comparison tools, deployment automation tools	A non-technical user can deploy changes at any time by applying packages exhaustively tested previously
Product owner	Audit change history	VCS Blame command, bug-tracking tools	Easily discover new changes, the version that introduced a change, and identify when and by whom each change was made

Table 8-2: Users and workflows.

The operations team, for example, since they are responsible for the availability, performance and general well-being of the "live" application, will generally be averse to deploying any changes that have not been very carefully tested and rehearsed. If the organization must conform to rigorous up-time service-level agreements (SLAs) or rigorous audit requirements, they are likely to favor the upgrade scripts approach, because this technique lends itself to an upgrade path that is easy to rehearse and perfect. When the time comes to deploy, the risk of failure is reduced because the exact scripts that will affect production have been flexed in other environments.

Conversely, if the team use **CREATE** script versioning, with a "push button" tool to generate the necessary transition script, they may be more inclined to leave testing of that script to the last minute, in which case it's more likely that difficult and complex changes will cause disruption and downtime.

Although it's important to consider everyone's needs as far as possible, it's also important not to get tied down in red tape, trying to build manual processes and policies to account for all the goals of all the users. We'd also generally advise against opting for the best-of-both-worlds approach of storing both the new **CREATE** script and the upgrade script, and each modification, in the VCS. In truth, it usually turns out to be the worst of both worlds, as it naturally creates a synchronization problem. What if the upgrade script doesn't yield the same final schema as the **CREATE** script? Which is right? What if the database developer forgot to commit one or the other?

Since the previous chapter demonstrated upgrade script versioning, for deploying database upgrades, this chapter will now focus exclusively on **CREATE** script versioning. However, pick whichever approach is best suited to your primary workflows and users and stick to it, and then implement the necessary automation and procedures that will smooth the rough edges and mitigate risk for others. For example, if you choose **CREATE** script versioning, or even the upgrade script approach, then mitigate risk to the operations team by deploying to environments that mimic production as early as possible in the development process, quickly spotting and fixing any potential issues with your migration scripts, as well as the product itself, long before it's time to go live.

Automation for CREATE Script Versioning and Deployment

We'd like our chosen toolset to provide a consistent set of techniques to ease and automate team-based database development, and then deployment of the new database to various target environments. Ideally, the tools will allow developers to save off the CREATE scripts as database developers finish their tasks, right from within their development environment (SSMS), and to upgrade their environments with the CREATE scripts of others, as they're ready. The same tried and tested techniques to deploy between development and test environments should also be available to operations staff to safely deploy new versions to production.

As discussed earlier, the major barrier when using CREATE script versioning is deploying schema changes, either to customers or to fellow developers. The CREATE scripts in the VCS represent the desired end-state of the database. If we're building a completely new version of the database from scratch, we can deploy them as-is, but what if a version of the database already exists in the target environment? To deploy them as-is, we'd need to tear down existing objects and replace them with their definition in the VCS. However, this is a bad idea for several reasons. It can become tricky and error prone when there are complex object dependencies, and it means we'll also need to re-create the data each time, exactly as it existed before.

Alternatively, a developer may choose to make the changes manually, looking through the VCS log and manually updating each affected table, column, view, stored procedure, function, and so on. This is simply a non-sustainable approach, and it isn't long before the developer starts looking for an automation solution.

Essentially, what we need instead is a "comparison engine" to automate the process of identifying differences between two schemas, and generate the **transition script**. This script is essentially a set of ALTER commands that will align the schema of the target database with that of a source database, or with the collection of CREATE scripts that form the latest revision in the VCS, while preserving all data.

The comparison engine could come in the form of a "roll-your-own" tool, or a third-party product. Whichever solution we choose, it will, ideally, allow manual intervention for delicate or complex database refactoring, such as splitting tables or changing a column's properties in a way that could affect the data it stores. This takes the form of a migration script, which will nudge the process away from the tool's defaults, when necessary.

Upgrades, transitions, migrations…

The terms for the various types of script can get a little confusing and are often used interchangeably so, to summarize their meaning in this book:

- *Upgrade script – a script describing a single database modification.*
- *Transition script – an auto-generated script to align a database with a set of files in the VCS.*
- *Migration script – a script used to steer the automated transition.*

We will, ideally, store the transition script in the VCS and then run it against the target schema. If there are any manual migration scripts, we could incorporate them into this transition script. When we have this process fully automated, the comparison engine will automatically compare the **CREATE** scripts and migration scripts stored in the VCS to the target server, infer the transition plan between them, and implement it.

Whatever our exact strategy, it is important that the approach we use to transition a database from its current state to the desired state should be the same in all environments. In other words, we should upgrade our database in development in exactly the same way as we would upgrade it in production, so that we fully understand and test the transition plan long before it comes time to execute it on a production system.

Automating the transition script

Our comparison engine, in whatever form it takes, needs to capture the database developer's intent, and build a transition script that takes the shortest path to the goal, while preserving user data.

Building our own tool to auto-generate a transition script from the **CREATE** scripts is not technically challenging, though some would argue that it's typically not cost-effective to build and maintain one to work robustly for every transition. Remember the panic-stricken DBA who is urgently trying to deploy this change while the software is offline?

Nevertheless, a home-grown tool need only loop through each schema object on both sides, diffing the details. Tools such as SQL Server Management Objects (SMO) allow .NET programs to easily discover table details, views, stored procedure content, and so on. Looping first through each schema object type, then through each object, then through the details of each object can quickly produce a list of what's different between two databases. It is a bit more difficult to build this tool when we're pulling the desired schema state from source control, as it is in the form of a set of SQL **CREATE** scripts rather than an actual schema. To solve this, simply let SMO write **CREATE** scripts for the database, then use string comparison to identify differences. Alternatively run each **CREATE** script into a blank database, and use SMO to diff the two databases. However, we still need to apply our knowledge of the schema differences into a transition script that will transition a database into the desired state. If, we just **DROP** and **CREATE** each object, this doesn't bode well for preserving table data. Running **ADD COLUMN** and **DROP COLUMN** scripts for each difference is slightly better, but breaks down if the intent of the change is to rename a column.

Ultimately, if undeterred by licensing costs or "not invented here" syndrome, the process of migrating a schema from one state to another is where the professional grade tools shine, and we have quite a number of choices for both of the automation strategies. If we're looking merely to infer the differences and then manually run the script, we'll look to tools such as Atlantis Compare, dbForge, Red Gate SQL Compare, and Visual Studio Data Tools. If we're looking for tools that fit into a continuous integration and/or delivery pipeline, we'll look towards tools such as SQL Source Control, Entity Framework Migrations, and Rails Migrations.

Whichever tool we choose should have some or all of the following features:

- Dump a database schema into CREATE scripts – in other words, we'd like the tool to generate a set of CREATE scripts automatically by analyzing an existing database.

- Compare database schemas.

- Compare a database to a set of SQL CREATE scripts.

- Support versioning static lookup data.

- Infer the differences between schemas and create a transition script.

- Run the transition script, harvesting errors and reverting if necessary.

- Allow manual overrides, when necessary, using **migration scripts** (covered in the next section) to instruct the comparison engine exactly how to perform a certain database upgrade.

Migration scripts

There are times when any comparison engine can betray us. The goal of the engine is to infer the database developer's intent. It does this by analyzing the two schemas (or CREATE scripts and schema) and guessing what the developer had in mind. It calculates this direct transition path, and writes out the SQL script. For most cases, this direct path will be fine; we can simply test the generated script and run it. However, sometimes the most direct path is not the right path. For example, if we rename a column or rename a table, most schema comparison tools will auto-generate a transition script that drops the old column or table and creates a new column or table. This process doesn't preserve the user data.

In these cases, we need to instruct the tool to perform the proper transition that will ensure preservation of data. In other words, we have to insert into the automated process a **migration script** that instructs the comparison engine on how to handle any unusual schema modifications.

For example, if we were to rename the `Author` table to `Authors`, we need to instruct our comparison engine to use `sp_rename` for that upgrade step, rather than drop `Author` and create `Authors`.

Within these scripts, we'll not only execute the `sp_rename` but we'll also place an `IF` condition around it to ensure the transition is necessary. For example, what if the target database already had the destination `Authors` table? What if the source `Author` table didn't exist? In either case, the migration script doesn't apply, and we should not use it as we migrate the schema.

To facilitate both deployment and the potential to roll back , many tools help us build a set of related migration scripts: one "up" script that upgrades the system to the new version, and one "down" script that downgrades the system or reverts the change. Though we'll want to account for this potential rollback process, the process of automating these "down" scripts is out of scope for this book. Instead we'll focus on creating and automating the "up" scripts, and inserting these migration scripts in the automation pipeline.

Automated Versioning and Deployment for Bookstore

It's theory-to-practice time again, for the final time in this book. The examples in the section will demonstrate just one possible toolset that will allow the team to:

- **Unify their versioning strategy around CREATE scripts**, which will be used for deployment to all environments.

- **Improve developer interaction** – saving a database developer's changes, and applying these changes to a co-worker's development environment, using Red Gate's SQL Source Control.

- **Improve our previous manual deployment process** – using Red Gate's SQL Compare to compare the **CREATE** scripts directory to the target server, and running the generated SQL script as a manual "push the button" process.

- **Allow the build server to deploy changes automatically** to a integration server using JetBrain's TeamCity and Red Gate's SQL Automation Pack (brief overview only).

Versioning databases with SQL Source Control

Up to this stage in the book, we've interacted with the source control repository almost exclusively through the respective users' working folders, developing scripts on a live SQL Server development instance, but then saving them manually over to the working folder and committing them to the repository. Likewise, if a developer needed to apply the change made by another team member, he or she would either need to drop the existing table and re-create it using the latest **CREATE** script, and reimport any data (not recommended) or generate manually the **ALTER** command to implement the required change (error prone).

Here, we'll look briefly at an alternative, tool-based approach, where every developer in the team uses Red Gate's SQL Source Control source control client, integrated with SSMS, to commit their changes and get the changes of others. To work through the example in this section, you'll need to install this tool.

SQL Source Control tool and references

- Version used in this book: 3.6.3

- Download (with 14-day free trial): HTTP://BIT.LY/1GFU18X

- Documentation: HTTP://BIT.LY/1JFFP0B

- Enabling Migrations v2 (in beta at time of writing): HTTP://BIT.LY/1OHXTGS

- Branching and merging support: HTTP://BIT.LY/1QONQKC and HTTP://BIT.LY/1P5NZJS

We'll assume each member of the team of developers works in their own sandbox copy of the database (the dedicated development model, see Chapter 3).

....

Best practice: dedicated development databases

With the right tools, I believe that it becomes a best practice for each developer to have their own sandbox database. We'd never open a Visual Studio solution from a shared network folder knowing a co-worker would also open the same solution from the same network folder. Why do this with your database? With the right tools, it becomes easy to keep the development database up to date without needing to call in a technician at every turn, and so the need to force database developers to experiment in a common development database lessens. Instead, put a copy of the database on each developer's machine, and use tools to keep it up to date.

....

Link database to repository strategy

In the most common mode of working with SQL Source Control, we link a database in a live SQL Server instance directly to the repository, using the appropriate repository URL. To do this, the first developer simply right-clicks the database and selects **Link database to Source Control**. SQL Source Control scripts out every database object, and when the developer commits, it auto-creates a specific folder structure in the repository, scripting every database object into a folder corresponding to its object type. Each subsequent team member creates their own local copy of the latest version of the database by creating an empty database, linking the database to the same repository URL and performing a "**Get Latest.**"

Thereafter, each team member simply right-clicks on the database in SSMS, and commits their database modifications directly to the central source control repository, for access by other team members. In a single commit, this will version all outstanding local changes made by that user. Likewise, all team members can simply click **Get Latest** to retrieve others' changes, as shown in Figure 8-1.

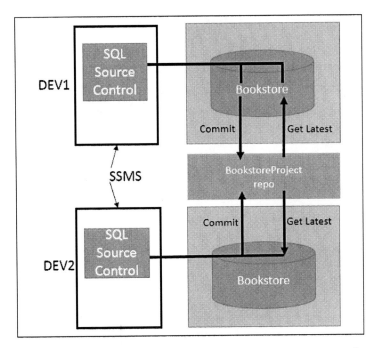

Figure 8-1:   Developer collaboration via SQL Source Control (repository strategy).

In addition, each developer can perform a check-out of the repository to their working folder. This is necessary because we still currently need to perform certain source control operations, such as creating a branch or performing most types of merge, through a native client such as TortoiseSVN.

For example, SQL Source Control supports linking to a branch, simply by unlinking from the current repository URL (e.g. the trunk) and relinking to the branch URL, or by creating a separate local database for the branch development work. However, we have to create and manage the branches through a native client. Likewise, SQL Source Control offers some limited support for merging, allowing developers to merge at the object level, either opting to keep "theirs" or "mine" in the case of a conflict. Recent versions of the tool do offer some line-by-line merging support by launching a third-party merge tool such as Beyond Compare (see the earlier *Branching and merging support* references). However, at the time of writing, line-by-line merging support was limited to stored procedures only.

Link database to working folder strategy

Given that we still need to use the working folder for certain source control operations, and since in this book we've become accustomed to interacting with the repository through our working folder, we'll use SQL Source Control in a slightly different mode, as illustrated in Figure 8-2.

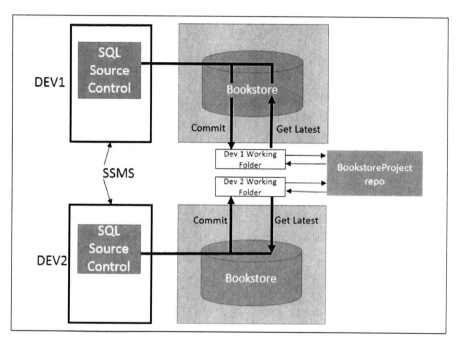

Figure 8-2:   Developer collaboration via SQL Source Control (working folder strategy).

In this strategy, SQL Source Control merely synchronizes the database content with a chosen directory in the working folder, and then the user can choose which changes to commit, and when. This is incredibly helpful when we want to commit both database and application code in a single, atomic commit to ensure the build server captures all content associated with the change. If we committed each separately, we could easily have a broken build between the two commits. The working folder strategy is a perfect tool to separate the concern of scripting and updating the database, from the process of storing and versioning these scripts.

Versioning the existing Bookstore database

We're now going to start the process of versioning the current version of the `Bookstore` database, both schema objects and static lookup data, as it existed at the end of Chapter 7, using SQL Source Control.

Setting up the initial Bookstore database in Development

If you've been following along with all the examples in the book so far then you'll already have a copy of the `Bookstore` database on your SQL Server instance. If not, in the code download for this chapter, we provide a backup of the database, as it existed at the end of Chapter 7, and you can simply restore it to your SQL Server instance to provide your starting point for the examples in this chapter.

An alternative is to deploy the `Bookstore` database from the VCS to your development SQL Server instance. Again, if you haven't been working along, we provide, in the code download, a backup of the `BookstoreProject` repository as it existed at the end of Chapter 7. The first step is to restore this repo backup to an appropriate location, from the SVN command prompt, as described in the *SVN merging precautions* section of Chapter 6. For example:

```
svnadmin load D:\Repositories\BookstoreProject < D:\SVNBackups\
BookstoreProject.bak
```

We can then deploy the database from the latest revision in the repository. We could do this using a PowerShell master build script, for example, as described in Chapter 7.

Once we've worked through this section, discussing how to use SQL Source Control to link this database to our `BookstoreProject` working folder, then more automated deployment possibilities will be open to us, using a comparison engine to compare the latest revision in the repository to an existing database (empty or otherwise) and deploy the changes.

Linking Bookstore to working folders

In Chapter 7, our team adopted a split versioning strategy, using CREATE scripts during development, but moving to upgrade script versioning after the first live deployment.

Ordinarily, if a team decided to adopt CREATE script versioning for all deployments, they would move the old upgrade scripts into a "legacy" or "old" folder, and ultimately delete them. However, for the purposes of this book, we'll instead just leave all existing scripts in place, and create a new folder to which SQL Source Control can store the CREATE scripts for our existing Bookstore database.

In previous chapters, our senior developer, Barb, checked out the BookstoreProject repository (**https://<server>/ svn/BookstoreProject/**) to **C:\SVNBarb\BookstoreProject**. The **\trunk\Databases\Bookstore** subfolder contained all the necessary content to create the database, tables, views, and data.

Let's now have Barb create a new folder within **C:\SVNBarb\BookstoreProject\trunk\ Databases** called **Bookstore_SoC** (where SoC forms a shorthand reference to SQL **Source** Control) and then commit that folder to the repository.

Barb needs to link this folder to the Bookstore database in her development instance, after verifying that her live database represents precisely the latest revision in source control. To do this, fire up SSMS, right-click the Bookstore database and select **Link database to Source Control** (or, choose the same link from the **Setup** page of the SQL Source Control tab, which you can open from the **Tools** menu).

Specify that we'll link the working folder, provide the URL to Barb's new **Bookstore_SoC** folder, and select the dedicated database development model, as shown in Figure 8-3.

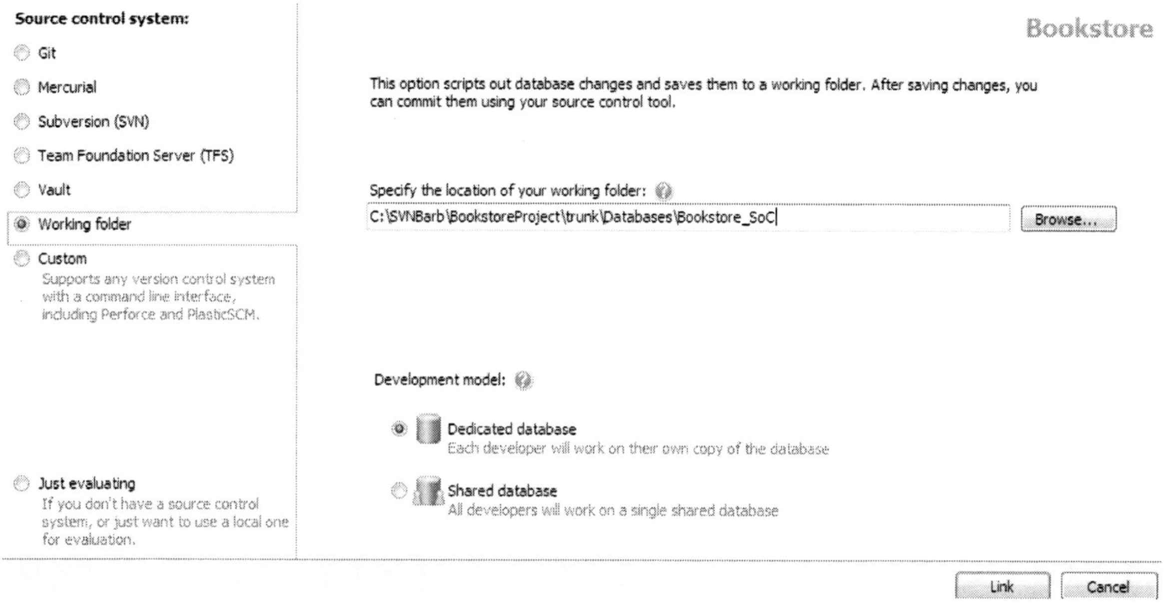

Figure 8-3: Linking `Bookstore` to Barb's working folder.

Now simply click **Link** to create the connection between source control and our `Bookstore` database.

Back in SSMS Object Explorer, we'll see a small blue globe icon next to all the database objects, indicating that SQL Source Control has discovered objects that are new, yet committed to our **Bookstore_SoC** folder. On the **Commit Change** tab, we see all these objects listed as **New**.

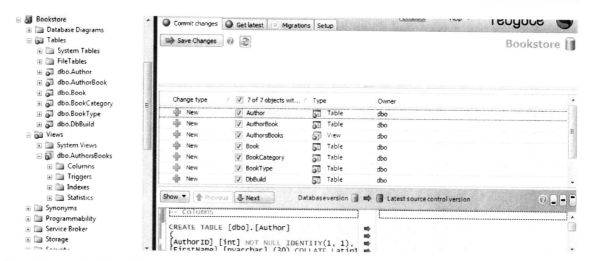

Figure 8-4: Database changes to save to the working folder.

Click **Save Changes** to write the scripts to our folder. Next, we can flip over to Windows Explorer to see exactly how SQL Source Control saved these scripts to Barb's working folder. SQL Source Control creates its own organizational structure for storing the scripts for each object, as shown in Figure 8-5. Note that it will create scripts only for the schema objects, not any reference data (but we'll fix that shortly).

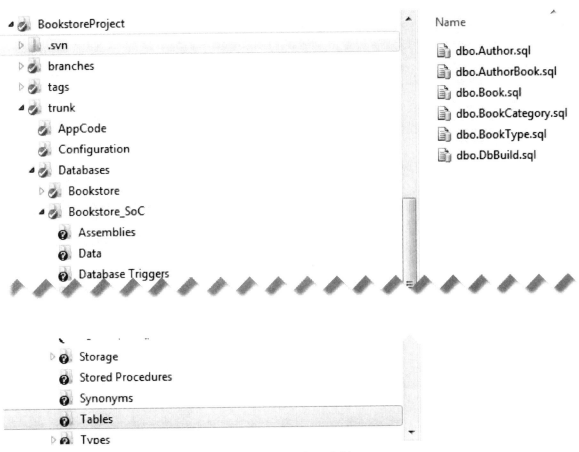

Figure 8-5: The SQL Source Control-generated working folder.

From Barb's working folder, let's have her commit all of this content to the repository.

Developer collaboration: linking further users

Our next user, Fred in this case, simply updates his working folder (**C:\SVNFred\ BookstoreProject\BookstoreDatabases**) to capture the changes Barb committed. Fred now needs to create the `Bookstore` database in his own dedicated SQL Server instance based on the latest revision in his working folder.

Of course, at this stage in the book, Fred likely already has an existing `Bookstore` database, but of course generally this process of linking working folder to source control would happen right at the very start of the project.

For the sake of this example, we'll have Fred create a new empty database called `FredBookstore` (see Listing 8-1) and then link this new database to his **Bookstore_SoC** folder.

```
USE master;
GO
CREATE DATABASE FredBookstore ON PRIMARY
( NAME = N'FredBookstore_Data', FILENAME = N'<your path>\FredBookstore.mdf' )
    LOG ON
( NAME = N'FredBookstore_Log', FILENAME = N'<your path>\FredBookstore.ldf' )
GO
```

Listing 8-1: Creating the `FredBookstore` database.

Right-click the new database and select **Link database to source control**, specify the working folder using the URL **C:\SVNFred\BookstoreProject\BookstoreDatabases\ Bookstore_SoC**, and select the dedicated database development model, as described previously.

Our first user, Barb, started with a live database containing all the required objects, and an empty working folder. Fred now has the opposite situation of a versioned schema in the repository, and an empty database. Switch to the **Get Latest** tab, and note all the schema objects that Barb committed and which Fred needs to apply to his live database. Click **Apply Changes** and in a short second, Fred should have a live development database with a schema identical to Barb's.

As mentioned briefly earlier, although Barb and Fred have synchronized schemas, Fred's database will not contain any static/lookup data, since versioning the data is a separate step and Barb linked in only her schema objects. Let's fix that now.

Versioning static data

In our application, there are a few pieces of data that are static. Perhaps the application duplicates these as an enumeration, or perhaps we're just confident this data doesn't change.

Throughout the book, we've added and modified a small volume of test data, as well as some static lookup data to our BookCategory and BookType tables, in order that we can display to users real book categories (such as "fiction") and book types (such as "paperback"), rather than meaningless IDs.

In this example, we'll version only the lookup data, in the BookCategory and BookType tables, and not the test data. With such a small volume of test data, we could version that too in this case, but in more realistic cases the test data is likely to be of a volume that makes source controlling it impractical.

Test data best practice

Some teams choose to have a seed database that mirrors production data, perhaps anonymized to protect customer privacy, perhaps a subset of the full database to avoid storage costs. You may find it helpful to refresh this seed database periodically so developers can experience production-like data as they work.

Having versioned this data, we can track changes to it, communicate with other team members, and restore to a point in time. In Barb's SQL Server instance, right-click the Bookstore database, and choose **Other Source Control Tasks | Link or unlink static data**, and then select the BookCategory and BookType tables, as shown in Figure 8-6.

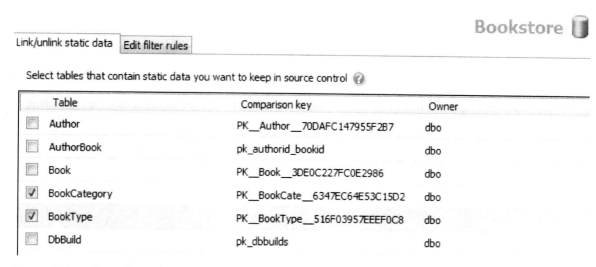

Figure 8-6:   Versioning the `BookCategory` and `BookType` lookup data.

Click **OK** and then switch to the **Commit Changes** tab in the SQL Source Control pane, which should report that there is a Data link change type to save to the working folder.

....

SQL Source Control filters

*You may have noticed the **Edit filter rules** tab in Figure 8-6. We won't cover filters here, but we can use them to exclude certain objects from source control (see* HTTP://BIT.LY/1O1F1R2).

....

Click the **Save Changes** button. In Windows Explorer, Barb's **Bookstore_SoC** folder should register changes that she needs to commit, so perform that commit now, with a descriptive commit message.

Now Fred can update his **BookstoreDatabases** folder and then, in SSMS, open the **Get Latest** tab in the SQL Source Control pane, and click **Apply Changes** in order to suck this lookup data into `FredBookstore`.

Updating the test data

Since we chose to version only the static data, Fred's new database won't contain any of the test data we added throughout the book. As discussed, most teams generate test data outside of the SQL Source Control process, perhaps using a seed database or perhaps using a data generation tool.

In this example, Fred can easily generate test data for his `FredBookstore` database simply by using the latest version of the `TestData.sql` script in his **BookstoreDatabases\Bookstore\TestData** folder. However, here he will run into a slight issue. In the previous chapter, the team added a new `BookTypeID` to the `Book` table and some test data to populate that column. However, the team added the data as a change script, and it's not included currently in the `TestData.sql` file. This illustrates one of the possible issues of switching database versioning strategy in this way.

To remedy this, Fred could update `TestData.sql` to incorporate the population of the `BookTypeID` column, and then run the script against his `FredBookstore` database.

Modifying Bookstore

Both of our developers now have a live `Bookstore` database, linked through their respective working folders which, in turn, link to a shared repository URL.

They can now proceed with the development effort, committing changing and getting the changes of others, and start preparing to deploy a new version out to testing, then on to Staging and Production environments.

Let's say that Dan, the new product owner tells Barb and Fred that the **Bookstore** application needs the ability to store the author's state and country of origin. Fred decides to add these columns to the `Authors` table of his `FredBookstore` database by running the script shown in Listing 8-2. Alternatively, right-click on the `Authors` table, and choose **Design** to add them through the Designer.

Generally, Fred would create a new AuthorLocation table for these state and country details and link it in to the Authors table, as we've done previously for book categories and types, but we'll keep things simple at this point, to focus on the collaborative source control processes.

```
USE FredBookstore;
GO
ALTER TABLE dbo.Author ADD
State NVARCHAR(100),
Country NVARCHAR(100);
GO
```

Listing 8-2:   Add State and Country columns to the Author table in FredBookstore.

At this point, Fred would run all the unit tests to ensure they pass, run the application, smoke-test critical pieces, and engage peer reviews to ensure the quality of the changes he's made.

We'll presume all this is complete and that Fred is ready to share this change with Barb. All he needs to do is jump to the **Commit Changes** tab in the pane and he will see that SQL Source Control detected the change and generated the new version of the CREATE script to save to his working folder, as shown in Figure 8-7.

Fred can click **Save Changes** and then, in Windows Explorer, commit the change with a descriptive commit message, in the usual fashion, to create a new revision in the repository.

At this point, Barb should update her working folder in Windows Explorer, and then back in SSMS use the **Get Latest** tab to incorporate this schema change into her development database.

Figure 8-7: Saving the new **CREATE** script for the **Authors** table to Fred's working folder.

Barb and Fred can proceed in this fashion, making changes to other schema objects or to the versioned static data as required, and saving the changes to their respective working folders directly from their sandbox SQL Server instances. They can visit the TortoiseSVN log to see the history of the database changes as it evolves. They can update their working folders and then apply the changes of other developers to their live database, as and when they are ready.

If they hit any merge conflicts during updates, they can resolve them using Tortoise-Merge, as described in detail in Chapter 6, or use the (currently limited) merge functionality of SQL Source Control, as discussed earlier in this chapter. Again, if developers commit and update early and often, it will minimize the risk of merge conflicts.

Deploying databases with SQL Compare

We've seen how a tool like SQL Source Control can help collaboration during development. Now, we're going to expand our toolset and see how to start automating the deployment process.

We're going to walk through an example of a basic database deployment of the latest revision of the Bookstore database in our VCS, directly to a new, empty database in the deployment environment, using a schema comparison engine. SQL Compare will infer the differences between the CREATE scripts stored in source control and the schema on the target database and generate a transition script. Later in the chapter, we'll see how to generate a database deployment package (such as a NuGet package) that our build server can use as part of a fully automated, continuous integration build and deployment.

In order to perform this basic database deployment, one of our developers will need a license for SQL Compare (or just a free trial download).

SQL Compare references

- Version used in this book: 10.7

- Download (with 14-day free trial): HTTP://BIT.LY/1J2TCYL

- Documentation: HTTP://BIT.LY/1KIJPQZ

If you also installed the SSMS Integration Pack as part of the SQL Source Control or SQL Compare (or another Red Gate tool) download, then you can launch a SQL Compare (or Data Compare) deployment directly from within SSMS.

Automating deployments with the SQL Compare command line

`sqlcompare.exe` *can do deployments without user interaction when you purchase a SQL Compare Pro license. If you need to perform more complex database deployment, such as deploying the same database version to multiple targets, consider deploying using the command line and PowerShell scripts, as described here:* HTTP://TINYURL.COM/NHEEHOL.

Deploying a new build of Bookstore

As we did in previous chapters, the team should branch or tag the content before or after this deployment, to mark that all content up to and including this version is deployed.

For example, following on from Chapter 7, the next minor release of our database could be v2.0.2. In which case, from Barb's working folder, she can create a new tag off of the trunk called **v2.0.2** (in **To path:** enter **/tags/v2.0.2**), from the **HEAD** revision in the repository (and then update the working folder to retrieve the tag).

Best practice: build numbers and deployments

Always have an easy way to relate the deployed database to the source that created it. Either store the source code revision number in the target production database (avoid using the build server's build number as this is by definition transient), or store the deployed revision as a tag in source control, or both. This way, if an issue arises in production, a developer should be instantly able to retrieve from the VCS the exact content that comprises the deployed version of the database.

Next, we need to create a "shell" database on the target SQL Server instance. To do this, Barb can connect to the target instance from SSMS and run Listing 8-1, adapted as appropriate to create a shell database on the target. In this example, she calls the new database `ProductionBookstore`.

Deploy the schema

Barb can use SQL Compare to auto-generate our transition script that will synchronize the current schema of `ProductionBookstore` (currently it is empty) with the latest revision of the database in source control.

Open up SQL Compare and start a new project. On the **New Project** dialog, we define the source and target for the comparison. We want to use the most recent set of `CREATE` scripts as the source and our new `ProductionBookstore` as the target. When we select the **Source Control** radio button for the source, we then have the option to compare direct from the source control URL or from a scripts folder. As a DBA or developer performing the deployment, we might opt to deploy direct from a repository location. However, a member of the operations team is much more likely to work from a script folder sent to him or her by the developer or DBA.

In this, case we're going to deploy from **Bookstore_SoC**, in Barb's working folder so, on the left side of the dialog, choose the **Scripts folder** option, and then enter the folder path **C:\SVNBarb\BookstoreProject\trunk\Databases\Bookstore_SoC** (or the same folder in the **v2.0.2** tag, if you created it).

On the right, choose the **Database** as the target, at the top, and then enter the details of the target server, specify the connection details, and select the `ProductionBookstore` database from the drop-down. Once complete, the screen should look something like what is shown in Figure 8-8.

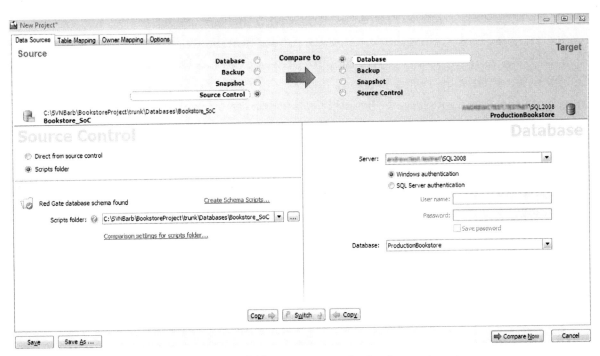

Figure 8-8: SQL Compare with a script folder as source and a database as target.

Click **Compare Now** and SQL Compare will generate a list of changes to synchronize the scripts folder and the target database. We should see six tables and a view that exist only in the scripts and not in `ProductionDatabase`. Select them all. We can click on each to find out exactly what changed and see the auto-generated script to perform the synchronization.

You may see objects that exist only in the target, for example if the target instance auto-creates certain custom users on all new databases. If this happens, don't select those objects.

With all necessary objects selected, click **Deployment Wizard**, at the top, and we get the options either to **create a deployment script**, or to **Deploy using SQL Compare**. We would generally choose the former, and then open up the script in SSMS to review and test it before running it.

However, here we're going to choose to deploy with the tool. Nevertheless, it's always a good idea to save the scripts that change the production database, so accept the option to save the transition script that SQL Compare generates to our **DeployScripts** folder. SQL Compare automatically assigns it a long name comprising the names of the source and target and the date. However, we'll simply call it **BookstoreTransitionScript_2.0.1To2.0.2**.

Click **Next** again, and we see the auto-generated transition script. Scroll through this script and note how table creation is carried out in the specific order that ensures dependent tables are created before the foreign keys that depend on them, that tables are created before views, and that SQL Compare wraps everything in a transaction.

Click **Deploy Now** to run this transition script against the `ProductionBookstore` database. In SSMS, connect to the target instance and verify that all the changes made it into `ProductionBookstore`. We didn't need to keep track of which things needed to be deployed or in which order we were to run these scripts. The tool inferred the changes, and built the SQL script.

SQL Compare will also have saved the transitions script into Barb's **DeployScripts** folder, so she should commit it to the repository.

Deploy the static data

Using the companion tool, SQL Data Compare, we can deploy the lookup data stored with the project. Earlier, we mentioned that with Red Gate's SSMS Integration Pack, we can launch schema or data comparisons right from within SSMS. Let's try that now for the static data (it you don't have the integration pack, simply launch SQL Data Compare separately).

In SSMS, right-click Barb's `Bookstore` database, select **Data Compare/deploy | Set as Source**, choose **Source Control** as the source, set `ProductionBookstore` as the target and then launch SQL Data Compare.

After that the process is the same as for the schema, and you'll need to choose the same source scripts folder as last time (**C:\SVNBarb\BookstoreProject\trunk\Databases\ Bookstore_SoC**). SQL Data Compare will generate a script to deploy the static data in the `BookCategory` and `BookType` tables to the target.

Deploying upgrades to Bookstore

Our database is now deployed and users are busily using it, and adding business data. The next time we deploy, to upgrade the `ProductionBookstore` database, we need to consider preservation of this business data.

Meanwhile, back in development, Dan, the product owner, comes to Fred and identifies a new business requirement. They want to modify the `Bookstore` application UI so that it is mandatory for users to enter an author's country of origin, and to modify existing entries in the `Authors` table to add any missing country data.

This is a change that requires a little thought. If the `Bookstore` application is not yet released internationally, we can presume all users in the system who haven't set a country yet are from the United States. In that case, we could just make the `Country` column `not null`, and set a default on it of "United States."

However, as soon as the application releases internationally, the `DEFAULT` constraint becomes invalid. A better fix that accomplishes the long-term goal, is to make an atomic change that modifies existing data as required and then immediately alters the column to `NOT NULL`. However, this is clearly not a change that SQL Compare can handle alone, with manual prompting from a migration script.

****

Enabling Migrations v2 in SQL Source Control and SQL Compare

At time of writing, Migrations v2 was still in beta, and you will need to enable it in both tools in order to run this example. For SQL Source Control, see HTTP://TINYURL.COM/LA7WARN. *For SQL Compare, start the tool, navigate* **Tools | Project Options** *and check the relevant option.*

****

Therefore, we're going to generate the migrations script that SQL Compare will incorporate into the transition script at deployment time. Unfortunately, at time of writing, SQL Source Control's migrations tooling only supports "up" (i.e. "apply this") scripts, and not "down" (i.e. "undo this") scripts.

In SSMS, select Fred's `FredBookstore` database and then hop to the **Migrations** tab in SQL Source Control, choose **Add Migration Script**, and paste in the script in Listing 8-3.

```
DECLARE @ShouldRunMigrationScript BIT
SET @ShouldRunMigrationScript = 1
IF NOT EXISTS ( SELECT   1
                FROM     Information_Schema.Columns
                WHERE    table_schema = 'dbo'
                         AND TABLE_NAME = 'Author'
                         AND COLUMN_NAME = 'Country' )
    BEGIN
        SET @ShouldRunMigrationScript = 0;
        PRINT 'Column [Country] in [dbo].[Author] could not be found -
            skipping migration.';
    END
IF @ShouldRunMigrationScript = 1
    BEGIN
        UPDATE  [dbo].[Author]
        SET     [Country] = 'United States'
        WHERE   [Country] IS NULL
        ALTER TABLE [dbo].[Author]
          ALTER COLUMN [Country] NVARCHAR(100) NOT NULL
    END
```

Listing 8-3:   The migration script.

Give it a descriptive name, such as **Set Author.Country Not Null**, along with a description, and click **Save and Close**. Run the migration script on the `FredBookstore` database and then switch over to the **Commit Changes** tab.

You should see changes to the following objects:

- **The affected table** – in this case, the `Authors` table. If it doesn't appear in the change list, you need to run the migration script against the local database.

- **`MigrationHistory` table-valued function** – tracks which migration scripts are applied and which still need to be run.

- **`RedGate` schema** – where the TVF is stored.

We should version these items in source control and deploy them to all databases including production. Click **Save Changes**, then switch to Fred's working folder in Windows Explorer, and commit the changes.

To update Barb's database using this migration, first update her working folder and then, back in SSMS, switch to the **Get Latest** tab, and click **Apply Changes**. This will run the migration script, and sets all the existing authors' countries to United States if they weren't specified.

The final step is to deploy the changes with SQL Compare, exactly as described previously. This time, the transition script should note that the Author table exists on both source and target but is different, and that two objects (the TVF ad schema) only exist in source.

Start the Deployment Wizard, and again we can either create a deployment script or perform the deployment directly through the tool. On the "objects you selected for deployment" screen, notice that it recommends deploying all dependencies (objects referenced by the changed object). Review the transition script, and note our "migration" should be one of the first actions in the script. On deploying the script, we should see the changes reflected in `ProductionBookstore`.

Auditing changes

Storing CREATE scripts that evolve over time makes auditing the database history as easy as automating the application code's history. We can use the SVN log, for example, to see which specific changes we made at each revision (see Chapter 4).

We can take auditing to the next level using the Blame view. For example, right-click on the Author.sql file in **C:\SVNBarb\BookstoreProject\trunk\Databases\Bookstore_ SoC\Tables** and choose **TortoiseSVN | Blame**. For each line of code in the file, the Blame view shows us the last revision that modified that line, and who made the change. We can mouse over a line, to see the commit date and time, the commit message, and other interesting details. This is a wonderful tool for understanding who changed what, and when. It's much easier to pull open this single view than to pull open each of a dozen transition scripts looking for which one introduced or modified a particular column.

Database Versioning and Deployment with Continuous Integration

We've seen how tools help us to commit changes to schema and data, making it much easier for other developers to update their databases with these changes. We've also seen how easy it is to make a migration script that can nudge SQL Source Control to care for data when its default drop/create methodology is insufficient. We also simplified the manual database deployment process, by using SQL Compare to compare the latest CREATE scripts in the VCS with the "production" database, and infer the transition script.

We can integrate these same tools and techniques into a continuous integration (CI) process whereby at regular intervals, such as at the end of each day (or even on every commit to our VCS, for some applications), the build server deploys a fresh build to the integration server for testing. In other words, instead of a developer running

SQL Compare to generate the transition script, the build engine will do so and use it, along with all the application source code and all other necessary build artifacts, all stored in the VCS, to run the deployment.

Installing the CI server and agent(s), configuring application and deployment build steps, and other continuous integration methodologies are beyond the scope of this book, so this section offers only a brief and broad overview of one possible approach.

Continuous integration tools and references

- Installing and configuring TeamCity:
  HTTP://BIT.LY/IJYO8KR

- Continuous integration using Red Gate SQL Automation Pack:
  HTTP://BIT.LY/IOIUZMU

- Automating database builds with TeamCity and SQL Automation Pack:
  HTTP://BIT.LY/RAC8MD

- Data synchronization with Team City:
  HTTP://BIT.LY/IJ4ZHN7

With TeamCity installed, download and install the Automation Pack (you may need to restart TeamCity to load the new plugin).

The reference above to *Automating database builds with TeamCity and SQL Automation Pack* provides worked examples for earlier and later versions of TeamCity, but in essence we need to open up a TeamCity build, add a new build step, choose the **Red Gate** runner type, and enter the CREATE scripts folder (**/trunk/Databases/Bookstore_SoC**) and the target database details. Since a CI build typically doesn't deploy directly to production, you could create a database called DevTestBookstore for this purpose.

With this build step in place, every time we commit code to the VCS, the build server will fire up to build, test, and deploy the content, including the database content. On each build, it will infer and execute the transition script. Together with unit and integration tests, this can give operations staff a high degree of confidence that the final deployment to production will work as expected.

Summary

This chapter demonstrated how tools can help us improve and automate the process of versioning and deploying databases, alongside the application. Right from within our database development tool (SSMS) we were able to modify our development database, and then (after testing) commit it to the working folder, or directly to the VCS, with a just a few clicks. We were also able to discover and apply others' schema changes by inferring the differences between the scripts stored in source control and the developer's local database.

With the same toolset, we could deploy new builds or upgrades directly to the target server, allowing our comparison engine to take care of most changes, but using migration scripts when we wanted to take specific steps to protect data integrity. We also explored how to incorporate such tools into a continuous integration and deployment pipeline.

None of this would be possible, without a version control system that stored the right version of every asset required for a successful deployment, including, of course, all of the relevant database objects and static data.

Choose the right VCS for your team, and then make the effort to find the right automation tools, whether home-grown, open source or commercial. Together, they can make the process of evolving, versioning and deploying a database far less painful.

Index

About Red Gate

You know those annoying jobs that spoil your day whenever they come up?

Writing out scripts to update your production database, or trawling through code to see why it's running so slow.

Red Gate makes tools to fix those problems for you. Many of our tools are now industry standards. In fact, at the last count, we had over 650,000 users.

But we try to go beyond that. We want to support you and the rest of the SQL Server and .NET communities in any way we can.

First, we publish a library of free books on .NET and SQL Server. You're reading one of them now. You can get dozens more from www.red-gate.com/books

Second, we commission and edit rigorously accurate articles from experts on the front line of application and database development. We publish them in our online journal Simple Talk, which is read by millions of technology professionals each year.

On SQL Server Central, we host the largest SQL Server community in the world. As well as lively forums, it puts out a daily dose of distilled SQL Server know-how through its newsletter, which now has nearly a million subscribers (and counting).

Third, we organize and sponsor events (about 50,000 of you came to them last year), including SQL in the City, a free event for SQL Server users in the US and Europe.

So, if you want more free books and articles, or to get sponsorship, or to try some tools that make your life easier, then head over to www.red-gate.com

CPSIA information can be obtained
at www.ICGtesting.com
Printed in the USA
FFOW02n0613200515
13433FF